Deconstructing Psychotherapy

edited by
IAN PARKER

SAGE Publications Ltd
London • Thousand Oaks • New Delhi

1004699 74 T

First published 1999

 SAGE Publications Ltd
6 Bonhill Street
London EC2A 4PU

SAGE Publications Inc.
2455 Teller Road
Thousand Oaks, California 91320

SAGE Publications India Pvt Ltd
32, M-Block Market
Greater Kailash – I
New Delhi 110 048

British Library Cataloguing in Publication data

A catalogue record for this book is available
from the British Library

ISBN 0 7619 5712 X
ISBN 0 7619 5713 8 (pbk)

Library of Congress catalog record available

Typeset by Mayhew Typesetting, Rhayader, Powys
Printed in Great Britain by Biddles Ltd, Guildford, Surrey

CONTENTS

NOTES ON THE CONTRIBUTORS

Nollaig O'Reilly Byrne is clinical director, a consultant child psychiatrist and family therapist, and on the senior faculty of the Family Therapy Training Programmes at the Department of Child and Family Psychiatry, Mater Misericordiae Hospital, Dublin.

Wendy Drewery teaches (among other things) counselling theory in the Counsellor Education Programme at the University of Waikato.

Vincent Fish is a psychotherapist and consultant in private practice at the Family Therapy Center of Madison and is a senior preceptor in the School of Social Work, University of Wisconsin-Madison.

John Kaye is senior lecturer at the University of Adelaide, where he established what is now the Masters in Psychology (Clinical Health). In 1994 he established the Discursive Construction of Knowledge Group and initiated its associated biennial international conference. With a major commitment to delineating the sociocultural determinants of thought and behaviour, he has graduated to a social realist and critical orientation toward psychology. This informs his work as a psychotherapist. He is accordingly not a narrative therapist, preferring to work within a frame he calls 'discursive therapy'.

Glenn Larner is a clinical psychologist and family therapist at Queenscliff Health Centre, Manly, Sydney. He has published several articles on the relevance and application of Derridean deconstruction to family therapy and psychoanalysis and is currently a doctoral student at Wollongong University researching a thesis on this topic.

Ian Law is a therapist and training provider who is based in Adelaide, South Australia. Over the last two years he has been with Yaletown Family Therapy in Vancouver, Canada. As well as editing *Gecko*, a family therapy journal, he has been writing and presenting on his development of a discursive approach to therapy.

Roger Lowe is a lecturer in counselling at Queensland University of Technology, Brisbane, Australia, where he teaches and supervises graduate students in the Master of Social Science (Counselling) pro-gramme.

Imelda Colgan McCarthy is Director of the PhD Programme in Families and Systemic Therapies, a Board member of the Family Studies Centre and a lecturer in the Department of Social Policy and Social Work, University College Dublin.

Wally McKenzie has been teaching narrative/postmodern ideas at the University of Waikato for the past six years as a part-time lecturer. He also has a full-time practice in the city as a therapist. Growing up with a strong Christian family environment led to an interest in developing an alternative respectful and spiritually supportive therapy for Christians which could be available from 'non-Christian' resources. It is a practice which seeks to honour Christian tradition but stand apart from theological debate.

Stephen Patrick Madigan is the Director of Narrative Therapy Training at Yaletown Family Therapy in Vancouver, and co-director of the Toronto Narrative Therapy Project in Toronto, Canada.

John Morss studied psychology in the UK, and taught at the University of Ulster before moving to New Zealand. He is currently senior lecturer in the Department of Education, University of Otago. His interests are in the critical psychology of development and he is now working on deconstructionist and anarchist approaches to psychology. His previous books are *The Biologising of Childhood* (Erlbaum, 1990) and *Growing Critical* (Routledge, 1995).

Maria Nichterlein studied psychology in Chile where she also did clinical postgraduate studies in systemic approaches to therapy. She is currently working as a family therapist at Children, Adolescents and their Families Mental Health Services, Dunedin Public Hospital, New Zealand. Before her immigration to NZ, she lived for eight years in Adelaide, South Australia where she worked as a family therapist, as a marriage counsellor and as a student counsellor at the University of Adelaide. During those years, she was also involved in the Management Committee of Migrant Women Emergency Services (a service focused on helping migrant women fleeing from situations of domestic violence) and in the formation of the Federation of Spanish Speaking Com-munities of South Australia.

Ian Parker is Professor of Psychology at Bolton Institute, where he is co-director of the Discourse Unit and programme leader for the MSc in Critical Psychology.

Eero Riikonen is a psychiatrist, and worked 1980–9 in the public mental health sector and as a manager of the Finnish Suicide Prevention Centre. In 1989–94 he was a researcher and 1994–6 a development manager in The Rehabilitation Foundation. From 1996 onwards he has been a development manager in the National Research and Development Centre for Welfare and Health (Stakes). His current work links with planning national mental health projects, outlining the European Mental Health Agenda and coordinating the activities of the European Network of Mental Health Policy.

Vanessa Swan has recently been appointed to the position of regional director of Women's Health at Adelaide Central Community Health Service in Australia, a position she will take up in 1999. She is currently working as a therapist and trainer at Yaletown Family Therapy in Vancouver, Canada.

Sara Vataja is a child psychiatrist, and has worked in clinical settings in both child and adult psychiatry. She has been involved with various research and development projects linked with solution and resource-oriented approaches. From 1994 she has been the manager of the VAK Project (centre for resource-oriented client work) funded by the Finnish Social Security Institute and based in Helsinki. Currently she is involved with a project funded by the Ministry of Social Affairs and Health that develops telematic applications for the social integration and promotion of mental health.

1

DECONSTRUCTION AND PSYCHOTHERAPY

Ian Parker

This book takes the narrative turn in psychotherapy a significant step forward. It includes a sustained reflection on the role of psychotherapy in contemporary culture, drawing on the writings of Jacques Derrida and Michel Foucault, and the development of critiques of language in psychotherapy that attend to the interweaving of meaning and power and which together unravel attempts to reveal hidden personal truth. These critical perspectives also show how it is possible to find a place for reflection, resistance and agency to create a transformative therapeutic practice. These tasks are intertwined, and we find aspects of each of them teased through in different ways from different vantage points in the chapters.

Our narrative is located in the context of discursive and postmodern approaches (e.g. MacDonnell, 1986; Weedon, 1987; Doherty et al., 1992). Although 'narrative', 'discursive' and 'postmodern' are often run together, as if they were equivalent or as if they led to the same kind of practice, we use them here to shift our attention away from narrative in the therapeutic encounter as such to include reflection on the way the therapeutic encounter itself is storied into being. We want to ask how psychotherapy is constructed moment by moment as people speak in certain ways *and* how the practice of psychotherapy is constructed as a kind of practice in which people believe they should speak like that (e.g. Siegfried, 1995; Pilgrim, 1997). An increasing attention to the range of narrative approaches in psychotherapy and the social construction of psychotherapy among practitioners and academics has provided the 'conditions of possibility' for these questions to be asked (e.g. McNamee and Gergen, 1992; McLeod, 1997; Monk et al., 1997). To address these questions we move from the construction of therapeutic discourse to its *deconstruction*.

Deconstruction is an intensely critical mode of reading systems of meaning and unravelling the way these systems work as 'texts'. Texts lure the reader into taking certain notions for granted and privileging certain ways of being over others. Forms of psychotherapy which take their cue from psychiatric or psychological systems, whether these are behaviourist, cognitive or psychoanalytic, also take for granted descriptions of pathology which often oppress people as they pretend to help them. Deconstructive unravelling works through a kind of anti-method which resists a definition or prescription, for it is looking for how a 'problem' is produced the way it is rather than wanting to pin it down and say *this* is what it really is (Derrida, 1983). As we read any text, including texts about 'deconstruction', we look for the ways in which our understanding and room for movement is limited by the 'lines of force' operating in discourse, and this invitation to attend to the role of power in defining problems leads many critical readers to connect Derrida's (1980) comments on these limits with Foucault's (1980) historical work. This also leads us to explore the way in which our own understanding of problems is *located* in discourse, and we must then reflect on how we make and may remake our lives through moral-political projects which are embedded in a sense of justice (Derrida, 1994) rather than given psychiatric diagnoses.

The conceptual apparatus of deconstruction in the theory and practice of psychotherapy is becoming increasingly popular amongst therapists working with 'problems' understood as narrative constructions rather than as properties of pathological personalities, and as embedded in discursive practices rather than flowing from developmental deficits (e.g. White, 1991; Lax, 1992; Parker, 1998a). It is also influential among a growing number of counsellors and helpers working in mental health support services generally who want to work with clients in ways that will facilitate challenges to oppression and processes of emancipation (e.g. White, 1991; McKenzie and Monk, 1997). Most of this work steps back from deconstructing the project of psychotherapy (e.g. White, 1991), but this step forward is one we think worth making. In this book deconstruction is brought to bear on the key conceptual and pragmatic issues that therapists face, and the project of therapy is opened up to critical inquiry and reflection.

I will start with a brief review of the connections between deconstruction and psychotherapy. This is not with a view to dismantling psychotherapy so that it can then simply be 'reconstructed', but with the aim of developing an account of something different, a 'deconstructing psychotherapy' as a practice that is always *in process* rather than something fixed, a movement of reflexive critique rather than a stable set of techniques. We will sometimes use the term 're-constructing', but this is as a provisional tactic to help us move forward rather than a grand strategy to solve all the problems and close questioning down. This kind of practice is already present in the world, and the chapters in this book thread their way through the ways it works.

Sources and Contexts

The contributors to the book thread together a picture of therapy as a practice that is both respectful and critical. This double-sided process is complex and contradictory.

On the one hand, deconstructing psychotherapy is profoundly *respectful*. The therapeutic practices that are woven together here attempt to do justice to the stories people tell about their distress, the experience they have of problems of living and the struggles they are already embarking upon when they first encounter a counsellor or psychotherapist. The task is to engage with a narrative that seems to all intents and purposes 'problem saturated' and to work *within* it (White, 1989a). Those working in this approach acknowledge the complexity of the narrative precisely so that the contradictions can be opened out and used to bring forth something different, some 'unique outcome' that was always hidden as a possibility but needed a particular kind of sustained reflection to find it sparkling in the undergrowth (White, 1991, 1995a).

Important here is an attention to *contradiction*, for as people struggle with and rework their problems and trace through the patterns they make in their accounts, they find themselves elaborating different competing perspectives. These narrative perspectives are sometimes aligned so that they seem to lie side by side and fit together, but there is a tension as they try and make us see the world in different ways at one and the same time. There is always, at least, a kind of narrative at work which takes up one kind of perspective which works from the standpoint of the problem and which is intent on holding the person in its grip. And against this it is always possible to find another narrative which takes up a perspective which flows from the standpoint of the person who is always trying to find ways of shaking the problem and perhaps escaping from it altogether. To be 'respectful', then, does not mean abandoning a standpoint, but it does mean acknowledging where we stand (Riikonen and Smith, 1997; Winslade et al., 1997).

On the other hand, deconstructing psychotherapy is intensely *critical*. Therapeutic practices are embedded in images of the self and others that systematically mislead us as to the nature of problems. Deconstruction in therapy does not presuppose a self under the surface, and a deconstruction of therapy alerts us to the way such a notion of the self can unwittingly be smuggled in as some people 'help' others. Narratives of mental distress can all too quickly lock us back into the problem at the very moment that we think we have found a way out. So, the task of the deconstructing therapist, and just as much so the deconstructing client, is to locate the problem in certain cultural practices, and comprehend the role of patterns of power in setting out positions for people which serve to reinforce the idea that they can do nothing about it themselves (Madigan, 1992; Allen, 1993). In this respect, of course, there is a close connection with the kind of work which has been developed by feminist therapists (Seu and Heenan, 1998).

There is also an attention to contradiction here, and it is only by working through the spaces of resistance opened out by competing accounts and alternative practices that it is possible to find a lever for change. We are always already embedded in a particular set of perspectives, operating from within certain positions when we try to understand ourselves and others. To be 'critical', then, does not mean finding the correct standpoint, but it means understanding how we come to stand where we are (e.g. Griffith and Griffith, 1992). This is where a concern with justice in therapy becomes intertwined with a concern for social justice in the world that has made therapy necessary. Critical movements in the deconstruction of power in therapy are also engaged in opening up their work to the broader sociopolitical realm (e.g. Chasin and Herzig, 1994).

Dialectics and Deconstruction: The Personal and the Political

We could say that the tensions that make 'respectful' work in deconstructing psychotherapy possible and which allow us to create something better in a narrative which is not problem saturated, and the tensions that make 'critical' work possible and make it possible to understand how we have been able to move from one narrative to another, are 'dialectical'. And the relationship between being respectful and being critical is also dialectical. These are dialectical relationships because they are contradictory and necessarily interrelated. The threads are knotted together in the picture we have of the problem and our practice such that they only take the tangled shape they do because they exist *together*, around each other. They exist as a 'unity of opposites', and they are played out in individual lives through certain idiosyncratic themes in a dynamic 'strategy of tension'. Like the disturbing interplay of dialogue and violence that pervades much contemporary politics, this strategy of tension is both the very condition for us being able to move in one direction or another in our relationships with each other in times of peace and, at moments in all our lives, it is the setting for a terrorizing arena of seemingly unending painful interpersonal conflict.

The advantage of this dialectical metaphor is that it connects the personal and the political. The development of this current of work raises once again the possibility, oft dreamt about in the feminist and socialist movements, of an approach to *individual* and *social* distress which links the two, and a view of relationships which understands the personal as political without reducing one to the other (Rowbotham et al., 1979). The search for a connection between these two spheres has led many psychotherapists from work with individual clients to an engagement with social structural problems, and it has also led many political activists into the realm of therapy to trace the ways oppression is reconfigured and reproduced at a personal level.

However, the problem with the 'dialectical' metaphor is two-fold. It can threaten to leave us with a detailed description of a complicated interrelationship with no practical suggestion for a way out. This has been the limitation of approaches from within Marxism that have attempted to engage with psychotherapy (e.g. Cohen, 1986), and practitioners in this theoretical tradition have often, as a result, been very suspicious of the whole enterprise of therapeutic professionalism (e.g. Pilgrim, 1992). The dialectical metaphor can also lead us to the comforting and paralysing thought that there is nothing we can do now, but that we will one day be able to trace our way through to the synthesis of the oppositions and resolve the contradictions. In this account, we would have to wait until a profound change in the social order, for a revolution, before we would be able to move from a description of the structure of the problem to its resolution.

But we cannot wait, and those working at the intersection of deconstruction and psychotherapy (and of course this intersection itself could be understood dialectically) are taking us through a way of working with the personal and the political which carries some of the force of socialist feminist visions of personal political activity which is always already 'prefigurative'; it anticipates forms of emancipated living that we hope to experience in the future, even after 'the revolution' perhaps, in the way we conduct our struggle to arrive there, the way we live now (Rowbotham et al., 1979). An assumption underpinning this 'prefigurative politics' is that, in any case, we will never be able to arrive at something better unless the *means* we employ are consonant with the *ends* we desire.

Perhaps the metaphor of 'deconstruction' is more apposite here then. That is the wager of this book, and for most of the contributors it invites a connection between the political and the personal which is *more* radical and practical than approaches derived so far from dialectics (cf. Dreier, 1997; Newman and Holzman, 1997). There are affinities between dialectics and deconstruction (Ryan, 1982), and it may be possible to quilt them together into 'a marxist feminist practical deconstruction' which simultaneously respects and carries forward the series of critiques that have emerged from postcolonial writing (Spivak, 1990). But deconstruction also promises us something more liberating, something open enough to respect our personal experience of conflict and the contradictions that we live as we either bend to oppression or try to break it.

So, how do we move between respect and critique, and how is deconstruction helpful in describing and unravelling this, and what should deconstructing psychotherapy look like? Well, there are different ways of telling the story about how we could answer these questions. This is not to say that we should plait the threads together to arrive at one place. We can find different stories about deconstruction and psychotherapy in different places, and those different stories lead us in different directions. The crossed paths of deconstruction and psychotherapy in two different institutional arenas, critical family therapy and critical psychology, will serve to highlight some common concerns.

Critical Family Therapy

The first path to deconstructing psychotherapy is in the broad field of family therapy. A sensitivity to the intentional and unintentional abuse of power in family therapy in the 1970s, and critical reflection on the unwillingness or inability of practitioners to address this issue has led to an influential current of work which promises something new and genuinely transformative.

Here the central defining problematic was one of *communication*. There was a critical impetus in this work toward questions of culture which we find marked at quite an early stage in the work of Bateson (1972) and Laing (1964), for example. Patterns of communication and miscommunication in families function in such a way as to produce complex systems of 'double binds' and unbearable 'knots' which lead to certain members being identified as the ones with the pathology. A pathological system can survive very efficiently if it can persuade one of its members that they are responsible and they themselves contain the problem. Traditions of 'structural' family therapy, which encouraged experts to operate as the saviours who might analyse and change alliances within the family (Minuchin, 1974), and then 'systemic' family therapy, which employed forms of questioning to reveal and reconfigure pathology in the family (e.g. Selvini et al., 1978; Cecchin et al., 1993), still tended to operate at the level of the family. This was the case even for the most radical anti-psychiatric sectors of this tradition, and the family itself was pathologized by the therapist as thoroughly as the family had pathologized its index patient (Jacoby, 1975). There was a way out, but it meant taking a step up and a step back.

MEANING AND POWER   First, the step up. The therapist had to be able to move up a level in their understanding of patterns of communication to see the family as part of a network of meanings. Families absorb and reproduce images of pathology that are present in the culture, and these images are held in place by patterns of meaning that are interlaced with patterns of power. The privilege that is given to certain terms in certain oppositions in patterns of meaning is something that had already been worried away at in literary theory and philosophy, particularly in the work of Derrida (e.g. 1978, 1981). And so the model of 'text', of the family as a text that could be read and rewritten in the context of the wider culture, was an important resource. It is to Derrida, for good or ill, that we owe the term 'deconstruction'. A de-construction is a process of critical reading and unravelling of terms, loaded terms and tensions between terms that construct how we read our place in culture and in our families and in our relationships, and how we think about who we are and what it might be possible for us to be. And so the province of literary theory, in critical reflection on reading and writing, and philosophy, in critical reflection on thinking and being, can be laced together in a profoundly practical way (Epston and White, 1989; White and Epston, 1990).

But there is more to it than this, for these family therapists were not engaged in a mere literary or philosophical exercise. To become a practical deconstruction in process in psychotherapy in the service of challenging pathology and changing lives Derrida himself had to be read alongside writers who were concerned with systems of communication as being embedded in systems of power. We can find in Foucault's (1971, 1977, 1981) work, at this point, a way of reflecting on the uncanny similarity between analyses of 'double binds' and 'knots' in families and paralysing contradictory messages that traverse a culture and position individuals within various discourses and discursive practices (Parker, 1989). At the level of the family we already had descriptions of the way that a 'schizophrenogenic' mother may simultaneously demand that her child show affection and then recoil at every embrace so that the child is attracted and repelled and so may be made mad (Bateson, 1972). Similarly, when we read Foucault (1977, 1981) we find descriptions of the way Western culture contains apparatuses which incite us to speak about our dirty depths and immediately shames us for speaking thus. We confess and are disciplined, and so then some of us are subject to 'dividing practices' and forms of incarceration which confirm that we must all always be frightened of falling into the realms of the mad (Foucault, 1971). Foucault also encourages a critical reflexive twist in this account so that we are able to understand better how 'madness' itself and 'bad mothers' who make madness are constructions which bewitch us into blaming the victims (Parker et al., 1995). This theoretical framework is invaluable for helping us understand the apparatus of psychiatry and the power of the 'spy-chiatric gaze' (Madigan and Epston, 1995).

Narrative approaches to distress which emerged from systemic family therapy in the 1980s have been linked in a number of recent texts with wider 'postmodern' debates across the human sciences (e.g. McNamee and Gergen, 1992). These developments have enabled practitioners in the fields of psychotherapy and counselling to draw upon theories of discourse and power in order to construct new forms of helping (Monk et al., 1997). The 'deconstruction' of the problem that the client presents has, in some of the variants of this approach, been the focus of therapeutic work (e.g. White, 1991). Some recent developments in narrative therapy have moved toward a 'solution-focused' approach to preempt the framing and reification of the issue of concern as a 'problem' (de

Shazer, 1985). Here any talk about 'problems' is eschewed, and the therapist deconstructs the categories the client may employ to make it seem as if there is a problem (de Shazer, 1991). Other more radical strands of work have preferred to take the problem seriously and to treat the problem as the problem. Instead of trying to deconstruct it away by refusing to talk about it, these strands of work focus on how the 'problem' is constituted in networks of discourse and power that position the client as helpless and as believing that the problem lies inside them (Chang and Phillips, 1993; White, 1995a).

REFLEXIVITY AND RESPONSIBILITY   So, second, the step back. At this point many family therapists came to see that they themselves were part of the 'system'. An engagement with a family in distress, an analysis of their pathology, an attempt to change patterns of communication, were each and all implicated in a kind of relationship which would serve both to reproduce and transform what was going on (Cecchin, 1992). Systems of one-way mirrors through which the family could be observed and reflected upon within the compass of the professional gaze hardly served to solve this problem. The position of the therapist as a reflexive critical participating actor had to be included in analysis, and so new practices of accountability started to be developed (White, 1995b).

These practices have included innovations like the 'reflecting team', in which the therapist becomes the object of study (White, 1995c). They have encouraged an opening up of professional psychiatric practice to make it visible (e.g. Pilkington and Fraser, 1992; Simblett, 1997). These practices have also led to reflections on the way issues of power and boundaries between client and therapist serve to warrant forms of professional abuse and mystification of 'experts' (e.g. Lobovits and Freeman, 1993). This then connects with debates about 'professionaliza-tion' and the way institutions which govern therapy protect the pro-fessionals under cover of a rhetoric of protecting patients (Mowbray, 1995; House and Totton, 1997). This stepping back has also, of necessity, required a reflection on the cultural assumptions that underpin the very task of 'psychotherapy', and the ways in which the therapist will always be reconstructing forms of pathology if they allow themselves to imagine that they are neutral disinterested professionals, and if they do not engage in a process of deconstruction with the communities they are part of (e.g. Tamasese and Waldegrave, 1996).

Readings and writings are always located in institutions, and the location of family therapy as an institution which was marginal to psy-chiatry permitted a flowering of critical work. The kinds of questions that have emerged within this institution have been framed by a par-ticular context. The critical impetus has been driven by an attempt to be more respectful. Instead of the index patient or the pathological family system being treated as an object of the gaze of the expert, these pro-gressive tendencies within family therapy have located the family in culture and located themselves in the same culture in order to construct an emancipatory feminist socialist humanist practice. These are the stakes of 'social justice' initiatives in this work, and the attempt to connect what goes on in therapy with what goes on in the world (e.g. Waldegrave, 1990; Grieves, 1997). A critical stance has been crucial here, and it has been in the service of respect for the lived realities of clients.

Critical Psychology

The discipline of psychology too has seen a progressive turn to narrative in the last twenty years. This has been manifested in a turn to language and then a turn to discourse which has shifted attention from what goes on inside people's heads to the way that the narrative positions they adopt constitutes them as 'having' certain psychological states (Gergen, 1985; Harré, 1986; Davies and Harré, 1990; Parker, 1997). Psychologists are then able to recognize these states as being the things they can predict and control, and this then constitutes individuals as subjects of the wider apparatus of surveillance and regulation in Western culture that psychology feeds upon and operates within. Each and every phenomenon that psychology takes for granted and uses to normalize and pathologize people can be shown to be socially constructed (Burr, 1995), and debates over what is 'real' now in critical psychology revolve around our understanding of the social context for the production of mental states rather than whether they are universal and essential (Parker, 1998b).

CONTEXT Foucault's (1977, 1981) work has been valuable here in showing how the twin tendencies of discipline and confession lock people together in such a way that the discipline of psychology becomes seen as a necessity, and is then able to pose as a solution. Psychologists are encouraged to think that they are able to change things, but they are part of a dense network, the 'psy-complex'. This network comprises the theories and practices which locate thinking and feeling inside individuals (Ingleby, 1985; Rose, 1985). Psychologists systematically delude themselves about their power in this apparatus, and this makes it all the more difficult for them to develop a critical reflection on the role power plays in people's experience of distress and their fraught relationships with professionals who are trying to help them.

The hope of many students early in their career in psychology is that they will be able to 'help' people. This is well-meaning, but we need to be careful about where it might lead. Why? First because there is the hope that 'help' is something that can be dispensed, and all the more effectively if an expert knowledge can be employed. The language that is used to frame the positions of those who 'help' and those who are 'helped' is deceptive (Gronemeyer, 1992). Even the word 'empowerment' betrays something of the position of the expert who thinks that they have been able to move an enlightened step beyond 'helping' people but cannot give up the idea that it is possible to bend down to lift someone lesser than themselves up a step, to give them a little empowerment (cf. Bhavnani, 1990).

Second, the idea that psychology can be used to help people is naive because it rests on the belief that the discipline is a neutral collection of tools which can be taken to help people if they are used wisely, or, perhaps, in rare cases, to harm people if used with ill intent. Psychology itself plays a paradoxical, duplicitous role here, for it both encourages the idea that it is best placed to help people suffering from mental distress, and we find this idea peddled with most enthusiasm in the attempts of the discipline to colonize therapeutic work through 'counselling psychology' (Woolfe, 1985). It then systematically crushes the aspirations of the well-meaning student as it repeatedly positions them as the 'experimentor' or 'researcher' who does things to other people (Burman et al., 1996a). The only way critical psychologists can tackle this problem is, as a first step at least, to read *themselves* into the problem.

SUBJECTIVITY   The role of subjectivity in critical psychology has come to the fore in the development of qualitative approaches (e.g. Banister et al., 1994; Henwood and Parker, 1994). This has made it possible for some psychologists to turn around and reflect on the way they tell stories about people rather than pretending that they are 'discovering' facts about behaviour. The research process is then opened up to the activity of interpretation, and an increasing number of psychologists are then able to realize that an interpretation calls upon their own place in the phenomenon. They are then no longer distanced neutral observers, but part of what they are studying, taking responsibility for the sense they are making.

The turn to language and discourse in qualitative research has been profoundly influenced by feminism, for feminists attend to questions of power as they flow from the big political arenas through to our experience of our own position as gendered subjects and back again. There has been a growth of critical reflection on psychological practice as gendered and as structured by images of culture and class (e.g. Burman et al., 1996b), and 'feminist psychology' itself has then been subject to critical reflection, to deconstruction (Burman, 1998). Critical psychology is then able to work with complex notions of power and subjectivity, and the link between social structural change and therapeutic work is then put on the agenda. This reflexive turn has thus been connected with the turn to discourse in the discipline, and they have together opened up a space for a reconsideration of the practice of psychotherapy (e.g. Hare-Mustin and Maracek, 1997).

The development of these critical tendencies in psychology has been conditioned by their institutional location. Just as critical family therapists were driven to ask certain questions about their practice because of the context they were working in, so critical psychologists have been profoundly affected by the way their discipline encourages them to think, and their particular arenas for resistance to those dominant practices. The attempt to find a way back to helping people and to respecting them has been through the development of critical work.

The emergence of deconstruction in different institutional locations has also served to remind us that 'deconstruction' is not a single thing, and cannot be summed up in a neat definition or be put to work as a discrete technique. Deconstruction is a form of questioning, a processual activity that defies definition, and it is marked by the very forms of *difference* that it theorizes (Derrida, 1983). Derrida (1994) has recently reminded us that deconstruction should not be reduced to simply talking about difference, and if we are to avoid getting bogged down in the quagmire of relativism in academic 'radical' psychology (e.g. Parker, 1998b) we also need to put deconstruction to work practically to really make a difference.

Theory, Practice and Critical Reflection

This book ranges across the various ways in which (i) deconstruction can be used *in* psychotherapy as part of the process of exploring problems and 're-constructing' how they function in the stories people tell, (ii) deconstruction can be used *as* psychotherapy in the reworking of the relationship between therapist and client to address issues of power, and (iii) deconstruction *of* psychotherapy can be developed to reflect critically upon the role of this modern enterprise of helping and exper-tise applied to the distress in people's lives. Let us take each of these in turn in order to present one version of the narrative of the book.

Deconstruction in Psychotherapy: Conceptual Frames

Ideas from the broad field of deconstruction have been used to support and extend the range of techniques in narrative therapy. Here 'decon-struction' appears in psychotherapy as a system of concepts that can be directly useful in conceptualizing what is going on and moving things forward (Madigan, 1992). We might even be tempted to think of these ideas as operating as discrete tactics, and indeed they are sometimes used in that way. They can appear as kinds of questioning and refram-ing, as the externalizing of problems (White, 1989b; Roth and Epston, 1996; Stacey, 1997) and internalizing of invisible friends (Epston, 1993). Here deconstruction itself is an invisible friend that has been taken into the process of psychotherapy and assisted a progressive reworking of the encounter and the institution. Instead of simply reconstructing psy-chotherapy, however, and moving from the use of critical ideas to the improvement of therapeutic practice, important though that may be, we are moving in the other direction, and we keep our 're-construction' at work as a provisional tactical activity. Our 're-construction' is in the service of deconstructing the resources that are already starting to be sedimented in narrative therapies, externalizing those resources to make them visible.

Part I of the book – 'Sources and Contexts for the Deconstructive Turn' – reviews the institutional settings and theoretical resources for the development of deconstruction in therapy. The five chapters focus, in turn, on Narrative Therapy, Foucault, Derrida, Postmodernism and Feminism. John Kaye sets out some of the foundations of the turn to narrative in family therapy, and traces the development of what might be called 'discursive therapy'. We are then able to appreciate connections between different versions of narrative therapy that have embraced deconstructive ideas. Glenn Larner explores the relevance of Derrida to psychotherapy, and his concern is immediately with questions of power, and the way 'deconstructing psychotherapy' operates as a form of intervention and the creation of an 'ethical-political space'. Vincent Fish focuses on the work of Foucault, and argues that any use of Foucault's work in psychotherapy as part of a progressive deconstructive approach must also employ 'a realist, historicist, anti-ideological lens'. Roger Lowe's examination of postmodernism as 'a transitional context' for critical work in psychotherapy makes it clear that any reading of deconstruction has to be reflexive, and we need to be ready to disturb it when it seems to be settling too easily into an existing institutional structure. Finally, Nollaig O'Reilly Byrne and Imelda Colgan McCarthy situate the turn to discourse and deconstruction in the context of feminist therapy and an insistence that an awareness of power must suffuse any perspective that aims to be critical. This chapter leads us to reflections on the ways theoretical resources and institutional contexts open up or close down possibilities for the development of deconstructive practice in therapy, and the way deconstruction can help us 'destabilize sites of oppression'.

Motifs of power and critique recur in the first part of the book on conceptual foundations of deconstruction in psychotherapy, and they reappear, of course, in our accounts of practice in the second part.

Deconstruction as Psychotherapy: Pragmatic Moves

These ideas could well be sedimented into sets of techniques, but then our understanding of power within the therapeutic encounter itself would be stripped away. So, we always keep the work of 'deconstructing psychotherapy' as a process, and Part II – 'Deconstruction in Practice' – provides practical examples of the way radical transformations of discourse and power can address, respect and question forms of identity, of gender, faith and identity. This part of the book elaborates critical reflections on the ways in which different cultural contexts and different notions of self and happiness provide a variety of resources for the development of helping narratives and practices in therapy.

Vanessa Swan reviews the way Foucault's work has been useful in her own work with a woman struggling with a story of worthlessness which dominated her conception of self, and the way contradictions could be opened up to bring to light 'previously obscured ideas'. She then argues, against some recent feminist critiques of therapy, that this approach is able to work at the intersection of the personal and the political without reducing one to the other. Ian Law takes up the other side of the task, 'to address and challenge the effects and practices of male privilege', and he shows how deconstructing psychotherapy can focus on forms of oppression that are relayed through the political and personal spheres, and how they may be made visible. The complex relationship between respect and critique is also an important theme in Wendy Drewery's chapter, written with Wally McKenzie, which focuses on therapy with Christian clients to explore how it is possible both to 'de-construct' the forms of narrative and practice that define a person's identity and to work with people as 'agents of their own lives'. Stephen Madigan also traces a narrative of agency in his account of the transition of a client in a difficult and pathologizing medical environment from being a 'Patient without Knowledge' to being a 'Person with Knowledge'.

We take care through the discussions and critical reflections that comprise the book to respect deconstruction as a strategy of reading which aims not to devalue the agency of the individual subject, but to *locate* it. However, we also need to locate our own practice, and we turn to this task in the third part of the book.

Deconstruction of Psychotherapy: Critical Reflection

We can use the notions explored so far reflexively to step back and explore the possibilities for linking deconstruction with political transformation, and questioning the role that the therapeutic encounter plays in that process. Part III – 'Deconstructing Psychotherapeutic Discourse' – explores the way deconstruction can operate to question traditional problem categories, and the degree to which deconstruction may be used to question the enterprise of therapy itself. John Morss and Maria Nichterlein warn against 'the temptation to emancipate' which always beckons a therapist using the old tricks and which still lies waiting for enthusiastic deconstructive therapists who think they have found the true path. Eero Riikonen and Sara Vataja then problematize the whole project of psychotherapy, including deconstructive versions, and move from outcome studies, which fail to show that psychotherapy is good for people, to accounts of language which seem to suggest that we are mistaken in thinking that any technique, deconstruction included, can lead us to 'happy dialogue'.

The contributors to the book come from Australia, Canada, Finland, Ireland, New Zealand, and the United States. Different institutional contexts pose different questions, and deconstruction in psychotherapy certainly takes different forms in different parts of the world. It would be possible, perhaps, to draw a strict dividing line between pragmatic pluralist ways of reading 'problems' (e.g. de Shazer, 1985, 1991) and the more radical interventions in discourse and power that are represented here. We could then see these as mapped, respectively, on to North American and European versions of deconstruction in literary theory (Eagleton, 1983; Cohen, 1996). These differences are important, and the book is concerned with externalizing the conceptual resources that have been important to all those working with narrative ideas so that we can bring out their radical character. There are also severe critiques of the more 'radical' forms of deconstructive work in psychotherapy from within the United States (e.g. Luepnitz, 1992; Fish, 1993). We do take seriously the pragmatic humanist impulse of North American therapeutic deconstruction, and this book should be read as a creative and critical deconstructive dialogue with friends who have paved the way for an attention to the construction of 'problems' and power.

You will find some of those critical readers writing in this book, and we hope you will join us and read their contributions critically too. There are, of course, tensions between the different narratives woven together in the following chapters, and they will appear sometimes as a latticework so they seem to interleave neatly as they move across each other. You will also notice direct contradictions, however, and be able to imagine a number of disagreements about interpretations of deconstruction. My account in this first chapter also pretends to synthesize some of the threads, and you can imagine the contributors reading it critically, disagreeing with its account of their work, and deconstructing its narrative of their narratives. And whatever route you take through the book, we imagine that you will construct your own picture of the process of deconstructing psychotherapy.

Note

Many thanks to Dan Goodley and Dave Harper for their practical deconstruction of an earlier version of this chapter.

References

Allen, L. (1993) 'The politics of therapy: an interview with Michael White', *Human Systems: The Journal of Systemic Consultation and Management*, 4: 19–32.
Banister, P., Burman, E., Parker, I., Taylor, M. and Tindall, C. (1994) *Qualitative Methods in Psychology: A Research Guide*. Buckingham: Open University Press.

Bateson, G. (1972) *Steps to an Ecology of Mind*. New York: Ballantine.

Bhavnani, K.-K. (1990) 'What's power got to do with it? Empowerment and social research', in I. Parker and J. Shotter (eds), *Deconstructing Social Psychology*. London: Routledge.

Burman, E. (ed.) (1998) *Deconstructing Feminist Psychology*. London: Sage.

Burman, E., Aitken, G., Alldred, P., Allwood, R., Billington, T., Goldberg, B., Gordo-López, A. J., Heenan, C., Marks, D. and Warner, S. (1996a) *Psychology Discourse Practice: From Regulation to Resistance*. London: Taylor & Francis.

Burman, E., Alldred, P., Bewley, C., Goldberg, B., Heenan, C., Marks, D., Marshall, J., Taylor, K., Ullah, R. and Warner, S. (1996b) *Challenging Women: Psychology's Exclusions, Feminist Possibilities*. Buckingham: Open University Press.

Burr, V. (1995) *An Introduction to Social Constructionism*. London: Routledge.

Cecchin, G. (1992) 'Constructing therapeutic possibilities', in S. McNamee and K.J. Gergen (eds), *Therapy as Social Construction*. London: Sage.

Cecchin, G., Lane, G. and Ray, W.A. (1993) 'From strategizing to non-intervention: toward irreverence in systemic practice', *Journal of Marital and Family Therapy*, 19: 125–36.

Chang, J. and Phillips, M. (1993) 'Michael White and Steve de Shazer: new directions in family therapy', in S. Gilligan and R. Price (eds), *Therapeutic Conversations*. New York: Norton.

Chasin, R. and Herzig, M. (1994) 'Creating systemic interventions for the sociopolitical arena', in B.B. Gould and D.H. DeMuth (eds), *The Global Family Therapist: Integrating the Personal, Professional, and Political*. New York: Allyn and Bacon.

Cohen, C.I. (1986) 'Marxism and psychotherapy', *Science and Society*, 1 (1): 4–24.

Cohen, T. (1996) 'The ideology of dialogue: the Bakhtin/De Man (dis)connection', *Cultural Critique*, 33: 41–86.

Davies, B. and Harré, R. (1990) '"Positioning": the discursive production of selves', *Journal for the Theory of Social Behaviour*, 20 (1): 43–63.

Derrida, J. (1978) *Writing and Difference*. London: Routledge & Kegan Paul.

Derrida, J. (1980) 'An interview', *The Literary Review*, 14: 21–2.

Derrida, J. (1981) *Positions*. London: Athlone Press.

Derrida, J. (1983) 'Letter to a Japanese friend', in D. Wood and R. Bernasconi (eds), *Derrida and Différance*. Evanston, IL: Northwestern University Press.

Derrida, J. (1994) 'Spectres of Marx', *New Left Review*, 205: 31–58.

de Shazer, S. (1985) *Keys to Solution in Brief Therapy*. New York: Norton.

de Shazer, S. (1991) *Putting Difference to Work*. New York: W.W. Norton & Company.

Doherty, J., Graham, E. and Malek, M. (eds) (1992) *Postmodernism and the Social Sciences*. London: Macmillan.

Dreier, O. (1997) *Subjectivity and Social Practice*. Aarhus: Skriftserie.

Eagleton, T. (1983) *Literary Theory: An Introduction*. Oxford: Blackwell.

Epston, D. (1993) 'Internalizing discourses versus externalizing discourses', in S. Gilligan and R. Price (eds), *Therapeutic Conversations*. New York: Norton.

Epston, D. and White, M. (1989) *Literate Means to Therapeutic Ends*. Adelaide: Dulwich Centre Publications.

Fish, V. (1993) 'Poststructuralism in family therapy: Interrogating the narrative/conversational mode', *Journal of Marital and Family Therapy*, 19 (3): 221–32.

Foucault, M. (1971) *Madness and Civilization*. London: Tavistock Press.

Foucault, M. (1977) *Discipline and Punish: The Birth of the Prison*. London: Allen Lane.

Foucault, M. (1980) *Power/Knowledge: Selected Interviews and Other Writings 1972– 1977*. Brighton: Harvester Press.

Foucault, M. (1981) *The History of Sexuality, Volume One*. Harmondsworth: Penguin.

Gergen, K.J. (1985) 'The social movement in modern psychology', *American Psychologist*, 40: 266–75.

Grieves, L. (1997) 'From beginning to start: the Vancouver Anti-Anorexia League', *Gecko*, 2: 78–88.

Griffith, J. and Griffith, M. (1992) 'Owning one's epistemological stance in therapy', *Dulwich Centre Newsletter*, 1: 5–11.

Gronemeyer, M. (1992) 'Helping', in W. Sachs (ed.), *The Development Dictionary: A Guide to Knowledge as Power*. London: Zed Books.

Hare-Mustin, R.T. and Maracek, J. (1997) 'Abnormal and clinical psychology: the politics of madness', in D. Fox and I. Prilleltensky (eds), *Critical Psychology: An Introduction*. London: Sage.

Harré, R. (ed.) (1986) *The Social Construction of Emotion*. Oxford: Blackwell.

Henwood, K. and Parker, I. (eds) (1994) *Qualitative Social Psychology*. Special Issue of *Journal of Community and Applied Social Psychology*, 4 (4).

House, R. and Totton, N. (eds) (1997) *Implausible Professions: Arguments for Pluralism and Autonomy in Psychotherapy and Counselling*. Ross-on-Wye: PCCS Books.

Ingleby, D. (1985) 'Professionals as socializers: the "psy complex"', *Research in Law, Deviance and Social Control*, 7: 79–109.

Jacoby, R. (1975) *Social Amnesia: A Critique of Conformist Psychology from Adler to Laing*. Hassocks, Sussex: Harvester Press.

Laing, R.D. (1964) *Sanity, Madness and the Family: Families of Schizophrenics*. London: Tavistock.

Laing, R.D. (1970) *Knots*. London: Tavistock.

Lax, W.D. (1992) 'Postmodern thinking in a clinical practice', in S. McNamee and K.J. Gergen (eds), *Therapy as Social Construction*. London: Sage.

Lobovits, D. and Freeman, J.C. (1993) 'Toward collaboration and accountability: alternatives to the dominant discourse for understanding professional sexual exploitation', *Dulwich Centre Newsletter*, 3/4: 33–44.

Luepnitz, D.A. (1992) 'Nothing in common but their first names: the case of Foucault and White', *Journal of Family Therapy*, 14: 281–4.

MacDonnell, D. (1986) *Theories of Discourse: An Introduction*. Oxford: Blackwell.

McKenzie, W. and Monk, G. (1997) 'Learning and teaching narrative ideas', in G. Monk, J. Winslade, K. Crocket and D. Epston (eds), *Narrative Therapy in Practice: The Archaeology of Hope*. San Francisco: Jossey-Bass.

McLeod, J. (1997) *Narrative and Psychotherapy*. London: Sage.

McNamee, S. and Gergen, K.J. (eds) (1992) *Therapy as Social Construction*. London: Sage.

Madigan, S. (1992) 'The application of Michel Foucault's philosophy in the problem externalizing discourse of Michael White', *Journal of Family Therapy*, 14: 265–79.

Madigan, S. and Epston, D. (1995) 'From "psy-chiatric gaze" to communities of concern: from professional monologue to dialogue', in S. Friedman (ed.), *The*

Reflecting Team in Action: Collaborative Practice in Family Therapy. New York: Guilford Press.

Minuchin, S. (1974) *Families and Family Therapy*. London: Tavistock Press.

Monk, G., Winslade, J., Crocket, K. and Epston, D. (eds) (1997) *Narrative Therapy in Practice: The Archaeology of Hope*. San Francisco: Jossey-Bass.

Mowbray, R. (1995) *The Case Against Psychotherapy Registration: A Conversation Issue for the Human Potential Movement*. London: Transmarginal Press.

Newman, F. and Holzman, L. (1997) *The End of Knowing: A New Developmental Way of Learning*. London: Routledge.

Parker, I. (1989) 'Discourse and power', in J. Shotter and K.J. Gergen (eds), *Texts of Identity*. London: Sage.

Parker, I. (1997) 'Discursive Psychology', in D. Fox and I. Prilleltensky (eds), *Critical Psychology: An Introduction*. London: Sage.

Parker, I. (1998a) 'Constructing and deconstructing psychotherapeutic discourse', *European Journal of Psychotherapy, Counselling and Health*, 1 (1): 77–90.

Parker, I. (ed.) (1998b) *Social Constructionism, Discourse and Realism*. London: Sage.

Parker, I., Georgaca, E., Harper, D., McLaughlin, T. and Stowell-Smith, M. (1995) *Deconstructing Psychopathology*. London: Sage.

Pilgrim, D. (1992) 'Psychotherapy and political evasions', in W. Dryden and C. Feltham (eds), *Psychotherapy and its Discontents*. Buckingham: Open University Press.

Pilgrim, D. (1997) *Psychotherapy and Society*. London: Sage.

Pilkington, S. and Fraser, N. (1992) 'Exposing secret biographies', *Dulwich Centre Newsletter*, 1: 12–17.

Riikonen, E. and Smith, G. (1997) *Re-Imagining Therapy: Living Conversations and Relational Knowing*. London: Sage.

Rose, N. (1985) *The Psychological Complex: Psychology, Politics and Society in England 1869–1939*. London: Routledge & Kegan Paul.

Roth, S. and Epston, D. (1996) 'Consulting the problem about the problematic relationship: an exercise for experiencing a relationship with an externalized problem', in M.F. Hoyt (ed.), *Constructive Therapies II*. New York: Guilford.

Rowbotham, S., Segal, L. and Wainwright, H. (1979) *Beyond the Fragments: Feminism and the Making of Socialism*. Newcastle and London: NSC/ICP.

Ryan, M. (1982) *Marxism and Deconstruction: A Critical Articulation*. Baltimore: Johns Hopkins University Press.

Selvini, M., Boscolo, L., Cecchin, G. and Prata, G. (1978) *Paradox and Counter-paradox*. New York: Aronson.

Seu, I.B. and Heenan, M.C. (eds) (1998) *Feminism and Psychotherapy: Reflections on Contemporary Theories and Practices*. London: Sage.

Siegfried, J. (ed.) (1995) *Therapeutic and Everyday Discourse as Behavior Change: Towards a Micro-Analysis in Psychotherapy Process Research*. New York: Ablex.

Simblett, G. (1997) 'Leila and the tiger', in G. Monk, J. Winslade, K. Crocket and D. Epston (eds), *Narrative Therapy in Practice: The Archaeology of Hope*. San Francisco: Jossey-Bass.

Spivak, G.C. (1990) 'Practical politics of the open end', in S. Harasym (ed.), *The Postcolonial Critic: Interviews, Strategies, Dialogues*. London: Routledge.

Stacey, K. (1997) 'Alternative metaphors for externalizing conversations', *Gecko*, 1: 29–51.

Tamasese, K. and Waldegrave, C. (1996) 'Culture and gender accountability in the "Just Therapy" approach', in C. McLean, M. Carey and C. White (eds), *Men's Ways of Being*. Boulder, Colorado: Westview Press.

Waldegrave, C. (1990) 'Just Therapy', *Dulwich Centre Newsletter*, 1: 6–46.

Weedon, C. (1987) *Feminist Practice and Post-structuralist Theory*. Oxford: Blackwell.

White, M. (1989a) 'The externalizing of the problem and the re-authoring of the lives and relationships', in *Selected Papers*. Adelaide: Dulwich Centre Publications.

White, M. (1989b) 'The process of questioning: a therapy of literary merit?', in *Selected Papers*. Adelaide: Dulwich Centre Publications.

White, M. (1991) 'Deconstruction and therapy', *Dulwich Centre Newsletter*, 3: 21–40.

White, M. (1995a) *Re-Authoring Lives: Interviews and Essays*. Adelaide: Dulwich Centre Publications.

White, M. (1995b) 'A conversation about accountability', in *Re-Authoring Lives: Interviews and Essays*. Adelaide: Dulwich Centre Publications.

White, M. (1995c) 'Reflecting teamwork as definitional ceremony', in *Re-Authoring Lives: Interviews and Essays*. Adelaide: Dulwich Centre Publications.

White, M. and Epston, D. (1990) *Narrative Means to Therapeutic Ends*. Adelaide: Dulwich Centre Publications.

Winslade, J., Crocket, K. and Monk, G. (1997) 'The therapeutic relationship', in G. Monk, J. Winslade, K. Crocket and D. Epston (eds), *Narrative Therapy in Practice: The Archaeology of Hope*. San Francisco: Jossey-Bass.

Woolfe, R. (1985) 'What is counselling? Counselling and counselling psychology as an ideology', *BPS Counselling Section Newsletter*, 3 (2): 4–16.

PART I

SOURCES AND CONTEXTS FOR THE DECONSTRUCTIVE TURN

2

TOWARD A NON-REGULATIVE PRAXIS

John Kaye

Can anyone do effective therapy without becoming an instrument of social control, without participating and contributing, often unknowingly, to the construction or the maintenance of a dominant discourse of oppression?

(Gianfranco Cecchin, 1993: ix)

Since its inception, psychotherapy has undergone seemingly dramatic changes in orientation, as have the models derived from these orientations. The most recent of these has occurred over the last decade, largely influenced by the notion that our realities are socially constructed and language-constituted. Language being seen as active and constitutive rather than simply representative, the therapeutic encounter has come to be thought of as a milieu for the creative generation of meaning and therapy itself as a process of semiosis – the forging of new meaning in the context of collaborative discourse (Gergen and Kaye, 1992). Whether this development is a discontinuous one – representing a revolutionary break from the essentialist notions of diagnosing and solving identifiable intrapsychic or intrasystemic problems – is open to question.

A related and equally important issue concerns whether this constructionist development has the potential to contribute to social well-being or whether psychotherapy remains implicitly immured in maintaining the social order, with all its inherent structural inequities. This is particularly pertinent given Hillman and Ventura's (1992: 3) impassioned contention that 'We've had a hundred years of analysis and people are getting more and more sensitive and the world is getting worse and worse'. While many problems reside in personal hurts or conflicts and others in dysfunctional relationship patterns, and while all are individually experienced, Hillman and Ventura's words point to the twin dangers of individualizing the problems people experience whilst ignoring their possible sociocultural base.

This consideration must lead us to question whether the enterprise of psychotherapy is largely trapped in a limiting paradigm by virtue of its focus on the intrapsychic causation of problems to the relative exclusion of a concern with the loss of certainty wrought by a changing world or by structurally ingrained inequities – of class, race, gender, economic deprivation and unfavourable living conditions. While it would be somewhat utopian to expect psychotherapy to attempt to find solutions to the injustices of the world, it is surely not too much to ask that therapists engage with issues of social context, together with the role of social inequities in the causation of psychological distress. It would also be remiss for therapists not to take these issues into account in their work, for as Judith Cross (1994) points out, if we ignore the role played by social inequity, we may inadvertently be acting to ask our troubled consultees to adjust to the unjust.

Further, in focusing on the amelioration of individual pain, we run the risk of implying that the sufferer is in some sense either deficient or responsible for the problem – a form of victim-blaming. At the same time, I question whether the language of psychotherapy is necessarily permeated by concepts of deficit as asserted by critics of modernist practices such as Drewery and Winslade (1997) and Gergen (1994). Similarly, I also question the tendency on the part of some critical theorists and those of a constructionist or narrative persuasion to portray those psychotherapies which locate the source of problems within the person as sinister organs of state control, clandestinely hegemonic, colonizing and reproductive of inequitable power relations.

Psychotherapy as a Normalizing Practice

Most psychotherapeutic practices both treat the individual as the locus of pathology (thereby diverting attention from the role played by socio-cultural factors in the genesis of psychological distress) and are informed by assumptions of:

1   An underlying cause or basis of pathology.
2   The location of this cause within individuals and their relationships.

3   The diagnosability of the problem.
4   Treatability via a specifically designed set of techniques.

Implicit in these suppositions are the concepts of normality and abnormality, the normatively good or bad and the presumption of a true root cause which can be objectively established, known and remediated. Within this frame, psychotherapy can be seen as an instrumental practice consisting of the treatment of what is judged to be mental disorder and abnormal or dysfunctional behaviour. Therapists working within these parameters seek to bring about a restructuring or reprogramming of behaviour in both individuals and families against some criterion of the normal, the deviant, the well-adjusted, the problematic and non-problematic. From this perspective, therapy is concerned with altering established behaviour patterns and belief systems and with the establishment of alternative, more functional or more socially acceptable patterns.

This model of practice has been questioned on both theoretical and politico-ethical grounds. Firstly, models based on notions of normality or abnormality are potentially pathologizing. As Gergen (1991) has pointed out, the assumption of a problem residing in the individual together with a language of deficit or deficiency can be iatrogenic, leading to what he calls 'a spiral of infirmity'. The act of helping too is problematic. Most psychotherapies incorporate a theory of function and dysfunction as well as an associated set of activities whereby it is assumed that change can be induced in another by the specially trained and accredited. Therapeutic activity in this frame:

1   Involves the exploration and examination of the consultee's story within the terms of the therapist's frame of reference.
2   Attempts to engage the other actively in the process of reinterpreting their narrative within the therapist's frame, developing new behaviours in accord with it.

As I have written elsewhere (Kaye, 1996), this conceptualization perpetuates the concept of the therapist as having privileged knowledge, a socially accredited expert who can both provide an authoritative true version of a problem and act according to a set of prescribed activities to correct it. In practice this gives rise to a top-down and instrumental therapist-centred activity – one in which the therapist acts instrumentally via dialogue on the 'client's' narrative and behaviour in order to change it rather than working collaboratively together with the 'client' toward new solutions which the 'client' finds fitting.

The issues thus far discussed raise valid questions about the relative innocence or sociocultural neutrality of therapy. For the issue of what constitutes the normal or the deviant, the functional or dysfunctional is as much a sociocultural variable as a medico-psychological constant. To understand this, one need only trace the changes in DSM categories over the years as these follow changes in socially constructed attitudes and mores. More theoretically, as Ian John (1998: 26) has cogently argued,

> psychological knowledge of any description, whether scientifically authorised or not, is itself in the world, or a part of the world. Like the psychological enterprise that revolves around it, it is shaped and constrained by social forces. It bears the marks of the culture from which it has arisen and is at the same time a constituent element of that culture. Neither the knowledge, or the enterprise, are part of a natural order that stands outside of society, and it cannot be assumed that they are necessarily benign, benificent or emancipatory.

Psychotherapy is not informed only by a technico-rational repertoire; it embodies both a moral-ethical discursive formation, prescribing what is socially normative, and a liberal humanist discourse, which instantiates the notion of people as rational autonomous individuals possessing a fixed identity, an essential self vested with agency and a consciousness which is the cause of their beliefs and actions. And just as psychological and psychiatric discourse treat the individual as the locus of pathology, so the moral-ethical and humanistic discursive repertoires make the individual the locus of responsibility. This then *does* justify queries regarding the role of psychotherapy as a normalizing, socially regulative discipline implicitly caught up in maintaining a given social order as well as queries regarding the consequences for those who seek psychological help.

Frames of Psychotherapy

Whatever the differences between the various models of therapy, all operate within two primary frames. One, a receptive helper frame, privileges the consultee's narrative and seeks to engage him or her in a process of self-discovery in partnership with an empathic listener who establishes a climate of trust and understanding. The other, a re-visioning frame, seeks to ensure participation in the therapeutic process by drawing on the authority vested in the therapist. This approach casts and directs the search for problem solution within the terms of the expert therapist's conceptual and linguistic frame – establishing a hierarchical relationship which privileges the therapist's perspective. These two alternate frames represent differences in emphasis – they are not incompatible opposites.

The Receptive Helper Frame

When we experience a problem, most of us, I think, hope that gaining some understanding of the problem or its cause will help resolve it.

Under these circumstances too, we might turn to another, hoping to be listened to with understanding and expecting that the other's perspective might prove helpful in providing us with insight or an explanation that would lead to a solution. Equally importantly, we also experience a need to be heard, understood and treated with understanding, to have our experience of events believed rather than rejected, to have our authorship of experience confirmed rather than disconfirmed.

The provision of a context in which one connects with the experiential world of another and in which that other feels their world of experience to be accepted and acknowledged as meaningful is a central element of the helping interview. Crucial to the provision of an accepting climate is what I have previously called the receptive stance (Kaye, 1993). The receptive stance is characterized by an openness to the other's experience, a readiness to learn about their world, a canvassing of multiple possible perspectives. It calls for an endeavour to immerse oneself in the other's story, to understand their point of view, to convey an understanding of how the gloss they put on experience makes sense to the person in the light of the premises themselves. It implies a form of interested inquiry which holds the premises open for exploration. In this way neither participant in the therapeutic dialogue is bound by the consultee's dominant story or its governing assumptions and presuppositions. Viewed in this manner, the active attempt to understand another's experience can involve its exploration as well as prompting alternative constructions to emerge.

Many therapists who work within this frame in seeking to understand and explore the problem as presented by their 'clients' adopt their frame of reference thereby limiting the range of possible exploration. While it is vital to gain an understanding of the other's world, change is likely to be limited to the extent that therapists limit their attention solely to the consultee's frame of reference. A focus on helping people to explore the presenting problem as they see it, on clarifying by means of empathic communication, or even on confronting them with contradictions in their communication, will not necessarily disrupt the behaviour patterns and belief systems which constitute their difficulty, let alone create new horizons of possibility. This is because by adopting the other's framework as their point of reference, therapists are in danger of being bounded or governed by the other's view of reality and thereby unwittingly ratifying it.

Again, while it is necessary to understand the other's perspective, an exclusive focus on understanding the content of their communication encourages a transactional dynamic whereby there is no mutual search for transformative understanding but rather the other determines the nature of the transaction, implicitly defining what is to be discussed, explored, or avoided. People seek confirmation of their beliefs; they try to elicit particular behaviour from others; they tend to avoid exploration of painful or threatening material. If this occurs in therapy, change or growth of understanding is less likely to occur – they are simply continuing to dwell within the belief system or mode of transaction which comprises their problem.

Unfortunately, many counsellors unknowingly collude in this, thereby limiting their potential effectiveness. By endeavouring to be understanding, to reflect understanding and to facilitate exploration of the 'clients'' chosen themes, they restrict themselves to their frame of reference, rather than responding to it from a superordinate framework. As a result, they are prevented from establishing a situation which would enable the other to examine their behaviour from a new perspective, to draw new distinctions which might trigger the evolution of new meanings. Rather, the 'clients'' narrative together with the discursive formations in which it is embedded remain unchallenged and a solution is sought within the story's terms – thereby circumscribing the teller's options.

Paradoxically, the activity of helping and launching the other on a journey of self-discovery may itself serve to reinforce the problem experienced by the consultee. The placement of a person in the subject position of patient or client implicitly locates the problem within the person thereby potentially attributing ownership of the problem to him or her. This can encourage interiorization of the problem thereby confirming the presupposition of the self as constituting the problem and the individual as responsible for it (or its amelioration). This individualizing focus set within a discourse of individual responsibility may render both therapist and consultee oblivious to the sociocultural constitution of the difficulty or its location in adverse social conditions. Further, the very practices prescribed by traditional therapies (self-evaluation, self-scrutiny) precisely parallel the practices whereby people are ushered into limiting subject positions.

The Re-visioning Frame and Meta-Communication

In the previous section, I suggested that therapeutic change is likely to be limited if the therapist remains immured within the consultee's frame of reference. What is required is a superordinate frame, one in terms of which the therapist responds to the other's narrative, in which the narrative is recontextualized, thereby triggering the development of new meaning and opening up visions of the possible. Specifically, problem dissolution and the evolution of new meanings is most likely to occur in a context which is both receptive and provides responses which:

1   Bring the other to attend *to* rather than *from* their beliefs and presuppositions.
2   Have them explore their assumptive world from a new perspective.
3   Prompt the emergence of new ways of construing experience and changed interpersonal attributions.

4   Promote a questioning of the restraints imposed by beliefs which
    have been taken for granted as true.

For this to occur, three superordinate skills seem necessary:

1   The ability to construct a transactional context which involves the
    participant(s) in the activity of being different.
2   The ability to focus beyond the 'client's' here and now communi-
    cation and behaviour by systematically relating it to a higher order
    framework, thereby reframing it and transforming its meaning.
3   The ability not only to communicate empathic understanding but to
    communicate about the consultee's communication, or comment on
    its connotations.

In this way, the therapist can maintain a receptive stance while also
offering statements, questions and frames which might generate new
distinctions and meanings – a form of meta-communication.

On the Therapeutic Importance of Meta-communication

Any communication can be treated as something to be understood in its
own right. It can also be responded to as a member of some other
category of behaviour. A person's request for a hug, for example, may
be responded to as such or classified as an instance of dependency.
Similarly, in therapy the helpee's communication may be responded to
with understanding or the therapist may adopt a meta-perspective – for
example by citing the communication as evidence of another category of
behaviour, an instance perhaps of a transactional style which might
cause conflict with others or of a misperception which contributes to the
person's distress.

As I have already indicated, to tacitly accept by responding understandingly to what another says serves to ratify it along with its attendant governing constructs. To examine the communication (however
understandingly) and to communicate about it does not have this effect.
To respond to a communication by treating it as an instance of a superordinate class of behaviour places that communication in a new context
thus tending to disrupt automatic patterns of interpretation, attribution
or transaction. While Haley (1963) discusses this as the imposition of a
therapeutic paradox, it can more simply be seen as changing the contextual embedding of a behaviour or of an interpretive attribution, and
thus its meaning.

The ability to 'meta-communicate' and to adopt a 'second-order'
perspective (Watzlawick et al., 1967) is therefore of particular importance in therapy. It enables the therapist to avoid becoming entrapped in
the other's world and triggers a shift in the way the person organizes

their world. Instead of their being allowed to attend *from* their constructs, thereby having these same constructs confirmed, by means of
therapeutic meta-communication people can be enabled to attend *to*
their constructions from an alternate perspective thereby bringing their
world-model and behaviour into question. The shift of perspective
necessitated by meta-communication serves to highlight previously
unnoticed connections between behavioural events, beliefs and feelings
as well as to disrupt previously automatic behavioural sequences.

Establishing a framework in terms of which the therapist commu-
nicates about the client's communication would thus appear to be of
central importance to the change process.

On Therapeutic Frames and their Implications

The ability to meta-communicate, or as Efran and Clarfield (1992) would
have it, to respond orthogonally, requires that the therapist work within
some framework of understanding or theoretical frame. One cannot,
indeed, not have a theory. All therapists act within the bounds of some
theory of human nature, of human problem formation, its genesis and
cure and within the parameters of some theory of therapeutic procedure.
Gergen (1994: 239) talks of how transaction within this frame necessarily
involves a process of hegemonic narrative replacement in which the
process must inevitably result in the slow but inevitable replacement of
the client's story with the therapist's. The client's story does not remain
a free-standing reflection of truth, but rather, as questions are asked and
answered, descriptions and explanations reframed, and affirmation and
doubt disseminated by the therapist, the client's narrative is either
destroyed or incorporated – but in any event replaced – by the professional account.

I find this an unconvincing overgeneralization, one which is based on
an over-literal translation of the narrative concept, and a confusion
between theories of problem formation on the one hand and therapeutic
practice on the other. It overlooks the complexity of meaning-generation
via conversational interchange, confounds the inevitability of working
within a frame with the imposition of a solution and flies in the face
of Maturana and Varela's (1988) concept of the impossibility of instructive interaction (the impossibility of any direct uninterpreted transfer-
ence of meaning from one person to another). It is overall a strangely
modernist statement for a constructionist to make suggesting as it does a
lineal conveyor belt notion of information transfer.

No school of therapy has an invariant narrative which it seeks to
impose on the client in a process akin to ideological conversion. Certainly we are inevitably involved in influencing the production of
meaning in our consultee's life and undoubtedly therapeutic interpretation is heavily laden with the presuppositions of the therapist as Gergen
avers (1992: 3). As one engages with another, his or her experience is

ineluctably reinterpreted within the frame of our interpersonal repertoire, utilizing words which emerge from or are sourced within the
constituent concepts of that repertoire. We cannot but shape that of
which we speak. However, the articulation of a response within this
frame hardly constitutes an imposition or the takeover of an other's
narrative – even if that other comes to use some of the same concepts.
And while therapeutic interpretations may be heavily laden with the
presuppositions of the therapist, this hardly constitutes narrative
replacement.

All therapies provide a conceptual frame which will hopefully enable
people to view their experience from a novel perspective thus opening
up opportunities for new ways of construing the events of their lives.
Gergen's point confounds this with the imposition of a solution, an
imperialistic colonization. The crucial issue is the nature of the frame
(some being more prescriptive, subordinating and limiting than others)
than the fact of there being a frame. The implied notion that one should
be somehow neutral and not allow one's viewpoint into one's engagement with the other, aside from its impossibility smacks of the very
hegemonic superiority that postcolonial critics are seeking to undermine.

A Note on Colonialism and Psychotherapy as Regulatory Praxis

My critique of the notion of narrative replacement is not to deny that a
process of colonization can occur in therapy. It is beguilingly easy for
therapists to create via their questioning the version they think they
perceive. At their best, if treated as possible hypotheses, where these
versions fit for the client, they allow for the drawing of new distinctions
or punctuations of experience which enables the client to generate new,
less problematic possibilities for him or herself. At their worst, they
represent a circular activity in which the therapist finds the patterns they
hypothesize to be there and attempts to impose these – a form of
intellectual colonialism (McCarthy and Byrne, 1988; Amundson and
Stewart, 1993; Hoffman, 1993). This can lead to a fixity or stereotypy of
both thinking and discourse which can potentially limit the consultee's
opportunity to forge alternative meanings, solutions and narratives for
themselves. As Amundsen and Stewart (1993: 113) would have it, 'If
under the temptation of certainty, specified knowledge and expertise is
held fast, the selection process becomes restricted'.

The problem of colonizing interaction is however yet more subtle.
Psychotherapy is inescapably a product of the ethos prevailing at a
given historical period and the theoretical conventions of the times. It
is a culturally constructed technology inscribed with the canonical
assumptions of the culture, its paradigmatic beliefs and disciplinary
practices. To paraphrase Jerome Bruner (1990), given that psychotherapy
is immersed in culture, it must be organized around those meaning-

making and meaning-using processes that connect the person to culture. As he writes,

> because it is a reflection of culture, it partakes in the culture's way of valuing as well as its way of knowing. In fact it *must* do so, for the culture's normatively oriented institutions – its laws, its educational institutions, its family structures – serve to enforce folk psychology. (Bruner, 1990: 4)

The word 'enforce' leads to a notion of psychotherapy as a normalizing discipline implicitly caught up in maintaining a given social order, as Foucault (1979) would suggest, and therefore implicated in the regulation of people. As Michael White (1991), drawing on Foucauldian concepts, has argued, modern psychotherapies are infused with ideologically saturated regimes of truth specifying particular power relations between consultant and consultee and which also govern the nature of the interaction – that is, what may be discussed *and* the mode of interaction. Not only is the consultee initially placed in a subordinate position, but the process can entail particular techniques of discursive regulation or practices of power which in turn produce and reproduce those rules and practices implicated in the maintenance of specific technologies of the self. Further the very practices prescribed by psychotherapy (self-evaluation, self-scrutiny, self-regulation) precisely parallel the practices whereby people are recruited into limiting subject positions.

In this light, psychotherapy may be regarded as at the very least potentially if not necessarily regulative. That is, it may position individuals to become complicit in their own subordination by implicitly inducing them to conform to specifications of personhood derived from dominant assumptions of normality, limiting role prescriptions or moral codes governing exemplary ways of being – discursive formations which problematized their experience in the first place. As Nikolas Rose (1990) asserts, therapy may well recruit people into engaging in practices or technologies of self in which they attempt to discipline, govern or change themselves in relation to socially mandated specifications of personhood while attention is drawn away from both the social location of difficulties and oppressive discursive practices.

If, as a socially sanctioned disciplinary technology, modern psychotherapeutic practice does unreflectively reproduce dominant discourses and mechanisms of control while masking inegalitarian regimes of truth, if the practice implicates the subjects of the discipline in their own subjection (Foucault, 1979, 1988), it thereby exercises limiting, subjugating and iatrogenic effects. Its very instantiation of self-scrutiny draws attention to the personal and encourages self-doubt while excluding attention to discursive positioning. In this way (and even taking into account the relational focus of family therapy), it embodies an individualizing ethic, simultaneously privileging liberal-humanistic notions of self, agency and autonomy on the one hand and a democratic, socially normative and conforming ethic on the other.

Within the above frame, psychotherapy may thus be plausibly construed as an ideologically driven practice which supports and is supported by the institutions of our society, may serve as an instrument of social control preserving the dominant culture, maintaining inequitable, disempowering or subordinating social conditions, practices and arrangements constitutive of the problems people experience (White, 1991). In this view, psychotherapy may act to perpetuate the causes of the problems it seeks to treat by confirming and normalizing oppressive or problematizing social beliefs, norms and mores.

From Narrative to Discursive Therapy

The remainder of this chapter will discuss the move to narrative therapies before exploring the idea of *discursive* therapy – one that privileges an exploration of the discursive regimes by which people are positioned rather than being reproductive of self-interrogative practices. The critique of modern psychotherapeutic practice has prompted the development of collaborative rather than top down or interventive approaches to therapeutic practice. These are deconstructive in spirit, and they avoid objectivist assumptions. Drawing on a range of postmodern and post-structuralist ideas, they are distinguished by a corresponding shift away from models:

1   Which attribute privileged knowledge to the therapist.
2   In which the therapist as objective expert acts on the other to produce change.

The stance toward therapy which informs the above quote entails what I have called a receptive stance and what Anderson and Goolishian (1992) thought of as working from a position of 'not knowing'. It implies a wanting to understand, a receptiveness toward and curiosity about the other's construction of experience, together with an active searching for (and openness to) the not-yet-said, the yet-to-unfold rather than a reductive reframing of the other's communication in accordance with some predetermined theoretical frame. The development of therapies consonant with this stance has been influenced by:

1   The language turn in the social sciences with its emphasis on the language-constituted nature of 'reality'.
2   The parallel thesis that human action is situated in a socially constructed world and that language provides the matrix for human understanding and experiencing.

The concurrent understanding on the part of therapists of a post-foundational persuasion is that they cannot directly know the 'cause' of a problem, and their role in producing a reading or version of that problem has prompted their realization that they are ineluctably working in the world of meaning – its siting in discourse, its construction and its interpretation. This has been accompanied by a focus on how people construe their lives and relationships as well as in seeking an understanding of this via the accounts they give of experience – their self-narratives.

Accordingly, therapists drawing on narrative and social constructionist concepts construe people as living out narratives negotiated in the social arena, actively constructed in discourse with others, drawing on culturally provided constructs and utilizing the genres, canons and rules of the culture for the negotiation of meaning. These psychotherapists have accordingly evolved therapeutic frames derived from hermeneutics, constructionism, literary and narrative theory. Within this framework, one prominent approach is to liken people's stories to texts, the meanings of which can be 'read' or interpreted in dialogue and which are amenable to deconstruction and restorying. In this way, the metaphor of the therapist as co-author of a new, less problematic narrative has been born (Schafer, 1981; Spence, 1982; White and Epston, 1989).

From this perspective therapy is viewed as a form of narrative construction with change inhering in the emergence of new personal realities and narratives. As Goolishian (1990: 4) put it:

Change in therapy as the dialogical creation of new narrative rests in the capacity to re-relate the events of our lives in the context of new and different meaning. We live in and through the narrative identities that we develop in conversation with each other. The skill of the therapist is the expertise to participate in this process.

On Narrative Prescriptiveness

The narrative commitment to viewing the therapeutic encounter as a milieu for the creative generation of meaning represents a major break from modern approaches based on diagnosing and treating identifiable problems residing within the person. The shift is from a preoccupation with veridicality to verisimilitude, from truth to narrative meaning and its effect on lives. Ironically however, the restorying metaphor employed in much narrative therapy retains the individualist cast in that the focus remains on the 'inside story' – an internal model of function or 'narrative' located within the mind of the individual person. The commitment to narrative can reinforce an ethic of individualism to the exclusion of the sociocultural. It also implies a narrative essentialism vested in a reification of self, its reconstruction and reformation or the discovery of a new true self or core identity via self-exploration and self-understanding.

To the extent too that the narrative construct is itself singular, it is potentially prone to a form of narrative rigidity. That is, it may promote the fashioning of a unitary, integrated identity or self-story within the bounds of conventional narrative roles which limit rather than expand choices or the capacity to operate flexibly across different contexts. Thus Ken Gergen and I have argued for a version of therapy which privileges narrative multiplicity over narrative singularity:

> Each narrative of the self may function well in certain circumstances but lead to miserable outcomes in others. To have only a single means to make self intelligible, then, is to limit the range of relationships or situations in which one can function satisfactorily. (Gergen and Kaye, 1992: 179)

The Disavowal of Expertise

Associated with the 'not-knowing' stance advocated by Harry Goolishian (1990) is a rather simplistic disavowal of expertise on the part of many professing narrative therapists which arises from a crass misinterpretation of his profound, hermeneutically derived dialogic position. Given the impossibility of gaining direct unmediated knowledge of any phenomenon, it is clear that we cannot 'know' another's experience and therefore we are in this sense not experts. Yet the very ability to formulate or understand this concept represents a form of specialist knowledge – or expertise. As 'constructionist' or narrative therapists this presumably enables us to construct a dialogic frame in which new meanings can emerge. The skilled therapist *is* an expert in this sense. To disown this, to disown knowledge (which is in any case socially constructed) or to disown that one works within the bounds of a given orientation is simply fraudulent.

The proposition that we cannot gain access to an objective reality does not require the abandonment of knowledge or expertise or of having an informed theory of helping. Further, as Efran and Clarfield (1992: 207–8) point out,

> To act as if all views are equal and that we-as-therapists have not favourites among them undercuts the very sort of frank exchange we want and expect to have with our clients. It patronizes them, compromises our own integrity, and treats open dialogue as if it was an endangered species needing 'hothouse' protection.

The contribution of the therapist's point of view is hardly in itself colonizing, nor does it deny either mutuality or respect for the consultee's world of reality. The withholding of one's viewpoint on the other hand is not merely a prescription for therapeutic impotence but itself constitutes a response – one cannot not respond. It can further be seen as disrespectful and condescending. What is required rather is the further expertise to develop a reflexive position toward our own stance, its implications and consequences.

The above points act as a counterpoint to the totalizing concerns raised by particular interpretations of post-structuralism and feminist critical theory that working with people from a base of 'expert knowledge' might be intrinsically oppressive and indeed that therapy may be reproductive of oppressive practices of power.

Perhaps an end to the overgeneralized ideological debates around therapy as a practice of power might occur if therapy were to be construed – and conducted – not as a top-down activity enshrining inequity but as a collaborative endeavour that relies on the interweaving of the particular 'expertise' and awarenesses of each participant, in a frame designed to promote the generation of new meanings. While hierarchy is unlikely to be eliminated in therapy, this frame allows one to view the therapeutic transaction as a process in which there is a shift from hierarchic skew to mutuality. It also displaces the notion of acting instrumentally on the other to change them in favour of the collaborative attempt to open up new possibilities and choices.

What is required however is the further expertise to develop a reflexive position toward our own stance, its implications and consequences.

Discursive Therapy

Implicit in the narrative metaphor employed by Goolishian (1990) is also a dialogic position which emphasizes meaning as being created via conversational interchange. According to Anderson and Goolishian (1988: 372) therapy is

> a linguistic event that takes place in what we call a therapeutic conversation. The therapeutic conversation is a mutual search and exploration through dialogue, a two-way exchange, a criss-crossing of ideas in which new meanings are continually evolving toward the dissolving of problems . . . Change is the evolution of new meaning through dialogue.

To employ the evocative phrase coined by Louis Sass (1994), therapeutic change does not merely rely on the malleability of reality but involves an active creation of meaning. In this sense, therapy may be construed as a generative and constructive (rather than simply remedial) process of meaning creation which seeks to forge new understandings via the juxtaposition of multiple perspectives in conversational interchange. It is a process which involves the reinterpretation or resymbolization of discourse in a novel context – one which

1   Differs from that which conventionally governs discourse in the
     area.
2   Creates novel distinctions and thereby generates new meanings.

In this way, generative inquiry can point to a possible world – 'something disclosed in front of the text rather than hidden behind it' as
Ricouer (1971) would have it; or in Goolishian's (1990) words, 'the not-
yet-said'. This process could not occur without the exchange of lin-
guistically and culturally available constructs. In the process of therapeutic interchange, we perforce use what Bruner (1990: 11) calls
'symbolic systems' already in place, already 'there', deeply entrenched
in culture and language. They constitute a very special kind of communal toolkit whose tools once used make the user a reflection of the
community. In this light a further set of concepts needs to be considered
in delineating a discursive therapy, the cultural specifications inscribed
in the socially constructed and historically situated networks of ideas,
meanings and beliefs acquired by virtue of membership of our
culture(s).

These networks of ideas and associated practices – discourses – make
us subject to normative cultural prescriptions thereby positioning us to
think or act in given ways and are in this way important determinants of
behaviour. That is, as Zimmerman and Dickerson (1994: 235) remind us,
'cultural stories, far from being neutral, lead to constructions of a
normative view, generally reflecting the dominant culture's specification,
from which people know themselves and against which people compare
themselves'. Indeed, as Bruner (1990: 58) avers, 'the very structure of our
lexicon while it may not force us to code human events in a particular
way, certainly predisposes us to be culturally canonical'.

Given this gloss, narrative and language-based approaches to therapy
with their implication that there is nothing outside the text are both
limited and limiting. For they de-politicize the broader social context by
which people are positioned – with a consequent lack of attention to
inequitable social arrangements, people's material conditions and indeed
power imbalances within a range of social groupings.

Thus Fish (1993) points out that changing a destructive narrative to a
more positive narrative within the same cultural discourse is not identical to getting free of that cultural discourse. Criticizing the tendency of
some narrative therapies to isolate the therapist-family system from any
social, historical, economic or institutional context, he writes:

> Splitting off a separate world of language divorced from any notion of a
> relevant social and material realm, they enforce a conceptual blackout which
> begins at the edges of the family's story or conversation. There is nothing for
> the therapist who operates solely within these models to mentally see, hear or
> touch but the content and arrangement of the words the family uses while in
> the therapist's office. (Fish, 1993: 228)

This argues for a greater sociopolitical awareness on the part of therapists, one which enables people to challenge the truth regimes to which they are subject and in terms of which they govern themselves. For example, to the extent that self-surveillance is implicated in the maintenance of problem-saturated subject positions, a therapeutic orientation embodying the above principle would shift the focus of interaction from an exploration of individual experience to examine its discursive location. From this perspective, while it may be useful to have people reclaim aspects of experience previously marginalized in the interests of conformity to a dominant narrative, it is equally important to set a context in which people are at the same time enabled to examine the effects of dominant socially constructed value constellations and behaviour specifications on their lives.

While showing no disbelief in the consultee's troubled story or its experiential veracity, this orientation would:

1   Seek to enable the consultee to examine the aspects of experience or action possibilities marginalized or excluded by the dominant story.
2   Put in question the practices of self associated with problem-saturated, limiting or impoverished subject positions.
3   Work toward exploring the dominant sociocultural discursive formations and associated practices by which the person is positioned rather than merely changing meanings within the dominant cultural frame.
4   Create the conditions which would enable consultees to question and take a position toward these discourses.

Overall, it offers a temporal narrative experience in which the author's positioning rather than the author is the centre of attention. This occurs in the context of an emancipatory therapeutic climate in which the therapist:

1   Is curious, receptive and ready to learn from the other.
2   Maintains awareness of the political, socially reproductive consequences of their practices.
3   Avoids imposition of limiting role prescriptions, rigid theoretical frames or practices in which are inscribed privileged versions of what constitutes the normal.

Toward a Socially Critical Position

The word 'psychotherapy' unavoidably carries overtones on acting instrumentally on another in order to remedy some psychological defect or deficiency. However in this chapter I have tried to advance some ideas informed by a post-structuralist and constructionist awareness which

provide a break from regulatory normalizing and socioculturally reproductive modernist practices. While this goal is partly realized in narrative
and collaborative approaches to therapy, I have argued for a discursive
therapy. The difference between this deconstructive socially critical
position and the narrative position is that the narrative still largely locates
problems within an individual meaning structure, whereas a critical
discursive approach seeks to examine the socioculturally constructed
discursive complexes and practices by which people are positioned or the
social conditions in which they find themselves.

My position clearly overlaps with that of theorists whose concern is
with the political processes of social control and who consider it an
imperative to explicitly redress discrimination, oppression or margin-
alization in their therapeutic endeavours. This can run the danger of the
top-down prescriptiveness criticized in modernist practices. The discursive approach creates a context in which both therapist and consultee
by examining their discursive positionings may become alerted to their
regulatory implications thus opening up new meanings, perceptions and
action options. However, removing the problem from the person and
placing it in their discursive position may not be sufficient. It still leaves
responsibility with the individual to change and locates the problem
with the person if not within. And this may position us as agents of
stasis. In Social Justice terms, might we not as Dulwich Centre in
Adelaide does and the Family Centre Group at Lower Hutt New
Zealand and the East Side Institute for Short-Term Psychotherapy in
New York do, work to create a context in which the marginalized gain
voice in a culturally congruent fashion? And strive to create a context in
which minorities are heard, become visible and able to make a difference
at least in their local communities rather than remaining submerged in
the dominant culture.

There will always be a cohort of therapists solely interested in working with individuals and their personal problems. In this way psychotherapy will be limited by its governing paradigm. However, many have
over the years worked with larger systems. While it would be grandiose
to think we should 'change the world' and its political structures, thus
righting all wrongs and ridding ourselves of all inequities, there is a
place for us to be involved in social change – for some of us perhaps by
alerting our colleagues or the public via our writings, for others,
working for change in sociopolitical structures.

Bearing in mind Sawicki's (1991) caution that no discourse is inherently liberating or oppressive, it behoves all of us as practitioners not to
blindly follow (or merely seek to refine) practice prescriptions, but
rather to scrutinize the institutional and disciplinary knowledges by
which we are positioned. While we may never be able to establish a
position outside the discursive field from which to accurately view our
practice, we *can* get outside particular disciplinary discourses in order to
question their (and our) practices of power. The readiness to adopt a

stance or meta-perspective toward the discursive prescriptions which regulate our practice might serve to at least partially mediate against unreflective and unwittingly iatrogenic practice.

In turn, an ongoing critique of its own power-knowledge may help prevent postmodern and post-structuralist deconstructive practice from forging a new hegemony with its own regime of political correctiness and certitude – a new superordinate and subordinating order of surveillance. Perhaps too, the paradigm shift mooted at the beginning of this chapter will emerge from a second order questioning and re-cognizing of therapy and its role as a socioculturally constructed enterprise rather than from a mere sharpening of its practices.

Bibliography

Amundson, J. and Stewart, K. (1993) 'Temptations of power and certainty', *Journal of Marital and Family Therapy*, 19 (2): 111–23.

Anderson, H. (1997) *Conversation, Language, and Possibilities: A Postmodern Approach to Therapy*. New York: Basic Books.

Anderson, H. and Goolishian, H. (1988) 'Human systems as linguistic systems: preliminary and evolving ideas about the implications for clinical theory', *Family Process*, 27 (4): 371–93.

Anderson, H. and Goolishian, H. (1992) 'The client is the expert: a not-knowing approach to therapy', in S. McNamee and K.J. Gergen (eds), *Therapy as Social Construction*. London: Sage.

Berg, I. and de Shazer, S. (1993) 'Making numbers talk: language in therapy', in S. Friedman (ed.), *The New Language of Change*. New York: Guilford Press.

Bruner, J. (1990) *Acts of Meaning*. Cambridge, MA: Harvard University Press.

Cecchin, B. (1993) Foreward in L. Hoffman, *Exchanging Voices: A Collaborative Approach to Family Therapy*. London: Karnac Books.

Cross, J. (1994) 'Politics and family therapy', *Dulwich Centre Newsletter*, 1: 7–10.

Drewery, W. and Winslade, J. (1997) 'The theoretical story of narrative therapy', in G. Monk, J. Winslade, K. Crocket and D. Epston (eds), *Narrative Therapy in Practice: The Archaeology of Hope*. San Francisco: Jossey-Bass.

Efran, J.S. and Clarfield, L.E. (1992) 'Constructionist therapy: sense and nonsense', in S. McNamee and K.J. Gergen (eds), *Therapy as Social Construction*. London: Sage.

Fish, V. (1993) 'Poststructuralism in family therapy: interrogating the narrative/conversational mode', *Journal of Marital and Family Therapy*, 19 (3): 221–32.

Foucault, M. (1979) *Discipline and Punish: the Birth of the Prison*. Middlesex: Peregrine Books.

Foucault, M. (1988) *The Care of the Self: The History of Sexuality Volume 3*. London: Allen Lane/Penguin Press.

Gergen, K.J. (1991) *The Saturated Self: Dilemmas of Identity in Contemporary Life*. New York: Basic Books.

Gergen, K.J. (1992) Introduction, in S. McNamee and K.J. Gergen (eds), *Therapy as Social Construction*. London: Sage.

Gergen, K.J. (1994) *Realities and Relationships: Soundings in Social Construction.* Cambridge, MA: Harvard University Press.

Gergen, K.J. and Kaye, J.D. (1992) 'Beyond narrative in the negotiation of therapeutic meaning', in S. McNamee and K.J. Gergen (eds), *Therapy as Social Construction.* London: Sage.

Goolishian, H. (1990) 'Therapy as a linguistic system: hermeneutics, narrative and meaning', *The Family Psychologist,* 6: 14–45.

Haley, J. (1963) *Strategies of Psychotherapy.* New York: Grune and Stratton.

Hekman, S. (1990) *Gender and Knowledge: Elements of a Postmodern Feminism.* Cambridge: Polity Press.

Hillman, J. and Ventura, M. (1992) *We've had a Hundred Years of Psychotherapy and the World's Getting Worse.* San Francisco: Harper.

Hoffman, L. (1993) *Exchanging Voices. A Collaborative Approach to Family Therapy.* London: Karnac Books.

Howard, G. (1991) 'Culture tales: a narrative approach to thinking, cross-cultural psychology and psychotherapy', *American Psychologist,* 46 (3): 187–97.

John, I. (1998) 'The scientist-practitioner model: a critical examination', *Australian Psychologist,* 33/1: 24–30.

Kaye, J.D. (1990) 'Toward meaningful research in psychotherapy', *Dulwich Centre Newsletter,* 2: 27–38.

Kaye, J.D. (1993) 'On learning to see through the eyes of another', *The Calgary Participator,* 3 (1).

Kaye, J.D. (1996) 'Towards a discursive psychotherapy', *Changes,* 14 (2): 232–7.

Maturana, H.R. and Varela, F.J. (1988) *The Tree of Knowledge: The Biological Roots of Human Understanding.* Boston, MA: Shambhala Publications.

McCarthy, I.C. and Byrne, N.O'R. (1988) 'Mis-taken love: conversations on the problem of incest in an Irish context', *Family Process,* 27: 181–98.

Monk, G. and Drewery, W. (1994) 'The impact of social constructionist thinking on eclecticism in counsellor education: some personal thoughts', *New Zealand Journal of Counselling,* 16 (1): 5–14.

Ricouer, P. (1971) 'The model of the text: meaningful action considered as a text', *Social Research,* 38: 529–62.

Rose, N. (1990) 'Psychology as a "social science"', in I. Parker and J. Shotter (eds), *Deconstructing Social Psychology.* London: Routledge.

Russell, R.L. and Van den Broek, P. (1992) 'Changing narrative schemas in psychotherapy', *Psychotherapy,* 29 (3): 344–54.

Sass, L.A. (1994) 'The epic of disbelief: the postmodernist turn in psycho-analysis', *Partisan Review,* 61 (1): 96–110.

Sawicki, J. (1991) *Disciplining Foucault: Feminism, Power and the Body.* London: Routledge.

Schafer, R. (1981) *Narrative Actions in Psychoanalysis.* Worcester, MA: Clark University Press.

Schon, D. (1983) *The Reflective Practitioner: How Professionals Think in Action.* London: Maurice Temple Smith.

Spence, D. (1982) *Narrative Truth and Historical Truth.* New York: Norton.

Tomm, K. et al. (1992) 'Therapeutic distinctions in an on-going therapy', in S. McNamee and K.J. Gergen (eds), *Therapy as Social Construction.* London: Sage.

Watzlawick, P., Beavin, J. and Jackson, D. (1967) *Pragmatics of Human Communication.* New York: Norton.

White, M. (1991) 'Deconstruction and therapy', *Dulwich Centre Newsletter*, 3: 21–40.

White, M. and Epston, D. (1989) *Literate Means to Therapeutic Ends*. Adelaide: Dulwich Centre Publications.

Zimmerman, J.L. and Dickerson, V.C. (1994) 'Using a narrative metaphor: implications for theory and clinical practice', *Family Process*, 33: 233–45.

3

DERRIDA AND THE DECONSTRUCTION OF POWER AS CONTEXT AND TOPIC IN THERAPY

Glenn Larner

Overcoming is not the end. One doesn't jump out of metaphysics one fine day, in order to go over to something else.

(Derrida, 1995a: 48)

The deconstruction of power in institutional settings, particularly as it bears upon issues of justice and ethics, is coincidental to the concerns of both contemporary psychotherapy and recent deconstructive philosophy. This chapter situates the topic of power in psychotherapy in the context of Derrida's (1992, 1994, 1995b) recent writings on matters of ethics, politics and justice. For Derrida (1995a: 49), a critique of power as justice or ethics, *is* deconstruction: 'Deconstruction is an affirmative thought of a possible ethics, of an engagement beyond the technology of the calculable. Concern for responsibility stands at the center of the deconstructive experience.' Elsewhere, Derrida (1992: 15) states: 'Deconstruction is justice.' For the latter Derrida, deconstructing is a *performative* activity, centred around questions of practice, responsibility, justice and ethics and not in terms of a *post*-modern agenda (Gasché, 1994). Justice is enacted through an ethical relation to the other which itself expresses the problem of power. As a textual intervention, deconstruction articulates the paradoxes and double binds inherent in discourses of power and institution, in order to minimize their violent repression of difference and the other.

Churvin (1996: 148) states the problem of power for psychotherapy clearly as follows: 'This power differential remains to my mind one of the unavoidable issues in understanding the therapy process, the problem of how to empower clients from a position of power as a professional "authority"'. To deconstruct power in psychotherapy is a powerful move, one that reinstates the power of the therapist. A therapist takes control of an interview in order to let the other have a voice, to be empowered. For both psychotherapy and deconstruction, the dilemma of power is how to take a *position* (for example, on ethics and justice) when such positioning itself involves a 'violence that founds or positions' (Derrida, 1992: 47). This is part of the postmodern quandary: how to think, act and know in the absence of transcendent grounds, reason, truth and foundations; how to critique an institution when no outside grounds or positions can be taken, and avoid one's position becoming institutionalized and used to support existing power structures (Nealon, 1993). The positioning of the therapist to empower clients may be a lesser violence no doubt, but it is a positional violence nonetheless. It is the position of not taking a position while taking one. There is a necessary impasse here: the deconstruction of power in psychotherapy requires the action of a powerful therapist to 'not know' (Anderson and Goolishian, 1992) and it requires a powerful knowing at another level, a 'not knowing' knowing (Larner, 1995). Therapy is violent in order to deconstruct the violence in people's lives at the social, political, legal, media-technological, sexual or physical levels. Somehow the therapist must be a master illusionist, making power inapparent in its apparence (Derrida, 1994). Thus in narrative therapy, the notion of 'co-constructing' includes the real power of the therapist to influence the authoring process, by not acting as a professional authority or expert while they are. To take a position on justice is to perform 'a power without a power' (Derrida, 1994: 17).

This is a paradox that cannot be grasped through reason and language, a paradox that one must learn to live with (Derrida, 1995b). Power is a problem precisely because it is a fact of everyday discourse and life. Power, structure and hierarchy make discourse itself possible, as to speak at all requires limits and decisions about what can be said and by whom. This means the discourse of psychotherapy is already a political institution which requires deconstructing from within. Nealon (1993: 88) describes the process this way: 'We begin to recognise aporias, gaps, fissures at its limits, while still inhabiting a discursive world made possible by the traces of this structure'. In this sense, the articulation of a deconstructing psychotherapy is the expression of a double bind around issues of power and knowledge, which as Derrida (1995a) suggests cannot be simply overcome. To deconstruct psychotherapy in the spirit of Derrida, is to purge the cultural idols of power, technology and mastery from therapy, while acknowledging that we can never quite leave them behind. As Derrida (1994: xviii) says, 'we learn to live with ghosts', or as the personal constructivist Miller Mair (1989: 225) warns: 'In all conversations there is a hidden patterning of power'.

This chapter touches on the inevitable struggle with power that psychotherapists must endure for the sake of their clients. It suggests that the problem of power does not have to be avoided, dissolved (in language), resolved or moved on from, but that it provides the very context in which deconstructing psychotherapy can proceed. Therapists working out of the paradoxes of power open themselves and psychotherapy up to difference, as an ethical position that expresses both power *and* non-power in a critical questioning of institutional grounds. In therapy, power is socially negotiated in the dialogic encounter. This is a 'power-in-process' in which the title of 'power' itself is deconstructed. Power is not the name of some *thing* we possess, but emerges out of the social situation. Power is the social, power is irreal, power is a condition for relationship and dialogue, power is haunted by its other, non-power. A deconstructing psychotherapy is obliged to be both powerful *and* non-powerful. It is the presence of this ambiguity of power in therapy which is conducive to change. That therapists can be powerful, but sacrifice themselves for the sake of the other, allows the power of the other to emerge. As Gibney (1996: 105) notes, 'we must accept our power, but aim at giving it away'. One way to think this paradox is to approach power in psychotherapy as Derrida (1994: 27) does justice, 'on the basis of the gift . . . as a gift of that which one does not have and which thus paradoxically can only *come back* or belong to the other'. As a gift, therapy expects of the other only that they be *other*, by participating in a dialogue, a 'back and forth' talk (Tedlock and Mannheim, 1995) that is mutual and reciprocal, despite the power hierarchy.

Deconstructing psychotherapy takes place at the level of *practice*, where it addresses issues of power, justice and ethics in relation to clients, and at the level of *theory*, where it deconstructs its own power and authority as an institution of psychotherapy. It asks certain deconstructing questions like: What is deconstructing psychotherapy and how is such a project possible? Within which networks of theory and therapeutic practices can it be located? Is there already an orthodoxy in psychotherapy which can lay claim to its title? Has a process of institutionalizing deconstructing psychotherapy already begun? What does deconstructing do to our understanding of therapy? and What does therapy do (if anything) to the activity or notion of deconstruction? The hope is that such enquiry will enable deconstructing psychotherapy, at its beginning, to remain innovative and open to its own possibilities, rather than being subject to closure under the regime and institution of theory.

Deconstructing 'Deconstructing Psychotherapy'

I have often had occasion to define deconstruction as that which is – far from a theory, a school, a method, even a discourse, still less a technique that can be appropriated – at bottom *what happens or comes to pass* [*ce qui arrive*]. It remains then to situate, localize, determine what happens with what happens, *when* it happens. To date it. Has deconstruction happened? Has it arrived? Of course it has, if you like, but then, if it has, so many questions arise: How? Where?

When? On what date exactly? Was it so long ago, already? Or perhaps not yet? (Derrida, 1995b: 17)

The notion of deconstructing psychotherapy, like a Mandelbrot equation in fractal geometry, suggests a repetitive process that is both creative and indefinite. Conceivably one could deconstruct psychotherapy and then deconstruct that deconstruction and so on, ad infinitum. Perhaps this illustrates that deconstructing is precisely *not* what we think it is, but like life, continually surprises, as *ce qui arrive*. In the spirit of Derrida and deconstructing, I raise certain deconstructing questions about the title of this book and the project to which it refers! For example, at the level of the institution of psychotherapy, how can we have a structural identity, a system of theory and practices in deconstructing psychotherapy that avoids totalizing and allows singularity and difference to be expressed?

The kind of deconstruction that interests Derrida (1995b: 24) is one that interrogates 'the justification and authority of the title'. This teases out the mystical or metaphysical foundations of names like 'justice', 'deconstruction' or 'psychotherapy' so they can be put 'back into play' in a language or discourse (and we should note that Derrida (1995b: 15) claims he has never identified his writings as 'deconstruction', a word which 'has always left me cold'). By displacing the institutional authority of the title, meaning once again becomes multi-referential and open to difference. This is why the *only* definition of deconstruction Derrida (1995b: 28) has dared to give is the following: 'both more than one language and no more of just one language'. Here the title 'deconstruction' is allowed to possess an excess of meaning, its reference becoming 'at once multiple, different and deferred' (1995b: 24). To have an indeterminate meaning does not mean a word lacks meaning, but that it has too much: 'an overabundance of meaning, of denotations and connotations, of words that mean many things at once, of words that remind us of other words, of things that are said and that are unsaid' (Yablon, 1992: 262). This multiplicity of meaning of titles continually fosters new networks of understanding both *within* discourses like deconstruction and psychotherapy and *between* them (Weber, 1992). For example, where these titles are fluid we can ask questions of mutual influence – what does deconstructing do to our understanding of psychotherapy, and vice versa? For Derrida, deconstruction is a 'proliferation of genres, styles, voices . . . a plurality that no concept of deconstruction could hope to totalise' (Gasché, 1994: 11).

The sort of deconstructing questions we can ask about deconstructing psychotherapy, paradoxically concern the very issues of power and institution by which it founds or titles itself, as a *post*-modern or discursive project. Pace Derrida (1995b) above: when and where and how, did or will, deconstructing arrive in psychotherapy, and is it in transit, just beginning or already in decline? Note that Derrida (1995b: 30) tells us that deconstruction has always been 'on the wane . . . from its

beginning'. Where many commentators today are quick to decry deconstruction as passé, for Derrida (1992) it is yet to begin, indeed it can
never begin and is always beginning, as an impossible enquiry into the
limits of power and knowledge. Impossible because with its possibility
comes an inevitable appropriation by political, economic and cultural
interests, turning it into another technology of power. Such institutionalizing of the activity of deconstructing would arrest the play of
difference and reduce it to a 'fashion, a school of thought, an academic
current, a theory, or a method' (Derrida, 1995b: 30).

Consequently, deconstruction explores how the knowledge of psychotherapy becomes institutionalized, how it is recognized, reproduced and
legitimized as a method or discipline of therapy (Gasché, 1994). In the
process of establishing the power and authority of a title, there is a
potential closure of limits upon theory and practice. For example, if we
say deconstructing psychotherapy is this *or* that, what ways of thinking
and doing therapy does this discourse exclude, and has the previously
excluded now become the excluding? Foucault writes: 'Discursive
practices are not purely and simply ways of producing discourse. They
are embodied in technical processes, in institutions, in patterns for
general behaviour, in forms for transmission and diffusion, and in
pedagogical forms which, at once, impose and maintain them' (quoted
in Nealon, 1993: 50). Under the authority of the title, professions and
disciplines, modern or post-modern, become inevitably involved in
networks of dissemination, such as the publication of books and journals,
the promotion of conferences and workshops, and the usual entrenched
positions in teaching departments or institutes, which pit one theory or
approach against the other (Nealon, 1993). In the attempt to supplant one
tradition with another (the new), power structures are perpetuated as yet
another institution with a title. This is why Derrida (1989: 222) can say:
'There is no such thing as a deconstructive *enterprise* – the idea of a
project is incompatible with deconstruction. Deconstruction is a situation.' The institutional power of a discourse as enterprise, an essentially
political activity which marks out borders, is what requires deconstructing. For this reason, the first responsibility of a deconstructing psychotherapy is to deconstruct itself as a site of intellectual privilege and
power. This is in order to prevent its institutionalization as yet another
totalizing discourse of truth, a deconstructive orthodoxy which is potentially violent in closing off difference and otherness. In effect, Derrida
sacrifices deconstruction by deconstructing its power, for the sake of
ethics and justice.

Aporias of Power

Derrida (1994) has recently advocated an ethical-political ground for
deconstructing in his book *Specters of Marx*. This is based on an idea of

justice as ethical relation to the other which is 'undeconstructible'. The book is a 'radical critique' in the spirit of Marx of the techno-media powers responsible for the many injustices of capitalist market economies. As Derrida (1992) explains elsewhere, this is a political 'position-taking' towards discourses of power, which aligns itself with the voices of the marginalized and the many. The book has engendered much debate about whether such an ethical-political *position* in deconstruction is tenable. Derrida's re-turn to questions of ethics and responsibility began in 1972 (see Kearney, 1993). Then again, 'ethical-political-juridical motifs run through *all* his writings' (Bernstein, 1993: 213). For a critical perspective see *Radical Philosophy* (1996). The problem is that Derrida's (1992, 1994) 'position' requires a kind of violence and force that mirrors the power it wants to deconstruct. As Derrida (1992: 11) says: 'a powerless justice is not justice'. How one adopts a position of power in order to deconstruct power is a paradox shared by both deconstruction and psychotherapy. Awareness of this paradox of power in psychotherapy, may be one indicator of the *arrival* of deconstructing in psychotherapy. It is part of the postmodern dilemma surrounding power and institution, which forms the subject of this chapter. In times of increasing institutional abuses (economic, political, cultural, technocratic, gender etc), how can deconstructionists and therapists take a *position* on ethics and justice, where there are no longer 'grounds' (in truth, meaning and reason) for doing so?

It is significant that Derrida does not attempt to either resolve or ignore the paradoxes of justice and power, but on the contrary, defines deconstruction in terms of them. As 'a certain experience of the impossible' (Derrida, 1992: 30), deconstruction explores the very movement between the possibility and impossibility of power as 'aporia'. 'Aporia' means the absence of a path, a barrier or roadblock to thinking; that is, *impasse*. It is a moment of undecidability in a discourse which marks the 'stress-point' for its logic, grammar and terms of reference (Norris, 1995). Nonetheless, for Derrida 'aporia' promises the thinking of the path or way ahead, as a thinking of the unthinkable (Cornell, 1992). As Derrida (1995c: 84) remarks, aporias in legal, religious, philosophical, ethical and political discourses have never stopped them from 'functioning', but on the contrary help them to operate 'so much better'. Deconstructing happens when the aporias of power inherent in discourses like politics, justice and psychotherapy lay bare their 'mystical' foundations and authority (Derrida, 1992). That is, deconstruction is not a harmless politically neutral technique for reading texts, but a real *force* for justice and difference. Derrida's (1994) *position* is against the abuses of techno-capitalist politics – privilege, reason, authority, violence. Deconstruction intervenes and changes things by destabilizing and complicating positions of power. The deconstruction of power is an examination of 'all the paradoxical situations in which the greatest force and the greatest weaknesses strangely enough exchange places' (Derrida, 1992: 7). Every positioning, deconstruction included, is a violence that legitimates and repeats itself by rejecting what has gone before. However, Derrida (1992: 49) deconstructs for the sake of justice: 'It is a matter of limiting the worst violence with another violence'. This is where justice and deconstruction as one and the same thing are *both* impossible. To say this is to illustrate the 'both/and' complexity of their titles, an 'irreducible plurality' which both contains and accounts for the paradoxes of power they express.

Thus for Derrida (1992), an ethical-political position is not only possible, but *is* deconstruction. The idea of justice as a non-violative relationship to the other, is what makes deconstruction itself possible and impossible in relation to the 'double bind' of power. Here it is apparent that critics of Derrida's (1994) stance on ethics and justice rely on a clichéd *post*-modern version of deconstruction, as a simplistic 'indeterminacy of meaning'. For Derrida, it is 'not interpretation all the way down' (Cornell, 1992: 178). Such a misreading of the complexity of Derrida's writings is driven by the inevitable conservative tendency of university and professional institutions towards closure and structure for their own purposes of power (Nealon, 1993). Deconstruction is a double 'both/and' reading which thinks opposites – for example, meaning and non-meaning, power and non-power – *together*.

What this suggests is that psychotherapy as a totalizing meaning or site of power can only be disrupted from *within* the tradition. To deconstruct power means to both preserve *and* critically question therapeutic practice and the institution of psychotherapy. The deconstructionist has one foot inside and the other outside the deconstructed system (Nealon, 1993). To step outside modernism and meaning completely, as in *post*-modernism, merely repeats the modernist move of violently replacing what has gone before (Larner, 1994a). Here deconstructing psychotherapy is not a critical discourse that moves beyond modernism, but enables it, that is, makes it possible by displacing its totalizing system (Nealon, 1993). This is because the *turn* to language, narrative, meaning and interpretation is itself a metaphysical *position*. Consequently, the flipside of the problem of power is the impossibility of *not* taking a position, the illusion that we can simply step outside foundations, power or the real. Here I suggest that deconstruction involves a *para modern* movement, both modern *and* post-modern. This describes a knowledge that is '"not-knowing" as a stable instability, a groundless ground, an uncertain certainty and a position of power that is non-powerful' (Larner, 1995: 212).

From the above, it can be said that deconstructing involves two stages: (1) deconstruction of the power and violence of institutional discourse, including its own, and (2) the enactment of an ethical relation to the other, based on a desire for justice and tolerance of difference. The first follows from the second, which means the primary requirement for deconstructing is ethical (Cornell, 1992). The deconstruction of the power and violence of totalizing discourse is a call to responsibility and ethics. For Derrida (1994), deconstructing is an ethical imperative to meditate on the problem of power.

Psychotherapy as Ethical Relation

> And yet nothing is more necessary than this wisdom. It is ethics itself: to learn to live – alone, from oneself, by oneself. (Derrida, 1994: xviii)

In this section, I develop the idea of psychotherapy as an application of deconstructive ethics. A deconstructing psychotherapy poses questions like: What is it to be a *responsible* therapist? How can we resist the influence of the culture to do therapy in a certain way? and Can we as therapists deconstruct ourselves so as to allow others to speak? Here the first subject of a deconstructing psychotherapy is the therapist, in the theory, ideologies, discourse and practices that inform his or her therapeutic approach. Deconstructing is itself a therapy which teaches therapists to say to the client: 'I would like to learn to live, I am with you, no better. I struggle with my demons too.' This is the power of non-power, humility and poesis where therapy becomes a narrative lived out in the session. This stance of being-with-the-other *is* politically empowering, as a human situation where a dialogue of meaning and sharing takes place. As Derrida (1992: 17) says, what constitutes justice is the desire to 'address oneself to the other in the language of the other'.

Therapy proceeds through the deconstruction of power as the enactment of an ethical relation to the other. The ethical relation involves 'the kind of person one must become in order to develop a non-violative relationship to the other' (Cornell, 1992: 13), one that sustains the other's difference and singularity. As Inger and Inger (1994: 49–50) write: 'Holding two or more points of view simultaneously is one of the central tasks of therapists, practising an ethically based perspective.' An ethical relation to the other is one that maximizes the difference that makes a difference, and this is the activity of writing, conversation, and the development of the person's narrative. Here each person's narrative is unique or other, and outside the bounds of any psychotherapy or its profession. Elsewhere I have proposed a notion of 'narrative destiny' whereby therapeutic-change occurs in the client's unique narrative time and not as a result of a narrative technology (Larner, 1998). What a deconstructing psychotherapy allows for is the therapeutic encounter as sacred and as 'wonder' (Gasché, 1994; Larner, 1994b). This is an attitude that inscribes a power that is not hegemonic, that allows the other to 'say everything' (as in literature), to think their own thoughts, to have their own feelings, to be their own subject, to write their own narrative (Chase, 1995).

To achieve the ethical relation, the therapist adopts a *double* gesture in relation to their own power and knowledge. Therapy becomes a way of negotiating an exchange of ideas and power. It is a politics of the voice which uses power and knowledge in a non-hegemonic way so as to open up power and difference. It is not the client's story that is deconstructed so much as the therapist's. The deconstruction of power in the therapeutic setting is what makes therapy possible, as a site where narrative develops through a tolerance of difference. It is the ethical relation which enables power to be deconstructed in the therapeutic setting. This is because in the face-to-face encounter of therapy, the therapist must use power to enable the client's empowerment in the telling of their story. Because the power base of psychotherapy is in late Western capitalism, it is also in the Marxist/Derridean critique when it questions the ethics of its own politics and power.

Deconstructing Face-to-Face

Deconstructing psychotherapy is involved in the process of ethical engagement in 'I-thou' relations (Inger, 1993). For Heidegger, the Greek 'ethos' was understood as 'abode or dwelling place' (Bernasconi, 1987: 132). The therapist in ethical relation to the other creates an abode or space for encounter and conversation. This occurs when therapy renounces itself, when it refuses to speak on its own behalf. This involves not so much the statement of an ethical system or philosophy, as the mutual working out of an ethics in the session, in the *saying* of therapy. The saying cannot be said because this would disrupt the dialogic moment, constraining it under the title of a psychotherapy. As a dialogue *between* persons, therapy involves a positioning towards the other in the present reality of an 'I-you' relationship (Inger and Inger, 1994). Where the saying is a spontaneous relational event, the said formalizes it in theoretical discourse, so the person becomes an object of therapy. In the 'face-to-face' talk of therapy, the other takes *precedence* in the relationship, a relationship which is intentionally asymmetrical or hierarchical. The therapist has a power that is invested by society as a representative of technology and expertise, but the ethical stance towards the other balances this hierarchy, tempering the violence.

To be in ethical relation to the other is to put the other first before yourself. This requires that others be recognized as *subjects* in their own right and not merely as a construction or idea of the therapist in their own image. For example, it requires a man to see a woman as separate, as herself. For Cornell (1992), this thinking of sexual difference is crucial to the ethical relationship. In other words, an ethical position requires a location not a dissolution of the subject. Derrida (1984: 125) reworks the ethical philosophy of his countryman, the philosopher Emmanuel Levinas, within a metaphysics of the subject, in order to counter a worse kind of violence: 'If the other was not recognised as, ego, its entire alterity would collapse.' The ethical relation requires humility before the otherness of the other as the basis on which dialogue can proceed. This is what Luce Irigaray calls 'wonderment', which recognizes for example, that man and woman are irreducibly different and that a man can never know, only wonder what it is like to be a woman, to have an abortion, etc. (Cornell, 1992). Respect and humility before the other in which their 'otherness' is preserved is a prerequisite for 'dialogue'. The therapist does not relate to the client in terms of a theory of the other, but as *strangely* other. This goes beyond social constructionist theory, and all theory. The other is not merely the 'socially constructed' other, but *other*, with a different existence. This non-violative relationship respects the otherness of the other as a separate being.

To respect the other as other, to listen to, rather than assimilate the other as one's construction (in imagination or theory), requires a hierarchy that is *for* or favours the other. However the social reality is that a client comes to a therapist for 'therapy', whether voluntarily or involuntarily; that is, the therapist is in a privileged, hierarchical position to begin with. The conscious movement of the therapist towards the other as an ethical stance allows a true dialogue of unequals, in which both therapist and client are powerful *and* non-powerful.

The ethical challenge in psychotherapy is to minimize the therapist's potential to violate the other through therapy, which is an issue for the 'post-modern' as much as the 'modern' therapist. This is the potential violence of theory, authority, expertise and technology to override the client's contribution to their life narrative. If a therapist takes a position, they silence the voice of the other, yet if they do not take a position, the already silent voice of the other remains silent and marginalized. To counter the injustice of violence, the therapist must be powerful *and* non-powerful simultaneously, powerful against violence in the ethical relation, yet non-powerful so as to allow the other to speak. To be non-powerful *is* to be powerful, *for* the other. To not take a position is itself an act *of* violence, implicitly condoning the injustices suffered by the client. The task of deconstruction, then, is to expose the violence inherent in the notion of 'therapy', therapy masquerading as 'therapeutic'. What is undeconstructible in theory is this ethics, the 'face-to-face' encounter, the *talk* of therapy as a being-for-the-other.

Where is Deconstructing Psychotherapy?

What is involved, of course, is knowledge, still, but above all the knowledge of how, without renouncing the classical horns of objectivity and responsibility, without menacing the critical ideal of science and of philosophy and thus without renouncing knowledge, the obligation of responsibility can be extended. How far? Without limit, no doubt. (Derrida, quoted in Weber, 1995: 60)

Where are we to locate a deconstructing psychotherapy today? Is it to be found in the pages of therapy journals, at work in the consulting rooms of narrative therapists, in books written by social constructionists, in teaching faculties and universities, clinical psychology and therapy training programs? Yes and no! Yes, because deconstruction as justice is to be found wherever therapists are responsible and ethically question their own foundations and institutions, where they are in non-violative relation to others and recognize the powerlessness of their power and the power of their powerlessness, and where they engage others as *others* and not as images or constructions of themselves. No, because 'deconstructing psychotherapy' is not some particular method, school, or doctrine of therapy that can be 'titled' as such. Derrida does not renounce knowledge, power and structure but links them to respon-sibility. Weber (1995) calls this a 'structural non-knowing'. Likewise in therapy, deconstructing power is an issue of maximizing the ethical-just response of the therapist. The therapist's power is called into question. Whose *interests* is it responding to – for example, the need for therapists to be successful, to establish a career and reputation in the market place, a professional niche; personal needs for control and power; the demands of a particular approach or ideology? (Larner, 1995).

The deconstructing therapist is a therapist in deconstruction, with an attitude of openness, enquiry, doubleness, responsibility to others, and a learning to live with ghosts and traditions. The deconstruction of power does not require its dissolution, which would be an abnegation of responsibility, but its humane and just exercise (Jay, 1992). It involves a certain questioning of therapeutic practice, which perpetuates a technocracy and consolidates the power of the therapist to the detriment of the client. Perhaps it can be said that where psychotherapy is for justice and ethics, it is deconstructing. When it seeks its own power and position as an exercise of technology, it requires deconstructing. But then this is a moment-to-moment challenge present in every therapeutic encounter, a 'deconstruction in process' that is never complete and always before us. Ethics involves an imperative, an 'I follow' which we aspire to but can never fulfil. As an ideal or horizon, therapy as ethics is yet to come or always arriving, here and now in relationship.

Deconstructing is a powerful intervention because it questions the limits of privilege, showing that pure power or non-power is impossible. The position the deconstructing therapist takes is both inside *and* outside power simultaneously. The therapist does not abandon knowledge and technology, but questions its use from an ethical-political perspective. For example, does what I say or do contribute to a just outcome in therapy, or does it merely repeat and sustain the techno-political con-ditions by which therapy as a commodity in the market-place can be consumed more smoothly? A deconstructing psychotherapy may be one ethical-political space where unavoidable hierarchies of power in human institutions and relationships can at least be resisted (cf. Hindess, 1996).

The primary requirement here is for therapists to acknowledge their own potential to abuse, whatever their theoretical orientation.

It is not as if the problem of power in therapy can be finally solved by its deconstruction. If anything, this adds to its complexity. Professional authority, power and social hierarchy in the therapeutic institution are *real* enough. What is illusory is to believe in their efficacy for change as part of a therapeutic technology (Larner, 1995). As McCubbin and Cohen (1996: 13) comment in relation to the power disparities between clients and mental health practitioners: 'Reduced power in the therapeutic context becomes isolation, within the social/political context.' Conversation that acknowledges its context of power is more open, reciprocal and conducive to self-understanding (Kögler, 1996). The power realities of postmodern culture are manifest in all psychotherapies, deconstructing or otherwise. This is the violence of institutional discourse which constructs opposition (for example, modern *versus* postmodern, real *versus* constructed) and frames certain thinking as foundational or legitimate. All positions are grounded in 'a kind of violent exclusion that must efface its other and eliminate difference to preserve its purity' (Nealon, 1993: 76). A therapist who is willing to resist this tendency and defer their preferred theory and technique of psychotherapy long enough to listen to the voice of the client, is in ethical relation to the other and therefore working from a deconstructing position.

The question of location can be put as follows: is deconstructing psychotherapy a deconstructed psychotherapy or a psychotherapy that deconstructs? That is, do deconstructing moments occur in all approaches to psychotherapy, or only in a therapy that titles itself as 'deconstructing'? For example, can a cognitive-behavioural therapist, a psychoanalyst or a structural family therapist ever be 'deconstructing'? Or is this title to be restricted to a *post*-modern, discursive approach such as in narrative therapy? This itself is a political question of the power and institution of 'deconstructing psychotherapy'. From a Derridean perspective, deconstructing does not attack disciplines like psychotherapy from the outside, but inhabits them in a certain way. In this sense 'deconstructing psychotherapy' can refer to *any* psychotherapy that is deconstructing of its own power and institution in ethical relation to the other.

This is a question of how to think within the tradition of psychotherapy rather than to *break* with it. Here we have to beware of word magic which supposedly gets us 'beyond' power and metaphysics in psychotherapy. All such *meta*-narratives in psychotherapy should be regarded tenuously. A deconstructing psychotherapy does not leave the therapeutic tradition behind, but reconceives it, rethinking concepts like 'mind', 'system', the 'real', and 'truth'. These are not replaced by new ones like 'narrative', 'voice', 'story' etc., which would be yet another form of metaphysics, but *reinvented*. Narrative discourse need not be opposed to the psychotherapy tradition but inhabits it from within as its marginalized other, providing new possibilities of inscription. (For an example of how psychoanalytic ideas can be interpreted hermeneutically see Larner (1996).) A deconstructing psychotherapy is ultimately open-ended, manifold, simultaneously inventing new approaches to psychotherapy while deferring to its tradition. To think within a tradition is to ask questions previously unasked and unthought within it, to challenge its canon of discourse, to open it up to other ways of thinking and speaking as questions that make a difference (Gasché, 1994). Deconstructing psychotherapy is a plurality, a performative work based on what therapists *do* rather than what they believe (in terms of theory) they do. As such it is centred on issues of practice and ethics.

Perhaps it can be said in conclusion that psychotherapy is the subject of a radical critique *while* we do it. By deconstructing the cultural and discursive forces that shape or constitute its profession it becomes a more powerful (and political) location for change. However psychotherapy is also the *other* or 'beyond' to deconstructing, testing its relevance or application to the limit. As a domain which encounters first hand the reality of a life narrative, psychotherapy offers a site from which to critique deconstruction as an investigation of the ethical and political. This book is not only an expression of the possibility of deconstructing psychotherapy, but also a challenge to justify its presuppositions and expose its naked power. In this sense, psychotherapy is a 'beyond within' (Cornell, 1995) the field of deconstructing, both inside and outside its system, questioning its right to speak on behalf of the other. But then this stance is itself deconstructing, which, as Derrida (1995b) says, is *what happens or comes to pass.*

References

Anderson, H. and Goolishian, H. (1992) 'The client is the expert: a not-knowing approach to therapy', in S. McNamee and K. Gergen (eds), *Therapy as Social Construction*. London: Sage.

Bernasconi, R. (1987) 'Deconstruction and the possibility of ethics', in J. Sallis (ed.), *Deconstruction and Philosophy*. Chicago: University of Chicago Press.

Bernstein, R.J. (1993) 'An allegory of modernity/postmodernity: Habermas and Derrida', in G.B. Madison (ed.), *Working Through Derrida*. Evanston, IL: Northwestern University Press.

Chase, C. (1995) 'Reading epitaphs', in A. Havenkamp (ed.), *Deconstruction is in America: A New Sense of the Political*. New York and London: New York University Press.

Churvin, P. (1996) 'To live more comfortably with difference: an interview with Peter Churchin by Maureen Crago', *The Australian and New Zealand Journal of Family Therapy*, 17 (3): 147–52.

Cornell, D. (1992) *The Philosophy of the Limit*. New York and London: Routledge.

Cornell, D. (1995) 'Rethinking the beyond within the real', *Cultural Critique*, 30: 223–33.

Derrida, J. (1984) *Signsponge*, trans. Richard Rand. New York: Columbia University Press.

Derrida, J. (1989) 'On colleges and philosophy', in L. Appignanesi (ed.), *Postmodernism: ICA Documents*. London: Free Association Books.

Derrida, J. (1992) 'Force of law: the mystical foundation of authority', in D. Cornell, M. Rosenfeld and D.G. Carlson (eds), *Deconstruction and the Possibility of Justice*. New York: Routledge.

Derrida, J. (1994) *Specters of Marx*. New York and London: Routledge.

Derrida, J. (1995a) 'Interview with Jacques Derrida', in F. Rötzer (ed.), *Conversations with French Philosophers*. New Jersey: Humanities Press.

Derrida, J. (1995b) 'The time is out of joint', in A. Havenkamp (ed.), *Deconstruction is in America: A New Sense of the Political*. New York and London: New York University Press.

Derrida, J. (1995c) *The Gift of Death*, trans. David Wills. Chicago and London: University of Chicago Press.

Gasché, R. (1994) *Inventions of Difference: on Jacques Derrida*. Cambridge, MA: Harvard University Press.

Gibney, P. (1996) 'To embrace paradox (once more with feeling): a commentary on narrative/conversational therapies and the therapeutic relationship', in C. Flaskas and A. Perlesz (eds), *The Therapeutic Relationship in Systemic Therapy*. London: Karnac Books.

Hindess, B. (1996) *Discourses of Power*. Oxford: Blackwell.

Inger, I.B. (1993) 'A dialogic perspective for family therapy: the contributions of Martin Buber and Gregory Bateson', *Journal of Family Therapy*, 15: 293–314.

Inger, I.B. and Inger, J. (1994) *Creating an Ethical Position in Family Therapy*. London: Karnac Books.

Jay, P. (1992) 'Bridging the gap: the position of politics in deconstruction', *Cultural Critique*, 22: 47–74.

Kearney, R. (1993) 'Derrida's ethical re-turn', in G.B. Madison (ed.), *Working Through Derrida*. Evanston, IL: Northwestern University Press.

Kögler, H.H. (1996) *The Power of Dialogue: Critical Hermeneutics after Gadamer and Foucault*, trans. P. Hendrickson. Cambridge, MA: MIT Press.

Larner, G. (1994a) 'Para-modern family therapy: deconstructing post-modernism', *Australian and New Zealand Journal of Family Therapy*, 15: 11–16.

Larner, G. (1994b) 'A miracle metaphor for family therapy', *Australian and New Zealand Journal of Family Therapy*, 15: 208–14.

Larner, G. (1995) 'The real as illusion: deconstructing power in family therapy', *Journal of Family Therapy*, 17: 191–217.

Larner, G. (1996) 'Child family therapy', *Family Process*, 35: 423–40.

Larner, G. (1998) 'Through a glass darkly: narrative as destiny', *Theory & Psychology*, 8 (4): 549–72.

Mair, M. (1989) *Between Psychology and Psychotherapy: a Poetics of Experience*. London and New York: Routledge.

McCubbin, M. and Cohen, D. (1996) 'Extremely unbalanced: interest divergence and power disparities between clients and psychiatry', *International Journal of Law and Psychiatry*, 19 (1): 1–25.

Nealon, J.T. (1993) *Double Reading: Postmodernism after Deconstruction*. Ithaca and London: Cornell University Press.

Norris, C. (1995) 'Jurisprudence, deconstruction and literary theory: a brief survey and critical review', *Res Publica*, 1 (1): 57–69.

Radical Philosophy (1996) 'Symposium: spectres of Derrida', *Radical Philosophy*, 75: 26–41.

Tedlock, T. and Mannheim, B. (eds) (1995) *The Dialogic Emergence of Culture.* Urbana and Chicago: University of Illinois Press.

Weber, S. (1992) 'In the name of the law', in D. Cornell, M. Rosenfeld and D.G. Carlson (eds), *Deconstruction and the Possibility of Justice.* New York: Routledge.

Weber, S. (1995) 'Upping the ante: deconstruction as parodic practice', in A. Havenkamp (ed.), *Deconstruction is in America: A New Sense of the Political.* New York and London: New York University Press.

Yablon, C.M. (1992) 'Forms', in D. Cornell, M. Rosenfeld and D.G. Carlson (eds), *Deconstruction and the Possibility of Justice.* New York: Routledge.

4

CLEMENTIS'S HAT: FOUCAULT AND THE POLITICS OF PSYCHOTHERAPY

Vincent Fish

It's true . . . that the circuits of psychiatricalizing and psychologizing, even if they pass through the parents, the peer group and the immediate surroundings, are finally supported by a vast medico-administrative complex. But the 'free' medicine of the 'liberal' doctor, the private psychiatrist or home psychologist are not an alternative to institutional medicine. They are part of the network, even in the case where they are poles apart . . .

(Foucault, 1989: 110–11)

One approach to understanding Foucault's work, and its importance for psychotherapy, is to see it as perhaps the most influential of a series of critiques of the Enlightenment project. Enlightenment philosophers conceived of *reason* as the means by which selves ('subjects') could autonomously attain to truth, and thus to freedom; as the firm foundation for developing not only valid systems of knowledge but also beneficial, egalitarian forms of government (as expressed, for example, in the American, French, and other revolutions), and as the basis for justice and social progress. Enlightenment assumptions of rationality, individualism, and progress continue to underpin the workings of modernity in Western culture, including the institutional network defined by its involvement with 'mental health/mental illness'.

In Foucault's view, however, the rationalism of the Enlightenment does not lead to emancipation or guarantee the autonomy of subjects, but instead results in new forms of domination based on the systematic ordering of knowledge about human life. Beginning in the seventeenth century, he argued, reductive theoretical constructions of various aspects of human existence cohered with modern forms of social regulation. These evolving discourses, these regimes of power/knowledge, continue to structure the field of human interactions while constituting the terms of individual experience.

Foucault, who was born in 1926 and died in 1984, was first trained as a philosopher (under the Hegel scholar Jean Hyppolite and the Marxist structuralist Louis Althusser), then studied psychopathology and psychology, and eventually took his doctorate in the history of science under Canguilhem. In his earlier writings, from 1961 to 1971, he employed an 'archaeological' approach, focusing increasingly on the analysis of discourses as rule-governed objects in themselves. In this way he examined the development of the modern discourses that constitute mental illness and its treatment, the nature of medical practice, and the human sciences. In 1970, moved perhaps in part by the events in France of May 1968 during his time in Tunis, Foucault began a shift to his 'genealogical' method. This approach emphasized much more the material conditions that embody and support the discursivities which archaeology identifies. In his genealogies, he investigated the formation of the subject within disciplinary institutions (e.g. prisons, schools, hospitals) and the historical subsumption and construction of sexuality within the discourses of biology, medicine, psychopathology, and others. During this period Foucault discussed the workings of power, especially what he called 'power/knowledge'. Foucault had come to see discourses as ineluctably implying and implied by particular institutional, societal arrangements. He used 'power/knowledge' to refer to the constant, ubiquitous effects of this conjunction of systematized knowledge and material arrangements upon both subjectivity and human interactions. In the 1980s, without abandoning his previous archaeological and genealogical positions, Foucault's attention turned to 'the care of the self' and ethics.

Opportunity and Context

Attention to Foucault's work within psychotherapy and related disciplines has created an 'opening' – one that allows for important examinations of the process and context of psychotherapy which are not bound by the usual, orthodox assumptions of the field. The opportunity for psychotherapists in studying Foucault's writings, presented particularly by the examples of Foucault's archaeologies and genealogies, is to explore psychotherapy as an institution; to further our understanding of the political, historical forces that have shaped, and continue to shape, in Foucault's terms, its discourses and practices. In Foucault's framework, these discourses and practices, in turn, define both clients' and therapists' experience and interactional options. I believe that it is critical for psychotherapists to keep in mind the immediate, inescapable connection between, on the one hand, clients' and therapists' subjectivity and behaviour and, on the other, historical, ongoing institutional and cultural processes. I think if one reads Foucault at all seriously, one cannot avoid making this connection and, in making it, understanding its *political* nature. Thus, especially for many in the United States,

Foucault has been able to broaden the definition of politics beyond what it is typically taken to be in the U.S. – the liberal pluralistic notion of overt campaigning and lobbying, and the activities of the official political parties – to include features of all social relationships and subjectivity itself.

But, if we stay within Foucault's framework, how far can we go with this connection between subjectivity and discourse? While pointing us toward certain understandings, I will argue below that his schematization of social processes also narrows our view sharply. Thus, I am deeply distrustful of Foucault's work at a number of points, even as I acknowledge its potentially positive significance. Some of this distrust, I must admit, also comes from the ease with which Foucault is appropriated or, like the Bible, selectively interpreted while disregarding the entirety of his work and its context. In this, of course, Foucault is like many other influential authors who, possessing a subtle and eclectic intellect, produce a sizeable, often contradictory and ambiguous, body of writings. More specifically, though, I will focus here on two of my reservations: the way Foucault consistently appears to value history while he actually obscures it, and appears to value political understanding while he undermines political agency.

Prior to reviewing these concerns, I wish to stress that Foucault wrote, and that we each read him, from within particular and often widely varying intellectual and political contexts. As an illustration in this vein, I want to briefly raise the question of why it is Foucault's work, rather than someone else's, that has been so successful in introducing the notion of politico-cultural discourse into our field. Since I am in the U.S. and am more familiar with developments here, my discussion will reflect this.

There are undoubtedly many factors involved in Foucault's recent ascension in the West; again for illustration, I will focus on just one possibility: the cultural valence of Marxism. Even in the U.S., in other fields such as literary criticism and sociology, the awareness of the limitations of liberal pluralism is usually associated with Marx, socialism, and with theorists who incorporate or elaborate such Marxist ideas as class-conflict, alienation, and the role of ideology in moulding consciousness. In the U.S., however, attempts in the first half of this century to establish socialist and class-conflictual perspectives from within the social sciences have ultimately failed (Gilkeson, 1995; Recchiuti, 1995). This has been true also for the discipline most related to psychotherapy – psychology (Nicholson, 1997). In American psychology since the 1950s, theorizing that incorporates Marxist or socialist concepts is simply seen as not viable.

Could the reception given Foucault's writings here in the overlapping field of psychotherapy be related to the fact that he eschews a focus on class-conflict or, indeed, on force, interests, or political agency? More generally, could his overt distancing from Marx be responsible for some of Foucault's acceptability both among those for whom Marxism has been outlawed and stigmatized, as in the U.S., and among those for whom the painful link of Marx's ideas with repressive Stalinist regimes may eclipse any other ways of looking at Marxist thought? If so, there is considerable irony in this, since in Foucault's academic environment, in contrast to circumstances in the U.S., Marx's writings were more than accepted: they were highly esteemed and routinely studied. So much so that, for Foucault and many of his academic peers, the problem was not whether to take Marx seriously but rather to find some way to move their political thinking beyond the generic Marxian assumptions which permeated it. Indeed, Foucault was a member of the French Communist party in the early 1950s. However, as he formulated his own approach to understanding society he made it clear that he viewed himself as stepping out of the Marxist tradition and criticizing it as he did other traditions, if not more so.

Thus, neglecting the intellectual and political contexts in which Foucault's work developed, and in which we react to his work, including the relevance of Marxism, would be misleading. Foucault, as his own theories would declare, did not operate in a discursive vacuum, nor do we. In challenging Marxist and structuralist tenets, for instance, he necessarily found himself operating in the same intellectual territory defined by these world views. The idea that subjectivity is constituted by particular aspects of the social world, over which individuals have little or no control, is thus not new with Foucault. What Foucault does is supplant the role of relations of production and ideology in constructing consciousness in Marx's conception with his own formulations of 'discourse' and 'power/knowledge.' The distinction and its implications are not trivial, of course. Nevertheless, Foucault, in this instance, follows in a conceptual tradition defined by Marx (1859). The 'shape' of the issue, if you will, is identical in Marx and Foucault, as it is in many other critical writers as well.

However one views the reasons for Foucault's relative appeal within psychotherapy, it is important to recognize that many others besides Foucault, including Marxists and socialists such as Althusser, Gramsci and Lukes, have worked with this theme – how subjectivity is constituted by power relations – as well. We need to be alert to characteristics of our own context that enable one perspective to capture our view while obscuring others. Investigating and criticizing other, related, non-Foucauldian approaches to subjectivity, social dynamics, agency, and resistance is an additional challenge and opportunity that Foucault's ideas ought to pose for psychotherapy.

History, Memory and Resistance

Now I return to two fundamental pitfalls that I believe are inherent in Foucault's ideas: the eradication of history and the loss of political agency. Although Foucault points to the workings of powerful cultural/institutional influences that underpin the individual's everyday experience, he at once mystifies and obscures these influences. Despite the exceptions to be found here and there in his writings, the main result of Foucault's apparent historicization and politicization of cultural processes – his archaeologies and genealogies – is, ironically, to de-historicize and de-politicize the relationship of the individual to these same processes. First, Foucault undermines a historical perspective by using historical data arbitrarily, mistakenly, and, he himself avers, fictionally. Sedgwick (1982) is among those who have documented some of the more blatant inaccuracies and misunderstandings in Foucault's *Madness and Civilization* (1965). Second, Foucault is, overall, vague and pessimistic about the possibility of individual agency and resistance. As Said has pointed out, 'With [his] profoundly pessimistic view went also a singular lack of interest in the force of effective resistance to it, in choosing particular sites of intensity, choices which, we see from the evidence on all sides, always exist and are often successful in impeding, if not actually stopping, the progress of tyrannical power' (1986: 151).

It should be observed that, especially in his later writings, Foucault did discuss the individual subject as an active agent and the inevitability of resistance to domination. He was, after all, in his personal life, an activist for a number of political causes. At the same time, however, he did not repudiate his more influential pronouncements and ideas regarding disciplinary power, e.g. 'the non-reversible subordination of one group to another' (Foucault, 1979: 222–3), nor did he ever explore the concept of resistance much beyond noting its faint, constant presence in the equations of power/knowledge. For Foucault, resistance destabilizes what is dominant; it doesn't stabilize anything different and better. His examples of resistance usually have to do with individuals or crowds *reacting against*, and these reactions are, in anything but the short-run, doomed. We don't find support in Foucault's world view for planned, long-term resistance, in cooperation with others and toward the installation of specific liberating social forms. He was candid about his hesitancy in this regard (Foucault, 1989: 281).

It might seem to some that Foucault, toward the end of his life, made important revisions or additions to his concept of power/knowledge and came to recognize the meaningfulness of individual agency in the 'care of the self'. However, I believe that a careful reading of his later pronouncements indicates that Foucault did not move very far from his original views about power/knowledge. In an interview in 1984, a little over six months before his death, Foucault attempted to clarify and, perhaps, amend his position on the relationship of truth and power:

> [W]hen I talk about power relations and games of truth, I am absolutely not saying that games of truth are just concealed power relations – that would be a horrible exaggeration . . . One can show, for example, that the medicalization

of madness, in other words, the organization of medical knowledge (*savoir*) around individuals designated as mad, was connected with a whole series of social and economic processes at a given time, but also with institutions and practices of power. This fact in no way impugns the scientific validity or the therapeutic effectiveness of psychiatry; it does not endorse psychiatry, but neither does it invalidate it. (1997: 296)

This passage illustrates one of Foucault's most persistent and pernicious tendencies: his ability to simultaneously valorize and efface historical reality. Here, he first implies that there is some truth to be spoken, beyond the connection of power and knowledge. But he then refers to a history – 'the medicalization of madness' – that he has also described elsewhere as fictional and which others have shown to be factually inaccurate. Next, he separates this history from the 'scientific validity [and] the therapeutic effectiveness of psychiatry'.

We may ask, though, how could any true history of psychiatry, or understanding of its practices of power, *not* involve its validity and effectiveness? For instance, if certain psychiatric situations entail domination by some totalizing discourse (remembering that Foucault viewed psychiatry primarily as a disciplinary institution: '. . . coercive practices – such as those of psychiatry and the prison system . . .' (1997: 282)), how could such domination not be connected to the validity and effectiveness of psychiatry for individuals? Does Foucault wish us to understand that dominating discourses and practices generally constitute subjectivity, yet are neutral in their impact upon precisely those aspects of subjectivity that we would call 'mental health'? This cannot be. Further, in decoupling his own history-telling from truth, and disconnecting psychiatric validity and effectiveness from history, Foucault displays a disconcerting indifference, on this theoretical level at least, to people's real struggles and experience.

His later position is indeed a continuation of the segregation of historical reality and 'scientific' truth that Foucault began in his earlier works. In the collection, *Power/Knowledge*, he responded to a question about the concept of ideology in this way:

The notion of ideology appears to me to be difficult to make use of . . . [L]ike it or not, it always stands in virtual opposition to something else which is supposed to count as truth. Now I believe that the problem does not consist in drawing the line between that in a discourse which falls under the category of scientificity or truth, and that which comes under some other category, but in seeing historically how effects of truth are produced within discourses which in themselves are neither true or false. (Foucault, 1980: 60)

For those who are oppressed, however, the problem of where to draw the line between ideology and truth, particularly historical truth, is the critical one. Vaclav Havel, writing prior to the 'Velvet Revolution' in Czechoslovakia, put it this way:

Ideology, claiming to base its authority on history, becomes history's greatest enemy. But the hostility is double-edged: if ideology destroys history by explaining it completely, then history destroys ideology by unfolding in an unpredictable way. Ideology, of course, can destroy history only ideologically, but the power based on that ideology can suppress history in real ways. In fact, it has no choice: if history, by unfolding unpredictably, were allowed to demonstrate that ideology is wrong, it would deprive power of its legitimacy (Havel, 1991: 336)

For instance, as Havel's countryman Milan Kundera begins his novel, *The Book of Laughter and Forgetting*,

In February 1948, Communist leader Klement Gottwald stepped out on the balcony of a Baroque palace in Prague to address the hundreds of thousands of his fellow citizens packed into Old Town Square. It was a crucial moment in Czech history – a fateful moment of the kind that occurs once or twice in a millennium.

Gottwald was flanked by his comrades, with Clementis standing next to him. There were snow flurries, it was cold, and Gottwald was bareheaded. The solicitous Clementis took off his own fur cap and set it on Gottwald's head.

The Party propaganda section put out hundreds of thousands of copies of a photograph of that balcony with Gottwald, a fur cap on his head and comrades at his side, speaking to the nation. On that balcony the history of Communist Czechoslovakia was born. Every child knew the photograph from posters, schoolbooks, and museums.

Four years later Clementis was charged with treason and hanged. The propaganda section immediately airbrushed him out of history and, obviously, out of all the photographs as well. Ever since, Gottwald has stood on that balcony alone. Where Clementis once stood, there is only bare palace wall. All that remains of Clementis is the cap on Gottwald's head. (Kundera, 1994: 1)

A Foucauldian approach to this anecdote of Kundera's might identify the activities of the propagandists as an expression of a 'totalizing discourse', a 'regime of truth' which is resisted and destabilized by Kundera's passage. As Charles Taylor (1986: 70) points out, though, there is not room in Foucault's conception of power/knowledge for 'truth' as historical *accuracy*: 'There is no truth which can be espoused, defended, rescued *against* systems of power. On the contrary, each such system defines its own variant of truth. And there is no escape from power into freedom, for such systems of power are co-extensive with human society. We can only step from one to another.'

Nevertheless, in contrast to the enervated history of Foucault, the significance of this example of Kundera's 'resistance' is in its correction of purposely inculcated historical inaccuracy by referring to historical fact. Clementis *was* on the balcony, he *was* accused and hung for specific, political, reasons. It was the open discussion of the historical truth about Clementis that was potentially destabilizing, that would 'demonstrate that ideology was wrong'. That was why specific leaders ordered particular subordinates to airbrush certain photos, rewrite history books along definite lines, and so forth: in order to subvert memory and induce forgetting and silence.

This strategy for maintaining power by influencing people's awareness and speech is both ancient and common among those in charge. The airbrush, for instance, is not some new technique of power, just a new edition of an ancient tool, the chisel. After Thutmose III of Egypt began his reign in 1469 BC, he ordered the name of the previous ruler, Queen Hatshepsut, who, as his regent, had up to that point been able to delay his taking the throne, expunged from every public inscription. In its place he ordered his own name to be carved or the name of one of his ancestors.

On a micro-level, Faynik and I (Fish, 1990; Fish and Faynik, 1997) have discussed incest perpetrators' attempts to control aspects of their family's self-descriptive stories. Relatedly, on an institutional level in the mental health system, inquiries of clients about childhood sexual abuse are often not made (e.g. Pruitt and Kappius, 1992), and information about clients' abuse often is not recorded in their charts (Jacobson et al., 1987; Lipschitz et al., 1996). Frequently, individuals who meet the criteria for diagnoses that would reflect their history of childhood abuse do not receive these diagnoses (Craine et al., 1988). Human groups and institutions, including the mental health system, have many ways of dehistoricizing patients' problems in the service of ideology without resorting to airbrushes and chisels. 'The struggle . . . against power,' says the first protagonist in Kundera's novel, 'is the struggle of memory against forgetting' (1994: 1).

It is one of the most frustrating things for me about Foucault that he sees this issue very clearly at times and yet steps away from its import and implications in his major writings. In 1974, he remarked:

> There's a real fight going on. Over what? Over what we can roughly describe as popular memory . . . [P]opular history was . . . more alive, more clearly formulated in the 19th century, where, for instance, there was a whole tradition of struggles which were transmitted orally, or in writing or songs, etc.
>
> Now, a whole number of apparatuses have been set up ('popular literature,' cheap books and the stuff that's taught in school as well) to obstruct the flow of this popular memory. And it could be said that this attempt has been pretty successful. The historical knowledge the working class has of itself is continually shrinking . . .
>
> Today, cheap books aren't enough. There are much more effective means like television and the cinema. And I believe this was one way of reprogramming popular memory . . . So people are shown not what they were, but what they must remember having been.

Since memory is actually a very important factor in struggle . . ., if one controls people's memory, one controls their dynamism. And one also controls their experience, their knowledge of previous struggles. Just what the Resistance was, must no longer be known . . . (Foucault, 1989: 91–2)

Mapping the Social World

Foucault's archaeological and genealogical frameworks allow us to locate our work with clients in a much larger, more richly interconnected societal terrain than our training programs and intervention models have usually hinted at. His geography of this cultural landscape is selective, as are all such geographies – it identifies many significant features while omitting some and distorting others. Every intellectual construction of the social field inevitably has areas that become blurry, indistinct, impossible, and Foucault's is no exception. I have attempted to point to some of these difficult areas regarding history and agency on Foucault's map.

One of the virtues of Foucault's account of the social domain is that it indicates, or at least implies, a number of regions of relevance for psychotherapists. There are two that I will consider here, perforce very sketchily:

First, how should the therapist take into account the idea that important aspects of clients' subjectivity, including the problems for which they seek help, are constituted by discourses – that is, by the effects of power/knowledge and, I would add, by ideology? Second, how should we understand the nature of the power relations between therapist and client; what is the therapist's proper role in these?

The Client, Power/Knowledge, Ideology

How may the problematic discursive contexts of our clients' lives best be addressed? Foucault's neglect of history and agency leaves purely Foucauldian-based methods incomplete. Some sort of supplementation is required. In a book on the relevance of deconstruction, it is fitting then that I introduce here the approach to deconstruction of Michael Ryan (1982), which is targeted on the same structures and processes that occupy Foucault. Ryan, however, is more fastidious about historical truth and identifies the role of interests and ideology. Eagleton (1986: 85), reviewing Ryan's *Marxism and Deconstruction*, notes, 'Deconstruction, as Derrida and Ryan understand it, insists not that truth is illusory but that it is institutional'. He alludes to Ryan's (1982: 24) tenet that deconstruction ought to operate in relation to the '. . . weave of differ-ential relations, institutions, conventions, histories, practices . . . and . . .

the institutionality . . . of language'. In Ryan's interpretation, Eagleton says, 'To "deconstruct," then, is to reinscribe and resituate meanings, events and objects within broader movements and structures; it is, so to speak, to reverse the imposing tapestry in order to expose in all its unglamorously dishevelled tangle the threads constituting the well-heeled image it presents to the world' (Eagleton, 1986: 80). Yet, as Eagleton points out, 'Derrida himself has hardly been remarkable for his "institutional" as opposed to discursive analyses . . . It is Michel Foucault, not Jacques Derrida, who has occupied the "institutional" area' (1986: 79). One way of regarding Ryan's conception of deconstruction is that it provides a realist, historicist, anti-ideological lens through which to scrutinize the relational, institutional terrain that Foucault has mapped out.

Power and Ideology in Families

The abuse of 'local' power relations in families and couples is one potential target for such a hybrid deconstructive focus. Fish and Faynik (1997) describe a case in which an intervention that may be viewed in this light was employed in response to an incident during family therapy. Individual sessions, mother-daughter sessions, and couple sessions had been ongoing with a family in which long-term father-daughter incest had occurred. The father had been removed from the home and had had no contact with his daughter for some months. Eventually, a first family session was held to gauge the parents' ability to respond productively together to their six-year-old daughter. In the videotaped family session, in spite of the parents' apparent progress in individual sessions, it was evident that the father was still overly controlling and physically involved with the daughter while the mother appeared to be oblivious to this. In their following individual sessions, the parents' stated belief about what had happened in this session was that their 'mischievous' daughter had gravitated to her father for attention that the mother wasn't giving her. Neither parent's subsequent story about the family session included recognition of the father's controlling, intrusive behaviour with his daughter. In the following couple's session, therefore, with the parents' agreement, the therapists played the videotape of the family session, allowing them to compare their initial stories about the session with documentation of what had actually occurred. After watching the tape, both parents revised their previous stories, in which the father's abuse of his powerful position with his daughter had not been spoken and thus had effectively disappeared from view. They were able to see and describe the father's actual behaviour with his daughter which had, in fact, included multiple verbal and nonverbal commands to his daughter, previously unnoticed and unremembered by the mother, to sit in the same chair with him even as she was moving toward her mother.

This couple's story of the family session evolved to the point of addressing the father's misuse of the power relations between him and his daughter because they were willing to take into account the real history of the session. The parents' original construction had an ideological aspect, in that it supported the father's control by concealing it and weakened the mother's position by wrongly portraying her and her daughter as essentially in conflict. Once this 'local ideology' was proved wrong by the real history of the session, then the link between the family members' behaviour and experience in that session and the broader structure and history of the father's sexual abuse of his daughter became obvious. For example, prior to the abuse being discovered, part of the father's historic pattern had been to consciously overindulge his daughter against his wife's wishes. One result of this was that a certain amount of conflict between mother and daughter was set up, and had made it difficult for the mother to feel certain of their relationship despite their closeness in other ways. Although it was not discussed in Fish and Faynik's (1997) article, the events of the family session could also have been located in the 'weave of differential relations, institutions, conventions, histories, practices' that bear on gender, patriarchy, marriage, sexuality, and related issues.

Incidentally, because of Foucault's emphasis on the disciplinary nature of the mental health field and on surveillance, one might be tempted to categorize video recording as a technique of surveillance and discipline. Video can certainly be used as such, in a Foucauldian sense, in many situations, including therapy sessions. In this case, however, it established an historical record that was accessible to the family as well as the therapists. In addition, while it showed the family, it also showed the therapists as they were – unable to formulate an intervention during the session suitable to the complexity of the situation (which, for brevity I shall not explicate here) and so remaining, albeit temporarily and uncomfortably, passively complicit in the low-level, non-statutory but nonetheless real mistreatment of the daughter.

Memory and Oppression

Locating the line between ideology and truth, reclaiming history, and conserving memories, are pressing issues for many clients with a wide range of presenting problems – often these problems are associated with some form of obvious physical, sexual, or emotional abuse. At the same time that these are clinical issues they are also inevitably political issues. This has been made plain, for example, by the furious debate over the veracity of delayed memories of childhood sexual abuse that has been raging in the U.S. and has recently spread to other countries. The importance of truth, memory, and history is also evident for those whose psychological problems are connected to political violence. In his paper 'Addressing Human Response to War and Atrocity: Major

Challenges in Research and Practice and the Limitations of Western Psychiatric Models', Summerfield (1995: 26) observes that 'It is significant that, in El Salvador, people are worried that they have begun to forget all the names of those murdered by the military in the 1980s . . . As Primo Levi, a survivor of the Jewish Holocaust, wrote of what he had witnessed, "If understanding is impossible, knowing is imperative."'

However, as Foucault might have cautioned us, attempts to conserve memories of political violence are not themselves empty of political content or impervious to political, institutional forces. Julie Taylor (1994) demonstrates this in her discussion of the Nunca Mas ('Never Again') movements in Argentina, Brazil and Uruguay. After Argentina's return to civilian rule following the 'Dirty War' against its own citizens of 1976–83 (out of which came the term *desaparecido* – 'disappeared'), steps were taken to document the terrorism of that era. When oppressive military regimes subsequently fell out of power in Uruguay, in 1984, and Brazil, in 1985, similar efforts were initiated in these countries as well. Taylor quotes Wechsler (1990: 3–4) on one of the overt functions of the Nunca Mas projects: '. . . [T]he desire for truth is often more urgently felt by the victims of torture than the desire for justice. People don't necessarily insist that the former torturers go to jail – there's been enough of jail – but they do want to see the truth established.' The thorough, open acknowledgement of the truth became an end in itself; this acknowledgement, so public and supposedly so thorough, somehow guaranteeing 'Never again'. She points out, though, that the 'Never Again' movements were subsumed by juridical discourses and bureaucracies that reduced the story of organized state terrorism into a series of decontextualized, disconnected accounts of individual victimization and individual malfeasance.

In this atomization of coordinated, strategic violence and, quite frequently, collective resistance, certain kinds of memories were excluded. Asks Taylor, 'What of collective massacres, thought to be more representative of the working-class experience? What of whole provinces where mass death came in the guise of open military confrontations that fit the rubric of battles, except for the sinister fact that casualties were never reported or even recognized? What about the memory, significantly almost never voiced, of Tucuman's sugarcane fields in flames when the armed forces set them afire to destroy the hidden guerrilla?' (Taylor, 1994: 201). There was no place for these in the Nunca Mas process. In this way, the Nunca Mas projects became powerful tools for obtaining forgetting and silence about matters that might prove troubling to the current ruling groups.

Like the law, psychotherapy is an atomizing institution. We treat individuals, whether as isolated units or in couples, families, and artificially formed groups, within discursive frameworks (therapy models, psychological theories, medical definitions, business relationships, professionalism, government regulation of practice, and so on) that do not speak of collectivities, domination of one group by another, ideology, or the possibility of governmentally authored or sanctioned oppression. The legitimacy and necessity of institutions that address the individual case, like the law, psychotherapy, and medicine, are undeniable. The question is how to also integrate ways of explicating the connections between the individual situation and the context in which it occurs, including the nature of the institution itself. As Summerfield reminds us in the case of those psychologically traumatized by organized state violence, 'Posttraumatic symptoms are not just a private and individual problem but also an indictment of the social contexts which produced them' (1995: 26), and he criticizes the philosophy of treatment that solely individualizes and medicalizes without bridging these domains. As psychotherapists, we need to investigate and adopt models that link individual symptoms and social contexts. To the extent that Foucault's insights can help us with this, we are in his debt.

A Multicultural Note

In his intellectual lineage and in his historiography, Foucault is quintessentially parochial. He wrote from within the French academic tradition, and was rooted predominantly in Greek, Roman and Western European precedents. Nevertheless, his work has heavily influenced what is now termed postcolonial theory, through writers such as Bhabha (1994), Said (1978) and Spivak (Landry and MacLean, 1996). However, each of them has had to grapple with and compensate for various aspects of Foucault's thought, not least its innate Eurocentrism.

The growing focus on multicultural issues within psychotherapy could be profitably informed by Foucault's work. It would be even better served, though, by attending to the work of writers who are themselves deeply involved in postcolonial or subaltern studies and who have incorporated the ideas of Foucault and others, such as Gramsci and Derrida, into their own original formulations. Postcolonial theory offers frameworks for analysing, for example, the influential role of white researchers in the area of multicultural psychotherapy (Parham, 1993).

Power Relations between Therapist and Client

The argument, advanced frequently by therapists who espouse post-modern viewpoints, that it is both beneficial and possible to reduce or eliminate the role of power in the therapist–client relationship finds no support in Foucault. First, any acquaintance with his concept of power/ knowledge scuttles this idea at once. As White and Epston (1990: 29) correctly acknowledge:

. . . [W]e are unable to take a benign view of our own practices. Nor are we able simply to assume that our practices are primarily determined by our motives, or that we can avoid all participation in the field of power/knowledge through an examination of such personal motives.

Second, Foucault contradicts those, including White (1991), who suggest that therapists can and ought to mitigate the power inherent in their 'expert' knowledge by striving for communicational transparency with their clients. Foucault asserts:

The idea that there could exist a state of communication that would allow games of truth to circulate freely, without any constraints or coercive effects, seems utopian to me. This is precisely a failure to see that power relations are not something that is bad in itself, that we have to break free of. I do not think that a society can exist without power relations, if by that one means the strategies by which individuals try to direct and control the conduct of others. The problem, then, is not to try to dissolve them in the utopia of completely transparent communication but to acquire the rules of law, the management techniques, and also the morality, the *ethos*, the practice of the self, that will allow us to play these games of power with as little domination as possible. (1980: 298)

Further on he makes a remark that is specifically relevant to the therapist role:

I see nothing wrong in the practice of a person who, knowing more than others in a specific game of truth, tells those others what to do, teaches them, and transmits knowledge and techniques to them. The problem in such practices where power – which is not in itself a bad thing – must inevitably come into play is knowing how to avoid . . . domination effects. (1980: 298)

The power imbalance within the therapist–client relationship derives not only from the expert role of the therapist but from other sources as well, such as the nature of the emotional attachment that many clients make to their therapists, clients' frequent membership in disadvantaged groups, and the societally determined influence that clinicians have in other institutional arenas (particularly within the legal system). The therapist–client relationship, including its formal boundaries and the skewing of power toward the therapist, is the basis for therapeutic work. This can be seen especially clearly in those cases where clients, who in any other context (because of their superior intelligence, education, status, wealth, or skills) would overmatch the person who happens to be their therapist and be impervious to their influence, may be helped within the context of the societally constructed therapeutic relationship. The therapist's power should be confined within the therapeutic relationship, be used for therapeutic purposes, support the client's communication and adequate reciprocal influence with the therapist, be monitored by the therapist and others (such as supervisors, consultants, and institutional regulators), and be counterbalanced by the availability to the client of powerful means of redress outside of the therapeutic relationship. In the U.S., there are a variety of remedies, albeit imperfect, for clients who believe that therapists have abused their power, for example, through criminal and civil courts, state departments of licensing and regulation, and professional organizations.

The legal and administrative governance of psychotherapy, and the *ethos* of practitioners, require constant attention and improvement. But it is these things, as Foucault notes, that ought to frame our concern about power differences in therapeutic relationships. In this light, attempts by therapists, however well-motivated, to dispense with power that is inherent in the societally constituted structure of their role and which, in that sense, is not under their control, are vain and misplaced.

Conclusion

It is worth attending to Foucault, as Walzer (1986: 52–3) put it, '. . . not only because Foucault is influential but also because his account of our everyday politics . . . is right enough to be disturbing – and also because it is importantly wrong'. I have been explicit in my view that Foucault is importantly wrong, for example, in neglecting individual agency, historical accuracy, and the uses of ideology. I have made an issue of disappearances: the disappearances of people, collectivities, and histories that individuals, acting separately or in concert, have engineered by purposefully using and crafting ideologies backed by force. At times these disappearances are self-consciously and voluntarily resisted, successfully or unsuccessfully, by those targeted or by still other individuals and groups. These material processes themselves, however, disappear within Foucault's framework. The great risk for therapists who unquestioningly adopt a Foucauldian perspective is that they may become conceptually blind to the occurrence of such processes, and our participation in them, as they play out in the institutional context of our practice with clients.

As critical as I have been, I hope I have been just as clear about the importance of Foucault's work for psychotherapy. As Foucault himself remarked about the function of criticism, it is '. . . to show that things are not as self-evident as one believed, to see that what is accepted as self-evident will no longer be accepted as such. Practising criticism is a matter of making facile gestures difficult' (1989: 154). To be alert for the 'facile gestures' that define and underpin our everyday work and to be willing to trace their institutional roots and their effects on individuals – here the example of Foucault is invaluable.

References

American Psychiatric Association (1980) *Diagnostic and Statistical Manual of Mental Disorders* (3rd edn). Washington, DC: APA.

Bhabha, H. (1994) *The Location of Culture*. London: Routledge.

Craine, L.S., Henson, C.H., Colliver, J.A. and MacLean, D.G. (1988) 'Prevalence of a history of sexual abuse among female psychiatric patients in a state hospital system', *Hospital and Community Psychiatry*, 39: 300–4.

Eagleton, T. (1986) *Against the Grain: Selected Essays*. New York: Verso.

Fish, V. (1990) 'Abuses of power by father-daughter incest perpetrators in treatment: the necessity of the therapist-family coalition', *Journal of Feminist Family Therapy*, 2: 227–42.

Fish, V. and Faynik, C. (1997) 'Videotape feedback as an intervention in incest families', *Journal of Family Psychotherapy*, 8 (3): 15–34.

Foucault, M. (1965) *Madness and Civilization: A History of Insanity in the Age of Reason*. New York: Random House.

Foucault, M. (1979) *Discipline and Punish: The Birth of the Prison*. New York: Vintage.

Foucault, M. (1980) *Power/Knowledge*. New York: Pantheon.

Foucault, M. (1989) *Foucault Live (Interviews, 1966–84)*. New York: Semiotext(e).

Foucault, M. (1997) *Ethics: Subjectivity and Truth (The Essential Works of Michel Foucault, 1954–1984; v. 1)*. New York: New Press.

Gilkeson, J.S. (1995) 'American social scientists and the domestication of "class" 1929–1955', *Journal of the History of the Behavioral Sciences*, 31 (3): 331–46.

Havel, V. (1991) *Open Letters: Selected Writings 1965–1990*. New York: Alfred A. Knopf.

Herman, J.L. (1992) *Trauma and Recovery*. New York: Basic Books.

Jacobson, A., Koehler, J.E. and Jones-Brown, C. (1987) 'The failure of routine assessment to detect histories of assault experienced by psychiatric patients', *Hospital and Community Psychiatry*, 38: 386–9.

Kundera, M. (1994) *The Book of Laughter and Forgetting*, trans. H. Heim. New York: HarperPerennial.

Landry, D. and MacLean, G. (eds) (1996) *The Spivak Reader*. London: Routledge.

Lipschitz, D.S., Kaplan, M.L., Sorkenn, J.B., Faedda, G.L., Chorney, P. and Asnis, G.M. (1996) 'Prevalence and characteristics of physical and sexual abuse among psychiatric outpatients', *Psychiatric Services*, 47: 189–91.

Marx, K. (1859/1970) *A Contribution to the Critique of Political Economy*, trans. S.W. Ryazanskaya, ed. M. Dobb. New York: International Publishers.

Nicholson, I. (1997) 'The politics of scientific social reform, 1936–1960: Goodwin Watson and the Society for the Psychological Study of Social Issues', *Journal of the History of the Behavioral Sciences*, 33 (1): 39–60.

Parham, T.A. (1993) 'White researchers conducting multicultural counseling research: Can their efforts be "mo betta"?', *Counseling-Psychologist*, 21 (2): 250–6.

Pruitt, J.A. and Kappius, R.E. (1992) 'Routine inquiry into sexual victimization: A survey of therapists' practices', *Professional Psychology Research and Practice*, 23: 474–9.

Recchiuti, J.L. (1995) 'The Rand School of Social Science during the Progressive Era: will to power of a stratum of the American intellectual class', *Journal of the History of the Behavioral Sciences*, 31 (2): 149–61.

Ryan, M. (1982) *Marxism and Deconstruction: A Critical Articulation*. Baltimore: Johns Hopkins University Press.

Said, E.W. (1978) *Orientalism*. Harmondsworth: Penguin.

Said, E.W. (1986) 'Foucault and the imagination of power', in D.C. Hoy (ed.), *Foucault: A Critical Reader*. New York: Basil Blackwell.

Sedgwick, P. (1982) *Psycho Politics: Laing, Foucault, Goffman, Szasz and the Future of Mass Psychiatry*. New York: Harper and Row.

Summerfield, D. (1995) 'Addressing human response to war and atrocity: major challenges in research and practice and the limitations of western psychiatric models', in R.J. Kleber, C.R. Figley and B.P.R. Gersons (eds), *Beyond Trauma: Cultural and Societal Dynamics*. New York: Plenum Press.

Taylor, C. (1986) 'Foucault on freedom and truth', in D.C. Hoy (ed.), *Foucault: A Critical Reader*. New York: Basil Blackwell.

Taylor, J. (1994) 'Body memories: aide-memoires and collective amnesia in the wake of the Argentine terror', in M. Ryan and A. Gordon (eds), *Body Politics: Disease, Desire, and the Family*. Boulder, CO: Westview Press.

Walzer, M. (1986) 'The politics of Michel Foucault', in D.C. Hoy (ed.), *Foucault: A Critical Reader*. New York: Basil Blackwell.

Wechsler, L. (1990) *A Miracle, a Universe: Settling Accounts with Torturers*. New York: Pantheon.

White, M. (1991) 'Deconstruction and therapy', *Dulwich Centre Newsletter*, 3: 21–40.

White, M. and Epston, D. (1990) *Narrative Means to Therapeutic Ends*. New York: W.W. Norton.

5

BETWEEN THE 'NO LONGER' AND THE 'NOT YET': POSTMODERNISM AS A CONTEXT FOR CRITICAL THERAPEUTIC WORK

Roger Lowe

Imagine a time in the future when the term 'postmodernism' is no longer used, except as an historical footnote. Imagine that you had to explain to a much younger, perhaps disbelieving therapist what all the fuss was about: how postmodernism and associated concepts achieved celebrity status towards the end of the twentieth century, and affected our thinking about all aspects of psychotherapy practice. What kind of account would you give? Was postmodernism a fashion that came and went, leaving many devotees feeling faintly embarrassed and psychotherapy largely untouched (except that it gained a few new models and some strange jargon)? Or was it a kind of watershed, that future generations will continue to look back to with pride as a major turning point in the betterment of psychotherapy and society in general? If it was a watershed, what enduring changes did it inspire?

The Wake of Postmodernism: Gaining a Perspective

> Defining postmodernism is not easy – and it is probably not wise either. (Potter, 1996: 88)

It can be bewilderingly difficult to gain a foothold, let alone a vantage point, for discussions of postmodernism, and I have found the above exercise useful in trying to gain some sort of perspective for surveying the field. It is by now virtually pointless, and perhaps even counter-productive, to attempt to define postmodernism in any definitive way, and it is tempting to suggest that term may have outlived its usefulness. As is the fate of many influential 'isms', it has taken on many more meanings than it can comfortably hold, and has achieved celebrity status in the sense that the confusions and polemics it typically generates have tended to become the main issue in themselves. In short, the 'P' word has become a great conversation stopper. Nevertheless, postmodernism will be with us for some time, and there is still a sense that, despite the confusions and pretensions, there is something there that is of abiding importance for psychotherapy. In trying to attain a vantage point for this chapter, I will adopt a deliberately selective and metaphorical approach, in which postmodernism is evoked as a self-consciously transitional moment: the boundary between the 'no longer' and the 'not yet' (Blumenberg, cited in Lather, 1991).

The emphasis on postmodernism as a contemporary context and metaphorical boundary allows us to focus on the general question of what choices and directions are available in the *wake* of postmodernism, and which are to be preferred. A major aim is to avoid a simplistic and antagonistic either/or logic. Though the 'no longer' may be typified as the untroubled or nonreflexive adherence to modernist assumptions, it is not intended to be synonymous with a blanket repudiation of all forms, contexts and aspirations of modernist thinking. Likewise, the 'not yet' is not to be depicted as a utopian realm of equally untroubled post-modernist assumptions. By positioning postmodernism as a metapho-rical transitional boundary, we can see it as a site for critically rethinking therapy discourse, rather than as an obligation to take sides and declare allegiances. It is a safe bet that psychotherapy will easily outlive the current interest in postmodernism. Therefore, our speculations may focus on the potential legacy of postmodernism, addressing the realm of the 'not yet': psychotherapy *after* postmodernism.

By focusing on postmodernism as a context for critical transition, I have also sought to avoid a number of potential distractions and sticking points: becoming bogged down in attempting to define postmodernism, entering into (and remaining stuck inside) the modern/postmodern debate, assessing the desirability of the category 'postmodern therapy', and seeking to analyse or evaluate specific 'pomo' therapies (the verna-cular term typically used in email discussion forums to refer collectively to narrative therapy, solution-focused therapy, collaborative systems therapy, etc.). Instead, I will focus on the relevance to psychotherapy of what Linda Hutcheon has called 'postmodern problematics': issues that have been created by the various discourses of postmodernism . . . 'issues that were not particularly problematic before but certainly are now' (1988: 5). A number of relevant issues are discussed in relation to therapy discourse, and the concept of an *ethics of theorizing* (Game, 1991) is used as an umbrella term for major choices in the sketching of the 'not yet'. Two major themes relate to the questions: What, in the wake of postmodernism, should we desire to represent in therapy discourse?

and, How can a process of ongoing critique be used to ensure that future therapy discourses do not revert to modernist ways?

Distinctions and Preferences

If there must be a general definition, perhaps it should be suitably ironic such as the one used by 'Beryl Curt' (a collective pseudonym for the authors of this text, a uniquely postmodern approach to the problem of the author) who defines postmodernism tautologically as 'that which results from the presencing practices of self-defined or other-identified postmodernists' (1994: 241). Perhaps, also ironically, we may get better mileage from the term by actually using it less (Curt, for example, prefers to speak of a generalized 'climate of problematization' and to avoid altogether the buzz words of postmodernism and social constructionism which, arguably, themselves now need to be placed under erasure or within quotation marks). Rather than become stuck with the 'P' word, I will briefly distinguish some typical uses as a prelude to elaborating the ones emphasized for the purposes of the chapter. The most common distinctions and uses surrounding postmodernism are as follows.

Firstly, postmodernism can be used to refer to features of society. In this usage, the adjective postmodern (as in postmodern society, the postmodern condition, the postmodern family, etc.) is taken to describe actually existing social and psychological realities, and serves to demarcate these from previously existing realities.

Secondly, postmodernism can be used to denote an intellectual or artistic position taken in various disciplinary or artistic fields. In this sense, the adjective postmodern (or, sometimes, postmodernist) points to an orientation or allegiance rather than serving as a description of society (thus, *postmodern* anthropology, psychology, architecture, cinema, dance, etc.). The postmodern orientation is typically contrasted with the modern orientation in an adversarial modern/postmodern duality.

Lastly, postmodernism can be used more metaphorically to evoke a particular cultural and ethical Zeitgeist, or in Curt's terms, a contemporary 'climate of problematization' (1994: 3). Used in this way it can be seen as a context or site for critically rethinking the discourses of particular fields without being reduced to a competiton between modern and postmodern ideas. For example, Lather (1991) describes post-modernism as a self-consciously transitional moment, or quoting Blumenberg 'the boundary between the "not yet" and the "no longer"' (1991: 87). While the 'no longer' represents unbridled acceptance of modernist assumptions, the 'not yet' is not synonymous with unbridled acceptance of postmodernist assumptions. As Lather notes, the 'not yet' is a way of staying outside such binary oppositions, and seeking to avoid an infinite regress of demystification and deconstruction. This usage allows us to place debates in historical context and imagine life (and psychotherapy) *after* postmodernism (Fekete, 1988).

Needless to say, the major meanings described above are typically confused and tend to be used interchangeably. Though I have selected the third and broadest usage for the purposes of this chapter, I will necessarily draw upon the other uses in ways which I hope are clear. In addition, I will also emphasize two other important distinctions. Firstly, postmodernism can be used for purposes of revisionism or descriptivism (Lowe, 1995). For some, postmodernism is best used as critique – as revisionism writ large. In this sense, it should not serve as a descriptive theory in itself, but should act as a perennial question mark posed to *all* theorizing. However, others seek to use postmodern concepts as the descriptive basis for reformulating their disciplinary areas. It is the descriptive uses of postmodernism which tend to be the most contentious. In the field of psychotherapy, for example, critics such as Held (1995, 1996) have argued that solution-focused therapy, narrative therapy and other 'pomo' therapies would be conceptually and ethically strengthened by ridding themselves of the postmodern tag.

Secondly, important distinctions can be made in terms of the articulation of postmodern concerns with contemporary social and political theory. This may be depicted as the distinction between *ad hoc* and *Critical* strands within postmodern orientations (with this distinction drawing on Potter's (1996: 230) view of three different kinds of criticism: '*ad hoc* practical, Critical (with a big C) and reflexive'). For many, a disconcerting aspect of much postmodern discourse has been its political ambivalence, its tendency to both subvert and reproduce dominant aspects of culture, and its ability to be assimilated to virtually any position on the political spectrum. Consequently, a number of writers have sought to define more systematically critical or oppositional strands. For example, distinctions have been made between mainstream and oppositional postmodernism (Lash, 1990), between reactionary and progressive postmodernism (Jameson, 1991), between postmodernisms of reaction and resistance (Foster, 1983), and between sceptical and affirmative postmodernisms (Rosenau, 1992). More recently, Nicholson and Seidman (1995) have introduced the term *social postmodernism* to emphasize a reaction against the narrowness of much postmodern critique which focuses on representations and knowledges, but leaves unattended their social and historical contexts. Instead, they argue for a postmodern perspective which attends to histories, institutions and social processes, avoids the infinite regress of some strands of deconstruction, and has a transformative focus for its critical reflexivity:

> The problematizing of essentialised identities, the de-centering of the subject and society, the re-centering of the social around analyzing power/knowledge regimes, are major sources for critical analysis and a democratic politics . . . The critique of deconstruction, therefore, should not lead to its abandonment but to its absorption in a 'social postmodernism', as at least one strategy for

imagining a democratic social theory and politics as we approach the end of the second millennium. (Nicholson and Seidman, 1995: 35)

These two distinctions are central to the later sections of the chapter, where the emphasis turns to sketching the 'not yet'. The prospects for descriptive uses of postmodern thought in psychotherapy are examined, and the discussion is informed by a preference for a critical or social postmodernist perspective.

The 'No Longer': What Won't be the Same?

Modernism is a way of talking, a discursive option . . . To put it this way is to say that modernism provides a distinctive discursive repertoire. (McNamee, 1996: 121)

In a sense, this is the easy part, and precisely because it is now so familiar, can be covered concisely. Before focusing on psychotherapy, it may be useful to outline in general terms some of the major areas of postmodern problematics. As Maranhão (1986) suggests, the post-modern critique is aimed largely at the question of authority, the production and maintenance of knowledge, and the shortcomings of a representational view of language; and draws attention, instead, to what he describes as the 'trinity' of power/knowledge/rhetoric. This view accords with Lather's conception of the 'no longer' as modernity's 'central assumption of human capacity to shape ourselves and our world' (1991: 87). We can usefully adopt McNamee's description of modernism as a discursive option, a way of talking, which has a dis-tinctive conversational repertoire. This allows us to organize discussion around the general question: *In the wake of postmodernism, what ways of talking won't be the same?* We can examine the ways in which the conversational repertoire of psychotherapy has been fundamentally challenged by the rejection of modernist beliefs in: a referential-representational view of language; individual autonomy and rationality on the part of therapists or clients (knowers and the known); historical, scientific and disciplinary progress; the desirability of grand and uni-fying theories and singular forms of knowing; objective and dis-interested knowledge and professional expertise; and differentiated and autonomous spheres of society.

Repudiating the notion of correspondence between language and 'reality' renders problematic the discursive repertoire of objective and decontextualized assessment, diagnosis and intervention, the use of classificatory systems, and the very status of theory informed by a metaphor of scientific discovery. When joined with the critique of the unitary and autonomous self, it also troubles ways of talking which assume an objective distinction between the subject or knower (typically the therapist) and the object or known (typically the client). Rather than reducing either to singular and knowable essences, a postmodern reading suggests that neither the subject nor object can be afforded the status of already existing fact or essence. Instead, they are both seen as socially constructed and relational, 'as continuously (re)produced in discursive and (other) practices in the course of social activities' (Stenner and Eccleston, 1994: 89). In place of a referential-representational view of language, a relational or rhetorical-responsive view can be emphasized (Shotter, 1993). When this view is privileged, many conventional therapy 'realities' such as the classification of disorders contained in the *Diagnostic and Statistical Manual of Mental Disorders* or DSM-IV (American Psychiatric Association, 1994) are no longer seen as actual states of being, but as historically situated ways of talking which have constitutive effects in the way clients and therapists are positioned in terms of identities, obligations and entitlements.

Whereas modern ways of talking are rooted in the scientific metaphor, the postmodern option tends to favour aesthetic or textual metaphors. This serves to trouble the modern conversational repertoire of grand explanatory theories, singular forms of knowledge (e.g. rational knowledge) and claims of historical and scientific progress, whereby contemporary theorizing and 'insights' are seen as milestones on the way to a definitive understanding of the nature of mental health and illness. By contrast, postmodern readings tend to focus more on historical disjunctures, gaps, doubts, and local manifestations of the 'unholy' trinity of knowledge/power/rhetoric. Thus, rather than being seen as possessors of an objective, specialized and progressively accumulating professional knowledge, therapists may be seen to constitute a particular *discursive enclave* influenced by articulation with other prominent institutional enclaves which help to define and constrain what is sayable and doable in a particular place and time. This relates in turn to a critique of the assumption of differentiated realms of society, or what Goldner (1988) calls the doctrine of separate spheres. In the context of therapy, this doctrine assumes that the sphere of the 'psychological', 'emotional', or 'individual' exists as an autonomous domain or level of activity which can be distinguished from other spheres such as the financial, political or relational. Thus, the modernist conversational repertoire tends to speak into existence a specialized sphere of activity which is the appropriate 'business' of psychotherapy, and to demarcate this from non-therapeutic spheres. By contrast, postmodern and feminist perspectives have pointed to the constructed nature of these demarcations. For example, Hare-Mustin (1994) describes the 'mirrored room' of therapy in which only discourses encouraged by the therapist tend to be reflected and developed, while other discourses (e.g. those of gender, inequality and power) are kept outside. More generally, the profession of psychotherapy can be seen as an institution which gate-keeps the discursive repertoire of cultural standards and desired ways of being. Those adopting more critical and socially oriented postmodern perspectives point to the historical emergence of psychotherapy within a particular modernist discourse emphasizing the importance of cultural standards for individuals' emotional and reasoning abilities, and the need for preserving and adjusting one's selfhood. This has contributed to a distinctive individual and internal focus in the profession's conversational repertoire, rather than a cultural and relational focus (McNamee, 1996).

In this brief discussion, I have highlighted some major themes of the 'no longer', which I have sought to identify with modernist ways of talking. The major themes have developed from both philosophical and political strands of critique. However, as indicated previously, the use of postmodernism for critique and revisionism is the easy part. Its use for descriptive purposes is more problematic. It is tempting for therapists to react to the modernist discursive repertoire by swinging over to a postmodernist repertoire and attempting to represent therapy in these terms. However, thinking of the alternative future as the 'not yet' may allow us to pause and take stock before wholeheartedly endorsing such an enterprise. If there are to be descriptive uses of postmodern concepts and practices, how should they be deployed, and how can we avoid reinventing the modernist wheel? Put differently, how can we ensure that postmodernist ways of talking do not end up doing the same work as modernist ones?

Towards the 'Not Yet': Challenges for an Ethics of Theorizing

> What this points to is the constant tension between the desire for representation and the process of critique, and the importance of the notion of permanent critique to an ethics of theorizing. (Game, 1991: 187)

How might we begin to sketch the 'not yet'? How might psychotherapy's conversational repertoire be different *after* postmodernism? Ann Game's tantalizingly brief discussion of an 'ethics of theorizing' in the quotation cited above provides a suggestive theme for unifying several threads of discussion. Postmodernism points to a different conception of ethics. In addition to the modernist conception of an ethics of practice, there is also an ethics of theorizing: a consideration of how one's discursive artefacts and repertoires define and position people. There is no longer an assumption of modernist theoretical innocence, of wondering if this might be so. There is an emphasis on the distinction between declarative intent and constitutive effect.

Based on the key points from Game's quotation, the key questions become: (i) after postmodernism, what should we desire to *represent* in psychotherapy discourse (or, using Curt's terms, what forms of 'representational labour' and 'knowledge mongering' do we wish to engage in?) and (ii) after postmodernism, what should inform the principle of *permanent critique* of psychotherapy discourse?

Between the Shoals

What should we desire to represent in psychotherapy discourse? In a discussion of the relevance of French discourse theories for feminist politics, Nancy Fraser points to the importance of navigating safely 'between the twin shoals of essentialism and nominalism' (1992: 68). This is a suggestive way of putting the dilemma of the dialectic between constructionist and realist perspectives, which Shotter (1993) sees as the difference between emphases on *making* and *finding*. Shotter suggests there is a necessary tension between the construction of reality and the 'real' limits of construction, and that we must acknowledge and learn to live with the fact that, ultimately, the two poles entail each other. However, seeing them as shoals rather than poles may suggest more pointed directions for navigation. Fraser's perspective appears consistent with what I have called critical or social postmodernism. It emphasizes the importance of avoiding two extremes: the essentialist tendency to reify universal and unchangeable entities or categories; and, at the other end, the nominalist tendency to reduce all significant realities to language, with the implication that changing language is synonymous with changing reality. If postmodern concepts are to be used as the descriptive basis for psychotherapy, Fraser's strictures on discursive navigating may provide useful guidelines. Several examples can be briefly mentioned.

Discourses of 'Discursive Therapy'

If anything typifies the influence of postmodernism on psychotherapy, it is the attention given to *discourse* as a pre-eminent term. Curt, not altogether approvingly, uses the term 'discursive therapy' to describe therapies embracing a social constructionist perspective (1994: 223), and the term is convenient as an umbrella for therapies based in discourse-related concepts (e.g. deconstruction, text, conversation, narrative, etc.). However, it is clear that there are remarkably different discourses of discourse available for articulation in 'discursive therapy', with quite different implications for practice.

For example, it is important to distinguish between *discourse* used pragmatically to describe any ongoing process of interaction and *Discourses* in the Foucauldian tradition, pertaining to 'systematic and institutionalised ways of speaking/writing which form the objects of which they speak, *and* conceal their role in doing so' (Lowe, 1995: 52). While proponents of an *ad hoc* pragmatic version of postmodernism might be content with the first pragmatic use (and focus their therapeutic attention, for example, on minimalist endeavours such as staying within the client's current frame of reference and seeking to influence linguistic patterns), social or critical postmodernists would be more interested in the second use and might seek to bring 'non-therapy' discourses into the mirrored room. Critical uses of postmodernism would therefore suggest that if discourse is to be used as the descriptive basis for therapy, it is important to select versions which go beyond an ad hoc study of individual sites of languaging, and instead seek to develop connections with broader institutional and social analyses. Suggestive possibilities for the latter include the work of Fairclough (1992) on hegemony and contemporary orders of discourse, and Parker (1992) on the institutional and ideological aspects of discourse dynamics. Herein lies the reason for the ambivalence of Curt and others towards 'discursive therapy': the tendency to focus on the individual site of text rather than on the broader context of *textuality*. For just as Foucault insisted that there is more to sexuality than sex, it is important also to bear in mind that there is more to textuality than text.

Identity and Difference: The Dilemma of Categories

An enduring postmodern problematic concerns the status of categories. If therapy discourse is to move beyond discussion of individual actions and intentions, it is important to articulate theorizations of personal and group identity formation. Yet how can this be done without reverting to the modernist repertoire of essentialism and totalization? In any therapeutic discourse, explicit or implicit meanings will be given to particular categories of inquiry: families, men, women, relationships, subjectivity, therapy itself, etc. In attempting to navigate between the shoals of essentialism and nominalism, preferences can be developed for categories which are understood in relation to ongoing sociohistorical dynamics, and are viewed as historically variable rather than foundational or essential. For example, rather than representing families as abstract systems, or natural entities, we may choose to see them as shifting institutional spaces which define members in constitutive ways, and within which 'certain actions can happen, and . . . certain kinds of subjects live' (Varela, 1989: 22). Similarly, rather than restricting the notion of subjectivity to essentially internal states of being (as one side of a boundary which separates the individual from the social), we could choose to view it as the point of *connection* between the individual and the social, thus drawing attention to social dynamics and historical variability (Parker, 1992).

As a more extended example, I will mention the work of Young (1995) who develops a concept of 'woman' based on the concept of *seriality*, borrowed from the work of Jean-Paul Sartre. Her suggestion is that an individual's being is defined through membership of a number of serial collectives or gatherings: one 'is' a farmer, commuter, radio listener, shopper, mother, woman, etc., but the membership is anonymous and the unity of the series is blurred, shifting and amorphous. Whereas a *group* has defining attributes and a shared sense of identity or purpose, a *series* is positioned passively in relation to a specific local and material milieu. Thus, while one is aware of being a member of a collective of radio listeners or commuters waiting at a bus stop, there is no assumed common identity or attributes for membership. At the same time, however, there is the potential for such collectives to form a group identity when circumstances arise (when, for example, a favourite radio programme is under threat, or a bus route is cancelled), after which the group disperses once more into the anonymity of seriality. Though the particular milieu which gives rise to the collective both constrains and enables individual actions, it does not define or determine them in any universal way. Young argues that seriality may offer a way of avoiding the shoals of essentializing the category of 'woman' in the name of identity, or obliterating it entirely in the name of difference. It allows the analysis of systematic patterns, while tempering the modernist tendency to define universal attributes. Extending this further to therapy, we might speculate about the effects of regarding client or problem categories as serial collectives rather than groups. Might this allow us to describe commonalities without ascribing identities? Might it suggest a way of maintaining an anti-foundationalist stance, without sliding into an anti-realist position?

Relational or Relational Engagement Therapy?

If, after postmodernism, psychotherapy no longer pursues a modernist repertoire focusing on internalized individual experience, it seems clear that the alternative lies in a more postmodern relational or 'systemic' focus. Yet, as McNamee (1996) warns, there are important distinctions to be made between relational psychotherapy and relational *engagement* psychotherapy. Relational psychotherapy, at first glance, appears to be radically different from individual therapy in the sense that its focus is on couples, families, groups or other relationship systems. However, much systemic language ultimately tends to maintain modernist ways of talking which reify family or systemic dysfunctions, focus predominantly on events internal to 'the system', privilege the rationality of the therapist, and maintain an emphasis on delivering well-adjusted relationships to the prevailing culture. It is an extension of, or addendum to, modernist discourse, rather than being, in any sense, an alternative construction. A timely example of the tendency for the once 'radical' family systems approaches to be incorporated into modernist discourse is the recent publication of the *Handbook of Relational Diagnosis and Dysfunctional Family Patterns* (Kaslow, 1996), which arguably resembles a relational version of the DSM-IV (though it also includes voices questioning the use of relational diagnosis).

By contrast, McNamee prefers an approach which centralizes relational *engagement* and focuses on the processes by which people come to create particular modes of understanding and acting, rather than on the products of these modes. Thus, rather than being concerned with dysfunction and adjustment, psychotherapy may serve as a space for conversational opportunities (both in therapy contexts and beyond), a 'conversational arena for participants to explore the discursive traditions within which disparate views have evolved' (1996: 132). Rather than a therapist seeking closure and finality, he or she might invite an array of voices and relationships into an evolving dialogue, shifting between speaking, listening and reflecting positions, encouraging many voices rather than the domination of one, and sanctioning rather than pathologizing indeterminacy. McNamee believes that such an approach is needed if psychotherapy is to respond to the multivocal postmodern world of multiple rationalities, shifting identities and changing cultural standards, in which today's 'problem' may be tomorrow's 'exemplary performance' (1996: 134). By contrast, staying within the modernist repertoire may render psychotherapy obsolete in the sense that its emphasis on cultural adjustment tends to preclude its potential to assist in the construction of new relational possibilities.

Discursive Health Warnings

After postmodernism, what should inform a process of ongoing critique of therapy discourse? Curt uses the metaphor of a 'Discursive Health Warning' to bring home the point that though discursive interventions may seem the most innocuous mode of social intervention, they are not risk-free in either the moral, political or consequential domains (1994: 228). Developing this metaphor further, we could suggest an obvious analogy with the physical health warnings on cigarette packets. Perhaps all therapy discourses should contain built-in discursive health warnings, through which their role in rhetorically shaping the objects of which they speak is revealed rather than concealed. It seems unlikely, for example, that any discourse can be innocent of a degree of 'ontological gerrymandering', whereby some descriptions or assumptions are presented as problematic while others are implicitly presented as 'factual' (Potter, 1996). Game's notion of an ethics of theorizing suggests nothing less than an ethical obligation on the part of the producers of therapy discourse to actively participate in the deconstruction of their own texts, rather than complying with an external mandate as in the tobacco analogy.

   In critically reflecting upon our own therapy discourse and that of others, a number of directions can be pursued. However, in the context of the major themes of this chapter, I will limit attention to one particular focus of reflection: the potential for the declarative intent of a discourse to be subverted by its constitutive effects. A timely example will be the potential for postmodernist ways of talking to end up doing the same work as modernist ones (or, as Amundson nicely puts it, for postmodernist clinical practice to be 'sent up the modernist river' (1994: 83)). The example is timely given the undoubted success and increasing popularity of discursive therapies and the increasing proliferation of authoritative books, articles, videos, training programmes and conferences devoted to them. The attendant danger is that of professional institutionalization and re-assimilation to a modernist conversational repertoire based on objectivist knowledge and instrumentalism. As Godzich (1987) suggests, an institution is first and foremost a guiding idea which is adopted by a group of individuals who become its public possessors and implementers. The institution then achieves its distinct identity through the translation of its guiding idea into set procedures, common attitudes, common behaviour, consensus and error correction. In short, a pioneering path soon becomes a beaten one.

Keeping in mind the theme of institutionalization, we will most likely need to place discursive health warning signs near the most novel and appealing guiding ideas of these therapy discourses, for it is here that the desire for representation may get the better of us. For example, it is important to place warning signs next to influential concepts such as *narrative, conversation, social construction*, and, of course, *discourse* and *postmodernism*, as these terms are clearly susceptible to varieties of uses and effects. An instructive example is Amundson's warning about the easy slippage from having a narrative orientation, to engaging in narrative *fundamentalism*. Though the postmodern emphasis on stories or narratives (as opposed to theory or truth) is intended as a statement of modesty, there can be an easy slippage into the reification of Narrative as a foundational form of knowledge. This can in turn lead to implicit assumptions about 'better' and more 'appropriate' narratives for clients and to a notion of therapy as a form of story assessment and repair. In such a case, the appeal of postmodern plurality has been diverted back into modern singularity.

Another example concerns the commendable efforts which many therapists are making to be more collaborative, transparent and inclusive in their relationships with clients. Yet it is also important to pose warning signs near these guiding ideas. How collaborative can collaboration be, and how transparent can transparency be if they are institutionalized within a particular mode of practice? It is one thing to offer clients a voice within a professional therapeutic discourse, but it might be quite another thing to allow them a discourse of their own. The declared intent of collaboration sits uneasily, at times, with the development of discourse technologies used to 'induce' collaboration. Might this be an example of what Fairclough (1992) calls the 'democratization' of discourse, a contemporary trend in which overt markers of power in institutional relationships may be replaced by more subtle or covert markers. In similar vein, the problematics of expertise and instrumentality remain. Do discursive therapy practices (such as reflecting teams and Socratic questions) encourage therapists to surrender instrumentality and power or do they serve, instead, to make them more sophisticated? Is the increasing refinement of therapeutic language practices contributing more to client agency or to the therapist's repertoire of influence? Though the declarative intent of these ideas may be to empower clients, the constitutive effects might be quite the opposite, being not so much disempowering but what Potter (1996) calls *mis*-empowering: adding new tools to the armoury of the already powerful. On a broader level, we may wish to relate the interest in discursive therapies to the increasing professional interest in discourse evident across a number of societal fronts. Fairclough, for example, sees the progressive 'democratization', 'commodification', and 'technologization' of discourse as important contemporary tendencies which modulate social change and ongoing hegemonic struggle.

The kinds of questions and issues I have raised are not intended to be clever, dismissive, damning or easily answered. They are intended as examples of the kind of discursive health warnings which may be appropriate for an ethics of theorizing in the wake of postmodernism. They temper modern zeal with postmodern irony. Wary of tendencies such as ontological gerrymandering, they allow us to temper the desire for representation with a mode of inquiry which recognizes the power of discourse in terms of the constitution of social identities, relational positionings, and assumptions about what is real and important.

Beyond the Great Divide: Psychotherapy After Postmodernism

By choosing to view postmodernism as a transitional context I have used this chapter to articulate some explicit and implicit preferences for an enduring legacy which goes beyond the limits of an 'either/or' debate. While the 'no longer' can be identified with the modernist discursive repertoire, the 'not yet' is still there for the making. Rather than arguing for or against a general category of postmodern psychotherapy, I have preferred to keep my discursive options open and to outline preferences and dangers in the potential uses of postmodern concepts as the descriptive basis of therapy. Taking a long view, perhaps the contemporary discursive therapies can be seen as preliminary sketches or drafts of the 'not yet'. I began the chapter with an exercise in crystal ball gazing which many readers will recognize as a variation on the future-projection questions typically asked in solution-focused therapy. It is interesting to note that, in a recent reformulation of their assumptions about this model, Walter and Peller (1996) suggest that an exclusive focus on either problems *or* solutions is unhelpful, and suggest that therapy, instead, be seen as the storying of life *beyond* the problem/ solution distinction. I will end the chapter with an analogous speculation. Could it be that after all the polemical dust has settled, the most important contribution of postmodernism to psychotherapy might be to serve as a harbinger of the 'not yet' – the fashioning of therapy discourses which move, ironically, beyond the modern/postmodern distinction?

References

American Psychiatric Association (1994) *Diagnostic and Statistical Manual of Mental Disorders* (4th edn). Washington, DC: APA.

Amundson, J. (1994) 'Whither narrative? The danger of getting it right', *Journal of Marital and Family Therapy*, 20 (1): 83–7.

Curt, B. (1994) *Textuality and Tectonics: Troubling Social and Psychological Science.* Buckingham: Open University Press.

Fairclough, N. (1992) *Discourse and Social Change.* Cambridge: Polity Press.

Fekete, J. (ed.) (1988) *Life After Postmodernism: Essays on Value and Culture.* Basingstoke: Macmillan.

Foster, H. (ed.) (1983) *The Anti-Aesthetic: Essays on Postmodern Culture.* Seattle, WA: Bay Press.

Fraser, N. (1992) 'The uses and abuses of French discourse theories for feminist politics', *Theory, Culture & Society*, 9: 51–71.

Game, A. (1991) *Undoing the Social: Towards a Deconstructive Sociology.* Milton Keynes: Open University Press.

Godzich, W. (1987) 'Afterword: religion, the state, and post(al) modernism', in S. Weber (ed.), *Institution and Interpretation.* Minneapolis: University of Minnesota Press.

Goldner, V. (1988) 'Generation and gender: normative and covert hierarchies', *Family Process*, 27: 17–31.

Hare-Mustin, R. (1994) 'Discourses in the mirrored room: a postmodern analysis of therapy', *Family Process*, 33: 19–35.

Held, B. (1995) *Back to Reality: A Critique of Postmodern Theory in Psychotherapy.* New York: Norton.

Held, B. (1996) 'Solution-focused therapy and the postmodern: a critical analysis', in S. Miller, M. Hubble and B. Duncan (eds), *Handbook of Solution-Focused Brief Therapy.* San Francisco: Jossey-Bass.

Hutcheon, L. (1988) 'A postmodern problematics', in R. Merrill (ed.), *Ethics/ Aesthetics: Post-Modern Positions.* Washington, DC: Maisonneuve Press.

Jameson, F. (1991) *Postmodernism, Or, The Cultural Logic of Late Capitalism.* Durham, NC: Duke University Press.

Kaslow, F. (ed.) (1996) *Handbook of Relational Diagnosis and Dysfunctional Family Patterns.* New York: Wiley.

Lash, S. (1990) *Sociology of Postmodernism.* London: Routledge.

Lather, P. (1991) *Getting Smart: Feminist Research and Pedagogy With/In The Modern.* New York: Routledge.

Lowe, R. (1995) 'Family therapy and the uses of postmodernism: from revisionism to descriptivism'. PhD dissertation, University of Queensland.

McNamee, S. (1996) 'Psychotherapy as a social construction', in H. Rosen and K. Kuehlwein (eds), *Constructing Realities: Meaning-Making Perspectives for Psychotherapists.* San Francisco: Jossey-Bass.

Maranhão, T. (1986) *Therapeutic Discourse and Socratic Dialogue*. Madison, WI: University of Wisconsin Press.

Nicholson, L. and Seidman, S. (eds) (1995) *Social Postmodernism: Beyond Identity Politics*. Cambridge: Cambridge University Press.

Parker, I. (1992) *Discourse Dynamics: Critical Analysis for Social and Individual Psychology*. London & New York: Routledge.

Potter, J. (1996) *Representing Reality: Discourse, Rhetoric and Social Construction*. London: Sage.

Rosenau, P. (1992) *Post-Modernism and the Social Sciences: Insights, Inroads, and Intrusions*. Princeton, NJ: Princeton University Press.

Shotter, J. (1993) *Conversational Realities: Constructing Life Through Language*. London: Sage.

Stenner, P. and Eccleston, C. (1994) 'On the textuality of being: towards an invigorated social constructionism', *Theory & Psychology*, 4 (1): 84–103.

Varela, F. (1989) 'Reflections on the circulation of concepts between a biology of cognition and systemic family therapy', *Family Process*, 28: 15–24.

Walter, J. and Peller, J. (1996) 'Rethinking our assumptions: assuming anew in a postmodern world', in S. Miller, M. Hubble and B. Duncan (eds), *Handbook of Solution-Focused Brief Therapy*. San Francisco: Jossey-Bass.

Young, I. (1995) 'Gender as seriality: thinking about women as a social collective', in L. Nicholson and S. Seidman (eds), *Social Postmodernism: Beyond Identity Politics*. Cambridge: Cambridge University Press.

6

FEMINISM, POLITICS AND POWER IN THERAPEUTIC DISCOURSE: FRAGMENTS FROM THE FIFTH PROVINCE

*Nollaig O'Reilly Byrne and
Imelda Colgan McCarthy*

In situating Feminism, Politics, Power and Therapeutic Discourse as a title for this chapter, an attempt will be made to follow their uneasy engagement and affiliation. Implicit in the four terms is a recognition of a variety of practices that seek to destabilize sites of oppression, and to promote an ethic of reciprocity. The validation of these practices relies on the primary assumption that colonizing discourses produce stable hierarchies of devaluation across a range of social, cultural, and representational positions in society. The devalued 'other' – woman, non-white, working class, dis-abled, non-heterosexual – of this hierarchical structure occupies a marginal or subordinate status, limiting the potential for autonomy and self-determination, and in which the politics of its own production remains submerged (Kearney et al., 1989; McCarthy, 1991; Byrne and McCarthy, 1998).

Alternatively, practices based on reciprocity, as an ethics of human relationship, rely on the mobilization of a range of materials, linguistic and extra-linguistic that come into service as tropes and sites of resistance and freedom. These practices, within the systemic therapies, aim to increase the margin of liberty for subject positions in a particular arena, which discloses self to self, self in relation to others, and self in relation to various social discourses (Foucault, 1982, 1994; McCarthy and Byrne, 1988; Andersen, 1990, 1995; White and Epston, 1990, 1993; Epston et al., 1992; McNay, 1992; Tomm, 1993; Waldegrave and Tamasese, 1994; Penn and Frankfurt, 1994; Byrne, 1996; Anderson, 1997).

Essentialism and Relativism

The articulation of the constitution of subjectivities and identity politics in sites of protest and contest brings the dual perspectives of essentialism and relativism into an ambivalent play. Essentialism occupies the tradition of classical dualisms, in which difference is a bi-polar construct. Relativism, by contrast, is a postmodern perspective, which proposes difference as multiplicity, ambiguity and upheaval of dualisms (Shotter and Gergen, 1989; Shotter, 1993; Gergen, 1994). Deconstructive strategies as features of discourses of resistance are drawn on by these contrary perspectives. Essentialist dualisms of essences or stable identities are exaggerated in the exploration and restoration of their revalued specificity and difference. From the perspective of relativism, difference is a multiplicity, which denotes a space of proliferation, disrupting the confines of dichotomized dualisms. There are difficulties with both perspectives in grounding the commitment of political and ethical practices (Braidotti, 1989; Butler, 1990; Flax, 1993; Benhabib et al., 1995). Taken to extremes, a heightening of specific differences may become foundational and over-arching of other differences, while an exaggerated relativism undermines the possibility of any stable representation. It is around these contraries that tension in contemporary feminist theory emerges.

Therapeutic Discourses

A discourse is a network of theories and practices engaging with, colliding with or erasing other discourses. What marks a particular discourse as therapeutic in contemporary society is drawn from a broader professionalized binary form of relationship, i. e. help-seeker and help-giver. This implicit asymmetry produces practices with varying contents of inequality and non-reciprocity but if useful to the help-seeker for strategic ends they may continue to hold a normative status.

Therapeutic discourse specifies a multiplicity of practices which hold possibilities to bring into view the different contents of colonization that circumscribe autonomy and, hence, a derogation of the primacy of ethics as 'self-esteem' in an individual life. As an amalgam of several discourses, it is not immune from a colonizing potential of its own, to the extent that it projects a framework through which the client's narrative is filtered and reshaped. Good intentions, or the alleged absence of any framework will not prevent this in the absence of a critical appraisal of the positionality of the discourse as therapeutic rather than colonizing (McCarthy, 1991; Byrne and McCarthy, 1998). In our view a discourse can be said to be therapeutic to the extent that the exchange between participants foregrounds the potential for reciprocity of perspectives and mutual respect. This is the domain of liberty which is a *sine qua non* of therapeutic practice. There is a requirement of politics and ethics in establishing this positionality, referred to by one of the authors (IMcC) as 'the politics of listening and the ethics of speaking'.

Feminist Politics: Equality as a Trope of Resistance

While equality is the originary trope of resistance within feminist politics, it relies on the foundational narrative of patriarchy as the stable object to which it is opposed. Within this view patriarchy has generated a highly differentiated masculinity and femininity by a rhetorical detour through biological and sexual differences (de Lauretis, 1987; Belsey and Moore, 1989; McCarthy, 1990; Joeres and Laslett, 1996). Thus it is the erasure and denial of sameness, which oppresses women and which is resurrected by the equality argument. Feminism originated as a political position that advanced a social analysis about the specific character of women's oppression and thus claimed a universalist project. The equality argument within feminism is based on the potential sameness of the sexes. This argument dates back to Mary Wollstonecraft and the early suffragists and remains the cornerstone of liberal politics (Wollstonecraft, 1982). As the articulation of women's rights, it has made possible a range of equality reforms that materially improved the lives of women and rendered them as equal subjects under law. However, as a political agenda the overstretch of this claim is modified by a filtering social analysis that identifies the particularities and burdens of oppression across historical time and in different societies.

The specific mechanisms of oppression and subordination of women, it has been argued, are not invariant; they are a complex mediation of concrete cultural phenomena, both materialistic and non-materialistic, which are inscribed to varying degrees on sexual difference (Spivak, 1987, 1988; Benhabib, 1992; McCarthy, 1995). Thus while the demand for equality in male–female relationships is the justification for feminism, this is contested and circumscribed by attention to the weight of other colonizing markers of inequality, particularly those of racism, ability, sexual orientation and poverty. These markers constitute greater burdens of oppression for specific groups of women which the equality argument of Western feminism suppressed. These are salient differences which separate women from each other in the name of different contents of oppression and hence specify different political agendas, in which feminism as a large-scale identity politics is no longer realizable (bell hooks, 1990; Higginbotham, 1996).

Two issues arise within feminist politics. Firstly, feminism as a political struggle must revise its universalist aim, to take account of the concrete differences which separate women from each other and thus generate more local solidarities. Secondly, it is recognized that legislative equality alone cannot reach those arenas of everyday life in which devaluation is symbolically coded and secured: 'What is an act of resistance, given that the subject who needs to resist is already complicit in "technologies of gender", those linguistic and social networks in which gender is produced and re-produced' (de Lauretis, 1987).

Feminist Feminine Theories: Difference as a Trope of Resistance

Broadly speaking, these are separatist theories that radicalize women as a counter society to male privilege and domination. Drawing on divergent assumptions, what they have in common is an articulation of the specificity of female subjectivity and desire, suppressed or devalued under patriarchy (Chodorow, 1978; Daly, 1978; Ruddick, 1980; Moi, 1987; Braidotti, 1989; Grosz, 1989; Flax, 1993). In extending the analysis of the power axis of men–women relationships, not only as subjects under law, where sameness is accentuated, other postulates of difference emerge. While 'sameness', as a citizenship issue has legitimated the demand for equality between men and women, it is the philosophy of 'difference' which has come to structure feminism as an ambivalent interplay of separatist and pluralist discourses. In the internal feminist critique, in dispute is the fact that the feminine subject produced by these various feminist theories places an aggravated emphasis on gender difference to the neglect of other differences that significantly mediate subject positions.

There is an irony here in that it is sexual difference that legitimates the naturalized inferiority of the feminine and it is this distinction that radical feminists draw on to articulate and revalue an extreme difference feminism. The positing of extreme difference slides into an essentialism of universal and invariant status which paradoxically elides the real differences that exist between women in different contexts (McNay, 1992: 19). In attempting to excavate the founding sexual difference beneath other determinations, this 'leaves woman once again reduced to her body . . . rather than figuring as a culturally shaped, culturally complex, evolving, rational, engaged as noisy opposition' (Soper quoted in McNay, 1992: 19). However, it is also argued that, in revaluing the feminine, the patriarchal logic of the discourse of sexual difference is a deconstructive strategy. The rhetoric of the body as a feminine articulation is an ironic exaggeration which exposes the elimination and the derogation of the female body in classical dualisms (McNay, 1992: 13, 20).

Gender Specificity

The maternalist strand of feminist theories essentializes the body from the standpoint of reproduction, child-birth and child-care (Chodorow, 1978). It variably was seen as the inescapable cultural duty or biological destiny of women (Wollstonecraft, 1982). For the maternalists, the particular experiences of reproduction determine female sexual desire and essentially feminine values of care and protection. In mothering theory, the incompleteness of the mother–daughter separation is posited as the source of gendered feminine generative capacity and desire. Here, the feminine, positioned in a gendered genealogical chain of being born and giving birth, is the founding sociality which ensures a relational sense of self, now understood as a part of feminist ethics (Gilligan, 1982; Noddings, 1984; Clement, 1996).

Feminist ethics, drawing on Chodorow's mothering theory and the notion of a deep sense of gendered self formed in infancy, has ushered in what is known as the care-justice debate (Held, 1995). While radical and separatist, the conception of a culturally constructed, stable and constant gender identity emerging early in life (Chodorow, 1996) is at odds with the feminine, theorized as 'otherness', 'supplement', 'margin', by the 'new' French feminists. In the internal feminist critique, however, both conceptions are politically suspect to socialist feminists (Spivak, 1987; Barrett, 1988; Nicholson, 1983, 1990).

Sexual Specificity

Within this feminist explanation, division by sex as the elemental structure of living forms, and hence of human life, is an inescapable difference and specificity of a sexed human life. In the natural domain – outside history, culture, ideology and human consciousness – this elemental difference is offered as the *sine qua non* of continuity in complex organisms. For Luce Irigaray and Helene Cixous, both Lacanian psychoanalysts, language operates on corporeal sexual difference as the *a priori* structure of difference in which language unfolds as an articulation of binary oppositions (male/female) or 'the play of differences' (Cixous, 1976; Cixous and Clement, 1986; Irigaray, 1993, 1994).

The ancestral woman (Irigaray), the elemental woman (Cixous), and the symbolically marginal woman (Kristeva), are utilized, not only to articulate a feminine specificity, but to re-position the feminine as a contemporary positive evaluation. Irigaray deconstructs the ascription of interminable and heightened ambivalence of the daughter's separation struggle with a restorative genealogy; Cixous deconstructs the devaluation of the feminine implicit in classic dualisms by replacing the hierarchical structure of devaluation with the Derridean term of 'supplement'. Kristeva's relational description of the feminine, as a shifting positionality in relation to the socio-symbolic contract, establishes it as a sacrifice articulated in the margins. Here the margin is the double emblem of woman's sacrificial history and the site of self-knowledge which constitutes feminine desire. Thus she is attempting to undo the victim–oppressor axis of femininity–masculinity as the founding script of male and female relations. In retaining the masculine–feminine axis, her notion of positionality draws attention to the non-equivalence of different contexts and contents of oppression and resistance (Moi, 1986).

While Irigaray seeks specificity and equality within the symbolic order, Cixous, by contrast, theorizes the feminine as irreducibly other to the socio-linguistic symbolic order. Sexual difference exists, and masculinity as constituted symbolically, is fixed and stabilized; by contrast the feminine is constituted by 'otherness' rather than lack and circulates on the borders and the limits of the masculine as a deconstructive potential. Cixous proposes a textual practice of 'écriture féminine', a writing at the margins of logocentric texts (Belsey and Moore, 1989: 14). This, paradoxically, conjoins the essentially feminine as 'otherness' in Cixous's theory with Derrida's postmodernist theory of difference as textual supplement. For Irigaray we have lost our mothers; for Cixous we are dead and spoken for in male idioms and practices. Both however specify the body in terms of its elemental sexual difference as the critical location for the operation of patriarchal oppression. In essentializing sexual difference as both Irigaray and Cixous do, at the level of the body and of language, however, they are reclaiming a site for women that counters the existing linguistic domination, gaps and silences of women's experience.

A language that shatters the exclusion and silencing, which constitute the binary oppositions of the patriarchal order, is proposed as 'woman-speak' (Irigaray) or 'écriture féminine' (Cixous) (Belsey and Moore, 1989: 13). In this shattering Cixous proposes that, 'woman will return to the body which has been more than confiscated from her by patriarchy' (Belsey and Moore, 1989: 13). Specifying female sexual difference as 'otherness' rather than 'lack'/'absence' provides the escape from the claim of dichotomized oppositions in which one position of the binary pair is devalued and/or silenced. The (re)inclusion now configures a new interplay of opposites and unites their feminist project with the philosophy of deconstruction. These positions, lexical markers of sexed subjectivities opened the way for imagining and defining presentations of sex as a social construction. The term 'gender' now enters as an attempt to highlight the different ways women and men are re-presented throughout history (Nicholson and Seidman, 1995: 10). These writers provide a feminist anthropology to articulate a feminine specificity, now repositioned as a contemporary positive evaluation. They can also be read as a narrative of colonization which locates the death (Cixous), the loss/devaluation (Irigaray) and the marginality (Kristeva) of woman in the socio-symbolic contract under patriarchy. They provide textual anti-colonial strategies which resonate with emergences in other contexts of colonization. Native language revival (Cixous), restoration of mythic sources (Irigaray) and speech from the margins (Kristeva) mark the efforts of the colonized as narratives of emancipation.

For our part, we draw on these resources not for their anthropological merit but rather as literary exegesis in which the motif of colonization emerges. Radical, essentialist and separatist to varying degrees, what the various feminist positions have in common is an articulation of the specificity of women's experience and requiring the emergence of other subject positions and strategies of resistance beyond or in addition to that of political mobilization.

Multiple Feminisms: Differentiation

Within contemporary postmodern Continental philosophy the theory of difference was a critique of classical dualisms, and was proposed as a deconstructive strategy by Kristeva to undo the polarized terms of masculine/feminine (Braidotti, 1989; McNay, 1992: 16). However, moving in a different direction, Nicholson and Seidman (1995: 1) have recently pointed out that 'Difference feminism' has been most at fault in ignoring differences among women. Nicholson (1990; Nicholson and Seidman, 1995) goes on to argue that we need to get beyond explicit or implicit notions of biological foundationalism if we are to get beyond the erasure of differences which supplement the notion of similarities. In this she means that we need to acknowledge all the different criteria of what constitutes male and female subjectivities in diverse societies and cultures.

Writing from a different orientation Carole Pateman has stated, 'who a "citizen" is, what a citizen does and the arena within which he [sic] acts have been constructed in the masculine image'. She points out that even though woman have formal citizenship in Western countries their participation is still for the most part devalued (Pateman, 1987, 1988a, 1988b). To get over what she describes as the 'Wollstonecraft dilemma' (demanding equality under a patriarchal concept of citizen is to demand to be like men, which runs counter to the demand to be included as women in the first place), she proposes that the notion of sexual differentiation be embraced. A sexually differentiated concept of citizen and equality would acknowledge woman's embodied subjectivity in their ability to bear a child as of equal political relevance to man's 'willingness' to 'fight and die for his country' in defining citizenship (quoted in Mouffe, 1988: 8, 70–82).

However, Chantal Mouffe extends the previous propositions as to how women might be (re)entered into public space by proffering a deconstructed notion of citizen which stretches beyond sex divisions and gender differences (Laclau and Mouffe, 1985; Mouffe, 1988: 323). She argues that sexual difference should be irrelevant to political citizenship and looks towards a notion of citizenship wherein social agents would be viewed as subjects who are articulated through 'an ensemble of subject positions' which correspond to the multiplicity of social relations in which they are inscribed. This multiplicity would be constructed within specific discourses which have no necessary relation but only contingent and precarious forms of articulations. Within this schema, which is akin to Baudrillard's idea that subjectivity is created through the interactions of social discourses and networks of relationships (Baudrillard, 1988), she would argue that there is no reason why sexual differentiation would be pertinent to all social relations within what she calls a radical democratic conception of citizenship (Mouffe, 1988: 323–4).

Towards the New Millennium

As we enter the new millennium we have proposed that an 'identity politics' which appears to offer group membership for some political purpose calls for a rethink. In its early phases identity politics held out hopes of specifying the rights to social inclusion for marginalized groups, e.g. women, gays and lesbians, minority racial and ethnic groups, the differently abled and so on. However, while the issues that these groups campaigned on were in part taken on board by the dominant culture, those who defined themselves as belonging to them were continually judged according to personal embodiments. Therefore, those groups were not the same as other political groupings where one could join because of interest or inclination – one did not generally choose to be a woman, a Jew, a Muslim in the same way as one did to be a member of a political party (Gergen, 1995).

If language is purported to be a masculinist socio-linguistic system, then the idea of a feminine discourse makes sense as a way to shatter oppositions of identity-other in favour of irreducible differences (Cixous); to situate oppositions in a relational frame where marginality is articulated as the unrecognized sacrifice exacted by the symbolic order (Kristeva); to locate in the literary heritage of the ancient world those powerful mythic mother–daughter ancestors who were later suppressed (Irigaray); to revalue maternity and mothering as the historically constructed site for the development of a gendered sense of self and gendered values (Gilligan).

In this sense the women's movement has been a resistance movement either to claim power, as in the demand for equality, or, as in radical feminism, to propose a counterpower (Belsey and Moore, 1989: 205). However, the achievement of power, of money or status by individual women has not transformed sexual power relationships or created solidarity for women. What is masked in this consolidation of power is the identification by women with male values. Here the specificity of women's needs and interests remain unarticulated in what is essentially 'a man's world'. In the counter-society of counter-power, the refusal to be conscripted is an anti-sacrificial trespass on the socio-symbolic contract, the most specific of these being a refusal of the exclusive role of perpetuating and providing for the care of the species. However, before proceeding to comment on feminist critiques, as sites of resistance, within the systemic therapies we turn now to a brief discussion of the links between Foucault and feminism.

Feminisms, Postmodernism, Foucault and Power

In Foucault's analysis of power, he breaks with revolutionary theory and humanist assumptions of the individual, and hence with both Marxist and liberal politics (Foucault, 1982, 1994; McNay, 1992). It is his view that power, as a feature of postmodern life, is not a possession of individuals or the central apparatuses of the State. He draws attention to the forms of power as exercised in multiple networks of relationships at the microlevel of society 'that invests the body, sexuality, family, kinship, knowledge'. This is not to deny that state and institutional power exists, or that the forms of power exercised in some societies may be repressive or coercive. His interest lies in providing an understanding of the postmodern subject, postmodern forms of subjectivity and subjugation mediated by relations of power. In replacing ideology with discourse, the position of the subject as a site of accommodation and resistance is theorized as important to Foucault's microanalysis. Hence power and resistance could be said to have a cybernetic structure in the Batesonian sense (Bateson, 1972, 1979; McCarthy, 1997). Here, the discourse of power re-presents the full array of normative cultural interpretations and values while resistance, as the discourse of protest, occurs in a multiplicity of sites that challenge the given and the taken for granted in the name of individual or collective social change.

Thus resistance in postmodern society is in the first instance a self-determining protest by individuals against forces of over-determination that is 'the government of individualization' (Rabinow, 1994). The discourse of protest is a counter-discourse that mobilizes groups that are marginalized, silenced or made invisible in normative discourse.

In Foucault's genealogical critique of history, the dialectic of power and resistance plays itself out in an ambiguous and oscillating fashion in specific and local struggles. In this view, no large-scale social change or transformation can be produced in advance of the creative participation of subjects who will benefit or be disadvantaged by this change. For Foucault, freedom and self-determination cannot be an abstract universal of contingent inalienable rights, but is an action-context sustained by the desire of subjects to produce some effects while resisting others. It is this which is said to have impact on dominant networks. However, Foucault's emphasis is neither on large-scale networks or ideologies of domination, but rather on how the individual constitutes power relations and is in turn constituted by them. In his later work, he counters the constitution of the 'docile body' as the effect of modern disciplinary power and 'technologies of subjectification' with a theory of self that avoids the passivity implicit in his early work. 'An ethics of self' is a narrative of emancipation addressed to the colonized and 'docile body'. It is this later analysis that can be incorporated into feminist discourse and other discourses of resistance (McNay, 1992: 4; Foucault, 1994). On a general level, victimization is construed as only one of the subject positions, possible in relationships of power. Specifically in male-female relationships, the theory of the self as a self-fashioning and self-determining subject of freedom and constraint deconstructs any essentialist concepts that predicate male–female power differences.

Feminist Critique within Systemic Therapies

This considerable critique has drawn attention to the gender neutrality paradigm on which therapeutic practices were based and in which gender inequality was unarticulated (Goldner, 1985, 1991; Hare-Mustin, 1987, 1994; MacKinnon and James, 1987; Hare-Mustin and Maracek, 1988; McGoldrick et al., 1989; McCarthy, 1990, 1991; Perelberg and Miller, 1990; Jones, 1993; Burck and Daniel, 1995; Burck and Speed, 1995; Gorell Barnes, 1995; Van Lawick and Sanders, 1995). Here, as in the general social arena, the systemic feminist political analysis of divided spheres, public and private, provided the recognition for the emergence of the personal as an appropriate subject of politicization. The 'systemic model' as a theory of stability and change in social systems, indebted to bio-logical and cybernetic theory and relying on normative assumptions of dominant social theory, subsumed/elided gender asymmetry under the dominant frame of circular interaction.

Therapist 'neutrality' as a central methodological component of Milan Systemic Practice (Palazzoli et al., 1980) sustained the strongest critique as the unwitting political buttress of the status quo (Jones, 1993). These challenges, both theoretical and political, problematized the nature of power relationships and the status of determinism versus voluntarism as action contexts. For systemic practitioners what continues to survive from the Batesonian framework is the positing of the primacy of rela-tionship, i.e. sociation as the *a priori* in individual development (Gergen, 1994) in which emerges the intersubjective constitution of subject positions and the insertion of power as a circular interactive frame, i.e. a strategic game of influence among equals (symmetry) or a strategic game of domination and resistance among unequals (complementarity) (Bateson, 1972, 1979; Foucault, 1994).

Thus in systemic practice the theoretical narrative of relationship and interaction is no longer an abstract schema that can be observed, stabilized or changed for strategic ends. Rather what now comes into view, as an ethically informed emancipation project, is the discursive formation or unfolding of social realities and subject positions, the self as an ethical subject (determined and free), and identity as the unique narrative unfolding of the stories one lives by (Foucault, 1994).

Therapeutic Discourse: A Fifth Province Approach

The Fifth Province Approach was developed by the authors and a colleague, Philip Kearney (Byrne and McCarthy, 1988; McCarthy and

Byrne, 1988; Colgan, 1991). The approach takes its name from the ancient Celtic myth of the Fifth Province in Ireland. There is debate as to whether this province existed or not. Many say that it was not a geographical domain but rather a province of imagination and possibility, whose only existing trace is in the Irish language. In our native language the word for province is *cuaige*, which means fifth. Other versions of the story site the Fifth Province at the centre of Ireland where the four geographical provinces were supposed to have met. Here, it is cited, there existed a druidic place where kings and chieftains came to receive counsel and resolve conflicts through dialogue. Whatever the story, the metaphor of the fifth province has come to mean for us the creation of a dialogical and imaginative space wherein participants might create together opportunities for a polyphonic and polysemic interplay. The Fifth Province approach is our particular innovation within systemic practice, one that attempts to resist the primacy of essentialism and/or relativism with the repositioning of ambivalence as the paradigmatic structure of discourse and relationship (Byrne, 1996).

Colonization has been a guiding metaphor in our articulation of the Fifth Province approach (Kearney et al., 1989; McCarthy, 1991). In recognizing the binary structure of thought and language as paradigmatic to discourse, ambivalence is posited as that abstraction and movement which propels thought along binary axes into divisions, oppositions and exclusions. In a logo-centric critique, indebted to Derrida, the French feminist psychoanalysts describe division as death (Cixous), opposition as devaluation (Irigaray) and exclusion as marginality (Kristeva). In our view, death, devaluation and marginality can be understood as the productive effects of colonization. Thus in our approach, colonization is the overthrow of ambivalence, securing the claim to certitude. Ambivalence, on the other hand, is the movement in relations of power creating the possibility of reversed and/or re-versed perspectives constituting and constituted through new discourses. Without this quasi-structure of ambivalence the world of discourse would be a static place where the 'last word' becomes the final say.

Within this approach therapeutic discourse becomes a vernacular exploration and dialogue, economized by the movement of ambivalence which narrativizes provisional and coherent identities from the force lines of multiple constituent discourses. As a relationship of power and mutual influence, resistance is also bi-directional. Here the claim of pathologizing genres of discourses as significant closures attempts to be resisted by participants. In a politics of listening, one is searching for the form of colonizing discourses hidden in the apparent transparency of personal accounts (Hydén and McCarthy, 1994; Byrne and McCarthy, 1998). Such colonizing discourses leave the personal account with a singular form, a form of devaluation and imposition. Through questions which mobilize and intensify the colonizing impulse which deforms a personal account the latter is brought to the limits of affective tolerance and coherent intelligibility. This dialogical enquiry, referred to by us as *'questioning at the extremes'* brings back the movement of ambivalence and the binary form of the discursive field, previously suppressed (Colgan, 1991; McCarthy and Byrne, 1995). Listening thus requires an immersion in and prior reflection on the specific contents on the shared world of the participants, particularly those that constrain individual or collective liberty. Here is a duty to 'know' before one can adequately listen in order that one can 'know' more.

In an ethics of speaking, participants draw together in a commitment to speak the 'truth' for one's own sake and for the sake of the other. Therapeutic discourse is a pre-eminently recognizable and specific form of truth-making in which the primacy of reciprocity in discursive exchange resists the closure of dogmatic assertion. How then can the practice of 'questioning at the extremes' be considered as a form of truth-making? Of itself it has no truth content. Rather, it is situated dialogically from inside a discourse challenging its claim to truth and certitude. It is a deconstructive strategy that loosens the hold of singular discourses over a personal life. Personal freedom and increased auto-nomy does not eliminate the rhetorical and material presence of the discourse. It is merely muted and estranged by the return to individual recognition of the binary form and suppressed pole from which it became individualized and stabilized in place and in time. The ethical dilemma thus is not to substitute a dominant discourse with its sup-pressed other but to embrace their juxtapositioning as an ambivalent structure of thoughtful life and moving point for preferred actions and choices (McCarthy and Byrne, 1988, Shotter, 1989; Byrne, 1996).

The metaphor of the Fifth Province can thus be said to be a cultural resource that we invoke to sustain an ethical disposition towards rela-tional reciprocity among participants, and an openness to the contents of discursive binary forms in which subject positions are constituted. We have imagined that this juxtaposing of binary opposites creates possibilities for the emergence of resources, solutions and generative ideas and behaviours (Byrne and McCarthy, 1988; McCarthy and Byrne, 1988).

Re-Versed Perspectives

Interviewing constitutes the major activity of therapeutic conversations, and within the context of this chapter the products of interviewing are articulated as co-constructions emerging within *inter-views* or between views and voices. As one of the authors has previously stated, an inter-view is a joint product between the interviewer and the interviewee (Hydén and McCarthy, 1994). Thus it is a mutual endeavour between both parties within the interviewing process. Within the domain of therapy, however, this joint product presupposes a primacy in relation to the interests of the help-seeker and not the help-giver. The concerns and complaints of the help-seeker are privileged articulations. As therapists we are thus called upon to background our own issues in the service of those we work with. This apparently noble policy of privileging client discourse has however constituted a dilemmatic encounter between therapist and client. In backgrounding the therapist's experiential, emotional and theoretical world the client is and has been at risk of an unintended but exposing gaze of an objectifying professional expertise. In such an encounter both parties in such activities run the risk of being alienated from the other within the intended dialogic interaction. They are alienated, or one might say 'hurt', within these interactions by a listening to theoretical and emotional calls from outside of the dialogue (Salamon et al., 1991). It is as if a third voice has entered, drowning out the authentic voicings of both client and therapist.

Such silencing is also possible when we consider that each interview is also carried on within a discursive culture, sociopolitical and professional, which constitutes the process. The emergent process in turn constitutes the culture so that (a) nothing changes, (b) pathology is co-constructed, and/or (c) the interview has the potential to constitute the culture subversively so that the discursive culture in which the interview happens is changed both for the actors and in terms of a professional practice. The authors, in this chapter, imagine a subversively situated practice in relation to the dominant, pathologizing and professional narratives which can drown out the local narrative of the interviewee's lived experiences and which in turn form the 'tyrannising power of the therapeutic motif' (Ehrenhaus, 1993: 82). As such our practice is imagined as a double-sided activity pervaded with ambivalence, ambiguity, open-endedness and ethical concerns.

References

Andersen, T. (ed.) (1990) *The Reflecting Team: Dialogues about the Dialogues about the Dialogues*. New York: Broadstairs, Burgman.

Andersen, T. (1995) 'Reflecting processes; acts of informing and forming: you can borrow my eyes but you must not take them away from me', in S. Friedman (ed.), *The Reflecting Team in Action: Collaborative Practice in Family Therapy*. New York: Guilford.

Anderson, H. (1997) *Conversation, Language and Possibilities: A Postmodern Approach to Therapy*. New York: Basic Books.

Barrett, M. (1988) *Women's Oppression Today: the Marxist/Feminist Encounter*. London: Verso.

Bateson, G. (1972) *Steps to an Ecology of Mind*. New York: Ballantine.

Bateson, G. (1979) *Mind and Nature*. New York: E.P. Dutton.

Baudrillard, J. (1988) 'The ecstasy of communication', in H. Foster (ed.), *Postmodern Culture*. London: Pluto Press.

Belsey, C. and Moore, J. (eds) (1989) *The Feminist Reader. Essays in Gender and the Politics of Literary Criticism*. London: Macmillan.

Benhabib, S. (1992) *Situating the Self: Gender, Community and Postmodernism in Contemporary Ethics*. New York: Routledge.

Benhabib, S., Butler, J., Cornell, D. and Fraser, N. (1995) *Feminist Contentions: A Philosophical Exchange*. London: Routledge.

Braidotti, R. (1989) 'The politics of ontological difference', in T. Brennan (ed.), *Between Feminism and Psychoanalysis*. London: Routledge.

Burck, C. and Daniel, G. (1995) *Gender and Family Therapy*. London: Karnac Books.

Burck, C. and Speed, B. (eds) (1995) *Gender, Power and Relationships*. London: Routledge.

Butler, J. (1990) *Gender Trouble: Feminism and the Subversion of Identity*. New York: Routledge.

Byrne, N.O'R. (1996) 'Diamond absolutes: a daughter's response to her mother's abortion', in P. Stratton (ed.), *Children's Voices: A Special Issue of Human Systems*, 6: 255–77.

Byrne, N.O'R. and McCarthy, I.C. (1988) 'Moving statutes: re-questing ambivalence through ambiguous discourse', *Irish Journal of Psychology*, 9: 173–82.

Byrne, N.O'R. and McCarthy, I.C. (1995) 'Abuse, risk and protection: a fifth province approach to an adolescent sexual offence', in C. Burck and B. Speed (eds), *Gender, Power and Relationships*. London: Routledge.

Byrne, N.O'R. and McCarthy, I.C. (1998) 'Marginal illuminations: a fifth province approach to intra-cultural issues in an Irish context', in M. McGoldrick (ed.), *Revisioning Family Therapy: Race, Class and Gender*. New York: Guilford.

Chodorow, N. (1978) *The Reproduction of Mothering. Psychoanalysis and the Sociology of Gender*. Berkeley: University of California Press.

Chodorow, N. (1996) 'Gender as a personal and cultural construction', in R-E.B. Joeres and B. Laslett (eds), *The Second Signs Reader. Feminist Scholarship, 1983–1996*. Chicago: Chicago University Press.

Cixous, H. (1976) 'The Laugh of the Medusa', *Signs*, 1 (4): 875–93.

Cixous, H. and Clement, C. (1986) *The Newly Born Woman*. Minneapolis: University of Minnesota Press.

Clement, G. (1996) *Care, Autonomy and Justice*. Boulder, CO: Westview Press.

Colgan, F.I. (1991) *The Fifth Province Model: Father-Daughter Incest and Systemic Consultation*. PhD dissertation. University College Dublin.

Daly, M. (1978) *Gyn/Ecology: The Metaethics of Radical Feminism*. Boston: Beacon.

de Lauretis, T. (1987) *Technologies of Gender: Essays on Theory, Film, and Fiction*. Bloomington: Indiana University Press.

Ehrenhaus, P. (1993) 'Cultural narratives and the political motif: the political containment of Vietnam veterans', in D.K. Mumby (ed.), *Narrative and Social Control: Critical Perspectives*. London: Sage.

Epston, D., White, M. and Murray, K. (1992) 'A proposal for a re-authoring therapy: Rose's revisioning of her life and a commentary', in S. McNamee and K.J. Gergen (eds), *Therapy as Social Construction*. London: Sage.

Flax, J. (1993) *Disputed Subjects. Essays on Psychoanalysis, Politics and Philosophy*. London: Routledge.

Foucault, M. (1982) 'The subject and power', in H. Dreyfus and P. Rabinow (eds), *Beyond Structuralism and Hermeneutics*. Chicago: Chicago University Press.

Foucault, M. (1994) 'Ethics, subjectivity and truth', in P. Rabinow (ed.), *Michel*

Foucault: Ethics, Subjectivity and Truth: The Essential Works of Foucault, 1954–1984. New York: The New Press.

Gergen, K.J. (1994) *Realities and Relationships: Soundings in Social Construction*. Cambridge: Harvard University Press.

Gergen, K.J. (1995) 'Social construction and the transformation of identity politics', unpublished manuscript.

Gilligan, C. (1982) *In a Different Voice*. Cambridge: Harvard University Press.

Goldner, V. (1985) 'Feminism and family therapy', *Family Process*, 24 (3): 1–47.

Goldner, V. (1991) 'Toward a critical relational theory of gender', *Psychoanalytic Dialogues*, 1: 249–72.

Gorell Barnes, G. (1990) '"The Little Woman" and the word of work', in R.J. Perelberg and A.C. Miller (eds), *Gender and Power in Families*. London: Routledge.

Grosz, E. (1989) *Sexual Subversions*. London: Allen and Unwin.

Hare-Mustin, R. (1987) 'The problem of gender in family therapy theory', *Family Process*, 26: 15–27.

Hare-Mustin, R. (1994) 'Discourses in the mirrored room: a postmodern analysis of therapy', *Family Process*, 33: 19–35.

Hare-Mustin, R. and Marecek, J. (1988) 'The meaning of difference: gender theory, postmodernism and psychology', *American Psychologist*, 43: 455–64.

Held, V. (1995) *Justice and Care: Essential Readings in Feminist Ethics*. Boulder, CO: Westview Press.

Higginbotham, E.B. (1996) 'African-American women's history and the meta-language of race', in R-E.B. Joeres and B. Laslett (eds), *The Second Signs Reader. Feminist Scholarship, 1983–1996*. Chicago: Chicago University Press.

hooks, bell (1990) *Yearning: Race, Gender, and Cultural Politics*. Boston: South End Press.

Hydén, M. and McCarthy, I.C. (1994) 'Woman battering and father-daughter incest disclosure: discourses of denial and acknowledgement', *Discourse and Society*, 5 (4): 543–65.

Irigaray, L. (1993) *Sexes and Genealogies*. New York: Columbia University Press.

Irigaray, L. (1994) *Thinking the Difference*. London: The Athlone Press.

Joeres, R-E.B. and Laslett, B. (eds) (1996) *The Second Signs Reader. Feminist Scholarship, 1983–1996*. Chicago: Chicago University Press.

Jones, E. (1993) *Family Systems Therapy: Developments in the Milan-Systemic Therapies*. Chichester: J. Wiley and Sons.

Kearney, P.A., Byrne, N.O'R. and McCarthy, I.C. (1989) 'Just metaphors: marginal illuminations in a colonial retreat', *Family Therapy Case Studies*, 4: 17–33.

Kristeva, J. (1989) 'Women's time', in C. Belsey and J. Moore (eds), *The Feminist Reader: Essays in Gender and the Politics of Literary Criticism*. London: Macmillan.

Laclau, E. and Mouffe, C. (1985) *Hegemony and Socialist Strategy: Toward a Radical Democratic Politics*. London: Verso.

Lieblich, A. (1996) 'Some unforeseen outcomes of conducting narrative research with people of one's own culture', in R. Josselson (ed.), *Ethics and Process in the Narrative Study of Lives*. London: Sage.

McCarthy, I.C. (1990) 'Paradigms lost: re-membering herstories and other invalid subjects', *Contemporary Family Therapy*, 12: 427–37.

McCarthy, I.C. (1991) 'Colonial sentences and just subversions: the potential for love and abuse in therapeutic encounters', *Feedback*, 3: 3–7.

McCarthy, I.C. (1995) 'Women, poverty and systemic therapies', in I.C. McCarthy (ed.), *Irish Family Studies: Selected Papers*. Dublin: Family Studies Centre.

McCarthy, I.C. (1997) 'Power, circularity and social exclusion', plenary presentation at the 3rd International European Family Therapy Association Conference, Barcelona, Spain, October.

McCarthy, I.C. and Byrne, N.O'R. (1988) 'Mis-taken love: conversations on the problem of incest in an Irish context', *Family Process*, 27: 181–99.

McCarthy, I.C. and Byrne, N.O'R. (1995) 'A spell in the Fifth Province', in S. Friedman (ed.), *The Reflecting Team in Action*. New York: Guilford.

McGoldrick, M., Anderson, C.M. and Walsh, F. (eds) (1989) *Women in Families: A Framework for Family Therapy*. New York: Norton.

McGuirk, M. and Byrne, N. (1994) 'Just now I like to call myself Myra', in I.C. McCarthy (ed.), *Poverty and Social Exclusion*, a special issue of *Human Systems*, 5 (3/4).

MacKinnon, L. and James, K. (1987) 'The new epistemology and the Milan approach: feminist and sociopolitical considerations', *Journal of Family Therapy*, 14: 1–28.

McNamee, S. and Gergen, K.J. (eds) (1992) *Therapy as Social Construction*. London: Sage.

McNay, L. (1992) *Foucault and Feminism*. Cambridge: Polity Press.

Moi, T. (1986) *The Kristeva Reader*. Oxford: Basil Blackwell.

Moi, T. (ed.) (1987) *French Feminist Thought: A Reader*. Oxford: Basil Blackwell.

Mouffe, C. (1988) 'American liberalism and its critics: Rawls, Taylor, Sandel and Walzer', *Praxis International*, 8: 70–82.

Mouffe, C. (1995) 'Feminism, citizenship and radical democratic politics', in L. Nicholson and S. Seidman (eds), *Social Postmodernism: Beyond Identity Politics*. Cambridge: Cambridge University Press.

Nicholson, L. (1983) 'Feminist theory: the private and the public', in L. McDowell and R. Pringle (eds), *Defining Women: Sociation, Institutions and Gender Divisions*. Cambridge: Polity Press.

Nicholson, L. (ed.) (1990) *Feminism/Postmodernism*. London: Routledge.

Nicholson, L. and Seidman, S. (eds) (1995) *Social Postmodernism: Beyond Identity Politics*. Cambridge: Cambridge University Press.

Noddings, N. (1984) *Caring: A Feminine Approach to Ethics and Moral Education*. Berkeley: University of California Press.

Palazzoli, M.S., Boscolo, L., Cecchin, G. and Prata, G. (1980) 'Hypothesing, circularity, neutrality: three guidelines for the conductor of the session', *Family Process*, 19: 45–7.

Pateman, C. (1987) 'Feminist critiques of the public/private dichotomy', in A. Philips (ed.), *Feminism and Equality*. Oxford: Basil Blackwell.

Pateman, C. (1988a) *The Disorder of Women*. Stanford, CA: Stanford University Press.

Pateman, C. (1988b) *The Sexual Contract*. Stanford, CA: Stanford University Press.

Perelberg, R.J. and Miller, A.C. (eds) (1990) *Gender and Power in Families*. London: Routledge.

Penn, P. and Frankfurt, M. (1994) 'Creating a participant text, writing, multiple voices, narrative multiplicity', *Family Process*, 33 (2): 17–23.

Rabinow, P. (ed.) (1994) *Michel Foucault: Ethics, Subjectivity and Truth: The Essential Works of Foucault, 1954–1984*. New York: The New Press.

Ruddick, S. (1980) 'Maternal thinking', *Feminist Studies*, 6: 342–67.

Salamon, E., Grevelius, K. and Andersson, M. (1991) 'Beware the siren's song: the AGS commission model', in S. Gilligan and R. Price (eds), *Therapeutic Conversations*. New York: Norton.

Shotter, J. (1989) 'Social accountability and the social construction of "you"', in J. Shotter and K.J. Gergen (eds), *Texts of Identity*. London: Sage.

Shotter, J. (1993) *Conversational Realities*. London: Sage.

Shotter, J. and Gergen, K.J. (eds) (1989) *Texts of Identity*. London: Sage.

Spivak, G.C. (1987) 'French feminism in an international frame', in G.C. Spivak (ed.), *In Other Worlds: Essays in Cultural Politics*. New York: Methuen.

Spivak, G. (1988) 'Can the subaltern speak?', in L. Grossberg and C. Nelson (eds), *Marxism and the Interpretation of Culture*. London: Methuen.

Tomm, K. (1993) 'The courage to protest: a commentary on Michael White's work', in S. Gilligan and R. Price (eds), *Therapeutic Conversations*. New York: W.W. Norton.

Van Lawick, J. and Sanders, M. (eds) (1995) *Family, Gender and Beyond*. Heemstede: LS Books.

Waldegrave, C. and Tamasese, K. (1994) 'Some central ideas in the "just therapy" approach', in I.C. McCarthy (ed.), *Poverty and Social Exclusion*, special issue of *Human Systems*, 5 (3/4): 191–208.

White, M. and Epston, D. (1990) *Narrative Means to Therapeutic Ends*. New York: Norton.

White, M. and Epston, D. (1993) 'Deconstruction and therapy', in S. Gilligan and R. Price (eds), *Therapeutic Conversations*. New York: Norton.

Wollstonecraft, M. (1982) *A Vindication of the Rights of Women*. Harmondsworth: Penguin. (First published 1792.)

PART II

DECONSTRUCTION IN PRACTICE

7

NARRATIVE, FOUCAULT AND FEMINISM: IMPLICATIONS FOR THERAPEUTIC PRACTICE

Vanessa Swan

I am of Arab/English background, middle class and heterosexual. I have identified as feminist since I was in my early twenties and I have worked as a therapist in Britain, Australia and Canada. Until recently, I spent four and half years working in a South Australian, feminist, women's health centre. In my late teens I studied social work and following this, I spent a number of years unclear about the methods I could use in my work with individuals. I was searching for a therapeutic method that would be consistent with my political beliefs. In fact, I wondered whether such an approach actually existed. Would being a therapist always feel like compromising the political to attend to individual emotional experiences? I read much of what described itself, at that time, as feminist approaches to therapy. Although this was politically helpful I found it loose and non-specific when it came to therapy; and at worst, it seemed to contribute to the already long list of what was 'wrong' with women. In continuing this search, I came across narrative therapy. This approach has provided me with the sense that what I do day-to-day sits as an integral part of what I believe in politically and, moreover, contributes towards achieving my feminist, political goals.

In this chapter, I will describe narrative therapy and articulate its relationship with contemporary feminist aims. I take this to mean, quite simply, the liberation of society from the unequal distribution of power caused by societal ideas which support male privilege. I will discuss the relationship of narrative therapy to contemporary feminist aims by dividing it into three parts. Firstly, I will look at the theoretical ground narrative therapy shares with feminism. Narrative therapy is significantly informed by the work of Michel Foucault amongst others and this discussion will involve considering the parallels and departures between his work and contemporary feminism. In particular, Foucault's notion of power informs the approach used in narrative therapy. I will discuss Foucault's description of the operation of power in Western society and the relevance of this view to the oppression of women. Secondly, I will use a case study detailing the experiences of 'Jo' with the aim of illustrating how narrative therapy is not only consistent with feminist principles but it is also a mechanism for consciousness-raising and highlighting personal agency. Finally, I shall look at the practice question of whether therapy, regardless of its form, can be validly used as a tool of feminism. I will focus on one prominent feminist's, Celia Kitzinger (1993), critique of therapy. My focus on this critique is not necessarily to defend therapy as a whole. My aim is to highlight some important questions which feminist therapists must consider to ensure a degree of sensitivity to the potentially harmful aspects of therapy and, conversely, to highlight the opportunities for change therapy can maximize. Kitzinger's paper forms a very useful and important critical framework for considering what I do.

Narrative Therapy

Narrative Therapy is the name given to the approach initially developed by Michael White (1988, 1988/9, 1991) and David Epston (White and Epston, 1989). They drew from, amongst other influences, specific aspects of post-structuralist work, particularly the ideas of Michel Foucault (1979) and, to some extent, the ideas of Jacques Derrida (1977).

Narrative therapy uses Jerome Bruner's (1986) notion of story as a metaphor to understand the process of how discourse reproduces particular power relationships and how this acts to construct certain meanings around our lives and the events which take place in them. These stories are not individually written but are the consequence of societal discourses that influence our everyday relationships with others and which become the themes of our own individual narratives. For example, it is not by chance or as a result of some personal inadequacy that many women find self-doubt an unwanted part of our lives, but, within this framework, this is understood to be a direct consequence of the ways patriarchy operates in women's lives to undermine our sense of self and thus, through self-surveillance, maintain particular relations of power.

The themes within these narratives invite us to explain events in our lives in particular ways. This is not only a process which occurs retrospectively but it is also a productive force which constructs particular understandings and meanings of events as they take place. This can be understood by considering the simple experience of a person spilling a glass of water. The event has little inherent meaning, it may be disregarded as nothing more than a mess to clean, or, conversely, this event may be attended to and remembered. Within the narrative metaphor, the difference between the extent to which this event is given attention and what meaning it is attributed with, is seen to depend upon the wider context of a person's experience. For example, if clumsiness has become a theme in this person's life, this event may be thought about and considered to be yet another example of clumsiness in her eyes or in the eyes of others around her. The spilt water may then be regarded as a significant marker of who she considers herself to be as a person and to some extent, perhaps, a marker of her self-worth. Although this experience may be considered to be trivial, it demonstrates the generative force these themes can have in our lives. It shows in a day-to-day way, the means by which societal discourses, in this example, about what it means to be a successful, competent individual, are internalized into the ways we think about ourselves. The narrative metaphor is thus a way of conceptualizing the process by which wider societal discourse and the normative rules this constructs can be seen to operate and inform our sense of who we are in the world. By specifically looking in detail at how this happens, opportunities for change, many of which have already been taken up by the person but often without their conscious awareness, can be highlighted and thereby made available to them to use in the future.

The relationship of these themes to the wider societal discourses are in the everyday, the sequence of daily life events, the 'of courseness' of our lives, the 'that's the way it is' anecdotes of our existence. We see it in statements like 'women are more emotional than men'; or, 'she is not old enough to understand'; or, 'to fully recover from a loss, one must let out the tears of grief'. This is not an innocent list of facts, but ideas that connect to certain ways of seeing the world, or discourses, and these discourses support some perspectives and make others invisible. The insidious nature of the everydayness of such statements is that they are made to appear in isolation, without connection to the belief systems they represent. The first statement relates to biological theories of emotion, the second to traditional notions of developmental psychology and the last uses the illness metaphor of medicine and connects this to cathartic ideas of emotional expression. Once exposed through a process of deconstruction, a person is able to think about the ideas or discourses from which these statements emanate and consider the overall effect of these on their lives. Is this notion something I agree with or not? What effect do these ideas have on my life and others around me? And so on.

The process of exposing and making explicit the ideas which inform the beliefs commonly accepted within society does not create an alternative position, free of discourse, where we can situate ourselves. We cannot stand outside of discourse, but we can be selective about which discourses fit better with our values and have less harmful effects on the wider community, for example, by selecting feminist-informed discourse. The danger inherent in this consideration is the possibility of merely reproducing one regime of truth with another. But instead, by opening up new possibilities, space is made for dialogue and the local contestation of knowledge, as opposed to the universal or commonsensical construction of knowledge. It is not about defining singular, better and healthier ways of being necessarily, but problematizing the universal and privileged nature of some knowledges. It is their privileged position after all – their common sense – which makes them implements of exclusion and oppression.

Let us return to the narrative framework, and the metaphor of storied lives. If a person finds these themes and stories problematic to their lives, it becomes the therapist's role to bring their awareness to these difficult-to-notice stories and the ideas and beliefs in the wider context of our society that support them. Through objectifying these ideas and stories, a process of what has been called 'externalizing conversations' takes place. The networks of ideas in which problems are contained, are held out for the person to see in contrast to their sense of self. A person is therefore able to see themselves as separate from the problem and its effect on their lives and to better understand the influence of dominant ideas.

Foucault, Power and Feminism

As we have seen, narrative therapy uses a Foucauldian notion of power to understand how people's lives are discursively constructed. Feminism, in particular post-structural and postmodern feminism, uses a similar approach to understand how women's lives are contained and defined through discourse. In this section I will further articulate these ideas and draw out the links and disparities between Foucault and feminism.

I will begin by outlining Foucault's notion of power in more detail, and I shall describe recent feminist writings with regard to the question of whether Foucault's writings can be validly used to further feminist aims and what implications these ideas have for feminism (if any).

Foucault (1981: 89) describes the operation of power as '. . . not ensured by right but by technique, not by law but by normalisation, not by punishment but by control, methods that are employed on all levels and in forms that go beyond the state and its apparatus'. He also states that '. . . power is tolerable only on condition that it mask a substantial part of itself. Its success is proportional to its ability to hide its own mechanisms' (Foucault, 1981: 86). Power is therefore seen to exist *within* our community. It is not the government or some modern day ruler that dictates how we should be. It is in the much more potent interactions of everyday life that power operates to control what we do, who we are and how we see the world, ways of control which, for the most part, go unseen and unnoticed as such. They are invisible not in their effect on how we behave in the world but they are unnoticed as the mechanisms of the operations of power within our society. A woman stands in front of a mirror and sheds her clothing, complaining 'it makes me look so fat'. She compares and criticizes herself, she modifies her behaviour and her notions of desired appearance are confirmed. In such situations power to modify and change according to society's rules, can be seen to operate; an action which occurs without even the presence of another and under, in this case, the guise of conformity or self-care.

Vickie Bell (1993) argues that Foucault's thesis implies feminism has missed this understanding of power. She writes of Foucault particularly in relation to understandings of sexuality: 'He implicitly casts the feminist work as naïve, slavishly reproducing models of understanding power and freedom that fail to grasp the present operations of power around sex, and thereby falling into the trap of producing more and more talk on sex that, far from liberating us, ensnares us deeper into the web' (1993: ix). Binary oppositions have been frequently utilized by feminism as a shorthand means to convey understandings of unequal power relationships, for example perpetrator/victim dichotomies. Foucault considers these binary understandings to reinforce simplistic constructions of rulers and ruled. Ramazanoglu (1993: 4) summarizes the effect of Foucault's work on feminists which, she says, 'invites us to think differently about the nature of knowledge and power, and questions in particular the ways in which feminists have thought about men having power over women'.

Although conceding the value of Foucault's work, feminists such as Ramazanoglu (1993: 4) also voice their concern about his supposedly neutral analysis in which he does not acknowledge his own male perspective. Ramazanoglu speaks of the dangers of 'political relativism' through the use of post-structural perspectives and she describes these approaches as '. . . extremely abstracted and also insensitive to the political point of feminism' (1993: 8).

Susan J. Hekman (1996: 1–2) summarizes feminist critiques of Foucault. Firstly, Foucault was a man; secondly, he had little to say about women and gender specifically, therefore raising the question of as to whether it is valid to use his methods; and thirdly, he questions the validity of feminist politics and he goes further to deconstruct the universal subject which disregards the category of 'woman', again undermining traditional feminist positions.

The compatibility of Foucault's work with the feminist project continues to be debated (Martin, 1988; Hekman, 1990; Nicholson, 1990;
Ramazanoglu, 1993), however, although this is of some relevance to this
chapter, further elucidating these discussions would turn this chapter
from primarily a practical piece into a theoretical exercise. Therefore, I
shall depart from this larger debate and proceed by focusing on one
aspect of this discussion, how Foucauldian ideas can be of use to
feminism.

McWhorter, in Bell (1993: 39), describes how she thinks feminists
should use Foucault's analysis of power, '. . . not to seek the "origin of
tyranny"', but to examine 'the interactions and the histories of daily
occurrences that sustain systems of normalisation and control'. It is the
questions which are posed by this understanding of society that form
the major contribution which Foucauldian thinking can add to feminist
discussions and feminist therapy. We thus depart from discussions in
regard to the formation or 'what' of the subject, to focus on the more
useful *how* the subject is constructed, what discourses are operating to
create the potentialities or occlusions of potential for the self and how
these can be of use to feminism?

One example of a feminist utilizing Foucauldian analysis is Sawicki's
consideration of racist feminist practices. She refers to the critique of
white middle-class feminist universals by feminists of colour. She
describes her steps to appropriate Foucault for feminism, and, in doing
so, the need to '. . . analyse the politics of personal interactions and
everyday life, and account for our participation in reproducing systems
of domination despite our conscious protests against specific forms of it'
(Sawicki, 1991: 10).

Bell (1993: 41) speaks of the increasing convergence of feminist and
Foucauldian notions of power, as feminists begin to argue against
simple powerful/powerless divisions and she identifies the opportunity
this creates: '. . . if power is exercised not possessed, contingent rather
than static, feminist opposition to the various operations of power may
expect to identify more gaps and weaknesses in power's operations.' In
this way it will create possible focal points for understanding and action
to change these relations of power. Bell (1993: ix) uses Foucauldian
notions, for example, to describe 'how incest is "put into discourse"
within the "power-knowledge-pleasure" network that Michel Foucault
made his object of study'. Foucauldian ideas can become tools for
feminist analysis, contributing to detailed understandings of the
methods of patriarchy operating in the day-to-day of women's lives.

Women's Lives

Having considered the methodology of the therapy and discussed
philosophical questions of feminism and Foucault, I will now articulate

practicalities of this approach in the life of a particular woman I will call
'Jo'. For reasons of confidentiality, Jo is not one individual, but her life
includes the experiences of a number of women with whom I have
worked.

Jo came for counselling following a deterioration in her relationship
with her partner of five years. That partner had moved out over the
preceding weekend. She described her feelings during the previous few
weeks as confused. Although separation was what she wanted, she had
felt increasingly critical of herself and worthless over this same period.
When we talked more about the role that self-criticism and worthlessness had played in her life, Jo described how these seemed to relate
very closely to guilt. When she felt guilty and responsible, self-criticism
and worthlessness seemed to enter her life and made her feel hatred
towards herself and all that she did. 'Guilt's' presence was large when
she began counselling as she felt responsible for her partner and *his*
distress. I asked Jo whether this was the first time that these players had
entered her life, and she described their presence, off and on, since
her early adolescence when she had been raped by her father. Soon after
this abuse, her father had left the family. Jo had felt very guilty and
responsible for his sexual attraction to her. Jo's mother had known about
the abuse and, at the time, had been supportive of Jo and separated from
her husband. However, as Jo got older, her mother became increasingly
critical of her relationships with men, describing her as 'loose', she
criticized how Jo dressed, and frequently made comments like 'Jo, you
are asking for trouble'.

During our conversations many of the ideas captured in her experience became clear. I asked Jo about where she thought her mother's
ideas about how women should be in relation to their sexuality came
from, what effect she thought these ideas had on women and on men,
what these sorts of ideas implied about the different responsibilities of
the genders when it came to their sexual desires, and whether she
agreed with these attitudes or not? We also talked about what our
society expected of women's roles in relation to the happiness of men in
their lives.

In considering feminist-informed answers to these questions, it
became clear that patriarchal beliefs about women were behind her
mother's thinking. These were beliefs with which Jo did not agree and
she wondered, if seen in this context, her mother would even have
agreed with them.

Jo and I also considered the presence of self-criticism and worthlessness in her life. I asked her about what happened when they were
not in her life and more particularly, what her role had been in
excluding their presence? We discovered through this discussion that
she was able, at times, to see through the eyes of her aunt, who always
saw the specialness in her. Jo had learnt to say to herself 'What would
Aunty B have thought about this?' and 'What would she have said to

me?' By answering such questions, Jo was able to appreciate her actions and the strength in her that they reflected.

As therapy continued, Jo was able to speak of the things about herself she was coming to respect, such as her determination to improve her life, by which she meant that she 'stuck at things' until they worked in her favour. These were positive changes that she would previously have attributed to luck or chance. We spoke of how much of women's abilities and strengths are owned by good luck and how our own actions are made invisible by such attribution. We spoke of the effects of dismissing her strength as merely being down to chance as undermining the power of women and as being a way of seeing our lives as if we are leaves in the wind with little control over the direction we blow in.

Jo and I considered the two contradictory stories about her. The first told through the eyes of the abuse and the misogynist views of our society and the second told through the eyes of her aunt who saw her courage and knew of her survival. We considered these two versions of events in relation to her separation and she was able to again use her aunt's vision. In this way she came from a place of confusion, to a different place of choice from which she could see the methods of control used in society and the ideas which are woven together to form the near invisible fabric which trap women in situations of subservience. She no longer saw self-criticism and a sense of worthlessness as evidence of unhealed or unresolved damage created by the abuse inflicted upon her, or as a marker of personal weakness, or some sort of subconscious need to harm herself. She was able to recognize these as reflections of the tools of power within our society and her discomfort with this, and she saw the times she was able to escape it as markers of a journey of strength and courage on which she had embarked in her teenage years.

The process of therapy thereby reveals some of the methods of individual control operating in our society. It is too simplistic to think that with this vision one can just turn away from the previous vantage point. Although one hopes it will never look quite the same again, many of the methods used to maintain this view are still in place. Education systems, family relationships, the media and so on continue to direct our focus. However, Jo is now able to consciously bring to mind *other* ways of seeing her life, views which make clear her sense of strength and value in the world. Within her own life, she is able to act against these problematic ideas which she has identified.

In a final conversation with Jo about others in her life that share her and her aunt's vision of her, she brought to mind a number of people who she felt might be able to see strength in her. We actively identified an audience who could support her sense of strength and who knew about her abilities.

In this example one can see how narrative therapy can open up and localize discourse for discussion and contestation, bringing light to the previously obscured ideas which trap women and have us blame our-selves for problems in our lives.

Politics in Therapy

The importance of being able to critically appraise the effects of specific ideas and their relationship to wider networks of ideas or discourses has been outlined within the context of therapy in a previous section. The importance of utilizing a similar process to appraise the ideas and practices that form the basis of a therapeutic approach, I think, is equally important. And for me this consideration is particularly of value in relation to narrative therapy's relationship with the feminist aims of ending patriarchy and liberating women. I am now going to explore further the question of how narrative therapy can be used as a tool for ending women's oppression. I will do this by focusing on Celia Kitzinger's (1993) article 'Depoliticising the personal: A feminist slogan in feminist therapy' which raises important feminist questions for therapy.

Kitzinger argues that, regardless of qualification, *all therapy* is bad for women. Kitzinger uses the analogy of arguing for the inclusion of certain meats in a vegetarian diet in order to illustrate the absurdity of therapists who argue for the exemption of their particular therapy from Kitzinger's criticism of all therapy. Although I appreciate the nature of her ethical stand, I find the creation of such a dichotomy – flesh and vegetable – to be rigid, dismissive and theoretically problematic. Such a view repeats the problems of reducing issues to binary opposition. The danger is that feminism would thereby lose the opportunity to involve more women in our action, women who otherwise would be entirely missed. There are many women whose lives are riddled with self-blame and a sense of unworthiness which maintain their silence and separate them from other women. Self-blame and unworthiness are examples of the power of oppression operating at a very local level, a level over-looked by Kitzinger's analysis.

Let us look more closely at the points Kitzinger raises. She describes four interpretations of the feminist catch cry 'the person is political' as a framework from which to critique therapy. Firstly, she argues that therapy personalizes the political, rather than, as much feminist therapy claims, politicizes the personal. She describes the process by which political discourses of violence against women and racism are extricated from their political context and internalized as personal inadequacies, which therapy then seeks to remedy. This continues the process pre-viously described by which mechanisms of power, within society, are separated from understanding the sources and purpose for their pro-duction. Therapy contributes in this way to not only maintaining the status quo but it also provides an active momentum towards holding the individual responsible and mystifying the political context. Secondly, Kitzinger describes how she sees therapy fostering the idea of the revolution 'from within' at the expense of political change in the outside world. She criticizes the idea that merely by feeling better about our-selves as women, this, in itself, constitutes political action. In fact, the opposite can be seen to be true; accepting one's lot mitigates against political action to create any structural change. Thirdly, if therapy merely aims to uncritically 'validate women's experiences', as some do, social and political factors which shape experience are once again ignored.

Finally, Kitzinger criticizes the concept of 'empowerment' based upon the idea of liberating the personal to free us to act politically. She argues against other therapists who suggest, as I do, that the particular therapy that *we* engage in, can, unlike many others, contribute to feminist goals. Again Kitzinger employs the analogy of meat-eating animal activists in an absurd tautology which in itself reproduces the very structure of power relations from which the oppression itself emerges. I would, however, agree with her when she points out that engaging in therapy is not the same as spending one's leisure-time indulging in an innocent pastime: it is a potentially dangerous activity. One can very reasonably inquire as to why women should ever enter this potentially toxic environment?

To answer Kitzinger's criticisms let us reconsider some of the points previously discussed in this chapter. If we consider mechanisms of power and control to be implemented at a local, everyday level, for us to then merely consider political action as only being macro, structural action, we immediately miss the day-to-day, pervasive methods of control and oppression. The potency of misogyny remains strong, as we as women continue to spend too much time questioning our com-petencies, comparing ourselves to others, and feeling unhappy and inadequate. Much of what Kitzinger says is right and important to ensure we are wary of therapy. As much as I agree that it is one of the very important and potent tools for feminism, it also holds all of the potential dangers of juggling with fire! Therapy has in the past and continues, at times, to condemn and pathologize women, and to distract us from political causes. Therapy has been used to blame and hold us responsible for the ills of society. For example, these accusations have been justified by focusing on the presence of women as mothers in children's lives. Our wariness of therapy is justified, but despite this history and these dangers, I believe it can also hold an important key of great feminist value.

Kitzinger's criticisms have a universalist 'always will be' quality that allows for no response or action with regard to them and therefore, allows no hope for therapy or no possible momentum towards feminist goals. Therapy is condemned for always, not only in the past and present, but in all possible future developments and responses. She seems to go too far. If such a totalization of therapy was accepted and the social practice of therapy disappeared, the feminist cause would also lose. We would be bereft of one methodology with the potential, when critically applied, to understand and liberate women's lives in a dialogical and contextual manner.

Narrative therapy seems to me to be able to achieve the elusive end of politicizing the personal. Kitzinger's binary polarization of one or other dismisses the connection between these two processes, achieved through some therapies, of politicizing personal relations as a stepping-stone to political action. Political action can be an important *therapeutic* goal and politicizing the personal through a therapeutic process, which makes evident the mechanisms of power and control, is a means to this end. The question of what comes next or what form of political action a woman might next take, should be made visible by therapy and should be a question the therapist and the therapy holds dear.

Kitzinger's universalist criticism of therapy holds further theoretical problems in that it places the headquarters of power in therapeutic practice. Foucault and narrative therapy argue exactly the opposite, that power operates at the local level. To miss this reading is to lose opportunities for feminism. Despite my objection to the main point of Kitzinger's paper, I do however believe that the process of evaluating the relationship of therapy to feminist goals is still vitally important. One can make assumptions about action and their outcomes which stand in the way of critically questioning processes and relationships.

Conclusion

In this chapter I have discussed the relationship of narrative therapy to contemporary feminist aims by considering it in three parts. Firstly, I have outlined the theoretical ground shared by both narrative therapy and postmodern feminism. Secondly, I have given a detailed example of the process of narrative therapy in which I have articulated the ways in which this connects to feminist goals. And finally, I have focused on the question as to whether therapy can be validly utilized as a feminist tool.

Notions that construct power as applied rather than lived, are limited in their usefulness to both feminist and therapeutic aims. Narrative therapy maximizes the opportunities for change made evident by an alternative understanding of power that makes evident its application rather than its operation. Through the process of therapy, space for the local, day-to-day problematization and contestation of the oppressive effects of power is created. Such opportunities are lost when power and those who are seen to hold it, are objectified and seen as discrete from everyday life. Feminist aims can be furthered in the lives of some women through this therapeutic process. This would be a process which creates opportunities that might otherwise be lost to feminism for the politicization of these women's experience. The necessity of processes which create this space is emphasized by Shane Phelan (Nicholson and Seidman, 1995: 335) particularly with regard to lesbian experience, when she says 'without that problematization of the "inside", the hegemonic core of social structures, we will continually return to unsatisfactory choices'. I believe this statement captures the current dilemmas facing both therapy and feminism.

References

Bell, V. (1993) *Interrogating Incest: Feminism, Foucault and the Law*. London: Routledge.

Bruner, J. (1986) *Actual Minds, Possible Worlds*. Boston, MA: Harvard University Press.

Derrida, J. (1977) *Of Grammatology*, trans. G.C. Spirak. Baltimore, MD: Johns Hopkins University Press.

Foucault, M. (1979) *Discipline and Punish*. Harmondsworth: Penguin.

Foucault, M. (1981) *The History of Sexuality Volume 1: An Introduction*. Harmondsworth: Penguin.

Hekman, S.J. (1990) *Gender and Knowledge: Elements of a Postmodern Feminism*. Cambridge: Polity Press.

Hekman, S.J. (ed.) (1996) Editor's Introduction. *Feminist Interpretations of Michel Foucault*. Pennsylvania: Pennsylvania State University Press.

Hudson, A. (1989) 'Changing perspectives: feminism, gender and social work', in M. Langan and P. Lee (eds), *Radical Social Work Today*. London: Unwin Hyman.

Kitzinger, C. (1993) 'Depoliticising the personal: a feminist slogan in feminist therapy', *Woman's Studies International Forum*, 16 (5): 487–96.

Martin, B. (1988) 'Feminism, criticism and Foucault', in I. Diamond and L. Quinby (eds), *Feminism and Foucault: Reflections on Resistance*. Boston, MA: Northeastern University Press.

Nicholson, L. (ed.) (1990) *Feminism/Postmodernism*. New York: Routledge.

Nicholson, L. and Seidman, S. (eds) (1995) *Social Postmodernism: Beyond Identity Politics*. Cambridge: Cambridge University Press.

Ramazanoglu, C. (ed.) (1993) *Up Against Foucault: Explorations of Some Tensions Between Foucault and Feminism*. New York: Routledge.

Sawicki, J. (1991) *Disciplining Foucault: Feminism, Power, and the Body*. New York: Routledge.

White, M. (1988) 'The process of questioning, a therapy of literary merit?', *Dulwich Centre Newsletter*: 8–14.

White, M. (1988/9) 'The externalizing of the problem and the re-authoring of lives and relationships', *Dulwich Centre Newsletter*: 3–20.

White, M. (1991) 'Deconstruction and therapy', *Dulwich Centre Newsletter*, 3: 21–40.

White, M. and Epston, D. (1989) *Literate Means to Therapeutic Ends*. Adelaide: Dulwich Centre Publications.

8

A DISCURSIVE APPROACH TO THERAPY WITH MEN

Ian Law

Maybe the target nowadays is not to discover what we are but to refuse what we are.

(Foucault, 1982: 208)

Much of the time that I have spent working as a counsellor, family therapist and training provider has been with those who have been subjected to and/or have reproduced violence and abuse. Being a male therapist, attempting to address and challenge the effects and practices of male privilege in a way that does not inadvertently reproduce it, has constantly raised dilemmas. However, an awareness of these issues is not a guarantee against reproducing them. The judiciary and the history of its judgements in relation to men's abuse of women and children is a good example of the failure of men to 'self-regulate'. Historically there has been a tradition of secrecy, called 'confidentiality' by professionals, that has mitigated against the work of therapists being open to scrutiny. However, there has been, more recently, a development of approaches to therapy and counselling that attempt to bring a sense of 'openness' and transparency thereby allowing the practice of therapy to be viewed. This means that therapy can be held accountable, seen in relation to the politics of power and privilege by those who are in a position to view it. It is not my intention to write about the various ways that this has been done or even the various ways I may have attempted it. However, this apparent shift in the field of therapy, from invisibility to greater visibility, brings its dilemmas more clearly into focus. For me, the way in which some of these dilemmas appear has become increasingly evident through discussion with women and men on the issue of therapy with men and boys; engaging in therapy with men and boys alongside women co-therapists; having, at times, a reflecting team of women therapists; showing videotapes of my work, with the consent of those appearing in them, to training groups; and outlining the details of therapy in such writings as this.

Some of the dilemmas in this work that, I believe, require constant attention are: as a man, what are the best ways to take responsibility for addressing and challenging the abusive practices of the male gender? What is the best way to ensure that the aim of stopping men's violence and abuse of women and children remains the guiding principle of therapy? How can a man's experience of being subjected to abuse and violence be acknowledged and addressed whilst retaining a focus on his being responsible for reproducing abuse and violence? What are the most effective ways of challenging a man's practices of abuse and violence whilst still engaging him in taking responsibility for such practices? What are the most effective ways of avoiding complicity in engaging men in taking responsibility for their reproduction of practices of abuse and violence?

This list, of course, is neither comprehensive nor prescriptive but I constantly refer back to it in evaluating my therapeutic work with other men. This work focuses on conversations that question the meaning that men may make of their life, their feelings and their actions. This questioning creates the possibility of other meanings being considered, meanings that allow for the possibility of thinking, acting and feeling differently. These conversations constitute a discursive approach to therapy (Law and Madigan, 1992, 1998) which is informed by post-structuralist theories of the self. This chapter uses a description of the process of therapy over six meetings with one man, Don, to outline a way of working that is sensitive to the politics of gender, the politics of the constitution of the self and the politics of therapy. This discursive approach has theoretical underpinnings, drawing heavily from the work of Michel Foucault. The way in which this particular approach interprets and applies Foucault's (1972) notions of discourse and discursive formation are outlined below. The reader may prefer to read this paper in the sequence it appears or to return to this section following a reading of the description of the therapy meetings.

A Discursive Approach

There is a growing tradition of approaches to therapy that draw upon post-structuralist ideas and combine them with other influences such as narrative (White, 1995), feminism (Weedon, 1987), psychoanalysis (Parker, 1997) and Marxism (Newman and Holzman, 1997). Some have pioneered the application of Foucauldian theory to therapeutic practice (White and Epston, 1989; White, 1991). Within that tradition a discursive approach (Law and Madigan, 1998) focuses on Foucault's (1972) notion of discourse, discursive formation, archive, institutions, discursive and disciplinary practices (Foucault, 1977), and the way in which power is exercised. If we examine men's ways of being in relation to these ideas then we can consider the ways in which discourses of masculinity are formed; the way in which theories and ideologies of masculinity constitute a discursive archive; the way in which men become the site of masculine discursive formation and are at the same time its subject and object; and the ways in which power constitutes men's sense of self and identity and enlists men in perpetuating regulatory and disciplinary practices. Such an approach to therapy and counselling with men can create a context for the identification, evaluation and critique of the discourses and discursive practices operating in their lives. This therapeutic practice can engage men in bringing abuse into the discourse of ethics which can then be regulated through the practices of accountability.

Discourse

Foucault (1990) described discourse primarily in terms of the judicial, the political and the moral, linked to the state, the judiciary and the Church and located within a web of *'mobile power relations'*. Discourse refers to the connection between statements and the prevailing social and power relations in which they are either uttered or silenced (Foucault, 1982). This description refers, then, both to what can be said and thought, and also to who can speak and with what authority so that meaning results from institutionalized practices that maintain the given discourse (Law and Madigan, 1992). The discourses in question here centre around religion, gender and the biological basis of behaviour. Each of these discourses has an archive, a body of knowledge that constitutes what is and is not an 'appropriately' gendered person.

Archive

Much of the current archive of knowledge on what it is to be a man and a woman has been informed by the twin discourses of Romanticism and Modernism. The binary opposition constituted by these twin discourses is in the tradition of dualisms of liberal philosophy such as Kant's reason/emotion, Descartes's mind/body, social/biological, and indeed, masculine/feminine. As is the way of binary oppositions, they are interdependent and one never fully eclipses the other (Derrida, 1976). Although the Romantic/Modern binary opposition appears, at first, to represent different and competing constructions of masculinity they are, in fact, two sides of the same coin. That coin was minted in the ideology of the biological basis of behaviour. This ideology, crudely put, states that men and women are the way they are because of their biological differences. This coin has been spinning since the period known as the Enlightenment. At times it has landed one side up for a while, as in the Romantic period of the nineteenth century and throughout the dominance of Modernism for most of the twentieth century. But even as one side lies uppermost and on view, the other is ever present. Mostly though, it spins so that both contradicting sides are present. First, a Romantic representation flashes brightly before a Modern representation then attracts our attention. Regardless of whether it is a Romantic or Modern notion that lands face up it is always the same coin being tossed. Images that dominated the representation of masculinity in Romantic literature were typified by such fictional characters as Heathcliff in Emily Brontë's *Wuthering Heights*, and legendary characters like Lord Byron for whom the phrase 'mad, bad and dangerous to know' was coined. Modern literature provides images of man typified in the film *A Clockwork Orange* along with the modern methods of his control. Film provides a host of cultural representations of masculinity such as John Wayne, Rhett Butler's 'forced kiss' in *Gone With the Wind*, and countless others. Popular culture has generated a gender industry based on the sale of commodities and driven by the perpetuation of certain kinds of masculinity and femininity that are now allied with pop psychology. Magazines are filled with pseudo-psychometric tests, self-help bookstores are filled with pseudo-romantic versions of masculinity such as *Iron John* (Bly, 1990), and pseudo-modern versions such as *Men are from Mars and Women are from Venus* (Gray, 1994). Throughout the twentieth century developmental psychology has given a modern respectability to a very traditional gender discourse, providing scientific research that 'validates' gendered role distinctions (Burman, 1994). Men not fitting the requirements of manhood as contained in the discursive archive on gender are seen as not measuring up, as being less than a man, as not being in control, as being a failure, as not succeeding in 'attaining' a career, an 'attractive wife' or 'attractive children'.

Prior to the Enlightenment, Western Christian notions of femininity and masculinity were constituted by the religious discourse. The archive consisted mainly of the New and Old Testaments founded on the ideology of creationism. Gender discourse has been reproduced through such myths as Adam and Eve in the Garden of Eden. This was the word of God interpreted by men in office as representatives of the Christian institutions of the Church. Creationism, crudely put, states that men and women are the way they are because God made them that way. Like the biological basis of behaviour ideology, creationism demands our acceptance of fundamental and fixed differences between men and women which are defined and described in the 'expert' scientific and religious texts.

Institutions

Gender discourse and its archive are administered almost universally through institutions. The institutions of the professions, the judiciary, the media, the arts, the Church, medicine, politics, and popular culture are all imbued with gender discourse. At a more local level the main institutions for the maintenance and perpetuation of gender discourse are heterosexual couples and the institution of 'the family'. When the criteria of gender and religious discourse are applied, most relationships do not then qualify as being a 'family' and 'couple', though the image of what they should really be like operates still with full force to normalize or pathologize them. In Foucauldian terms, the family can be seen as a 'node', or a site of discursive formation (Law, 1998). That is, various discourses constitute families, define families and families reproduce and support those same discourses through the perpetuation of certain ideologies and certain practices. The family is the institution through which gender discourse is distributed in the socialization of boys and girls and the surveillance and regulation of women. Thus, if a man is not in a position of authority over women and children the gender discourse cannot be effectively maintained and perpetuated. As a result those configurations that do not conform to the discursive requirements of 'family' such as gay and lesbian families, 'single-mother' families and any other configuration that does not involve heterosexual men being in a position of authority over women and children are systematically disqualified through the various institutions of society. This disqualification is itself a discursive practice.

Power

For Foucault (1977: 27), power is *'exercised rather than possessed'*. The application of Foucauldian ideas may be a contentious issue, but the relevance of his notion of power to an understanding of the politics of gender is clear (see Swan, Chapter 7). Rather than men, as a gender, acquiring power, Foucault (1977: 27) invites us to see power as being *'the overall effects of its strategic position'*. Power is the collection of discursive practices performed that serves to maintain the strategic position of a given discourse and those persons who have access to its privileges. In terms of gender discourse this 'strategic position' could be equated with the term 'male privilege', with 'power' being the performance of this privilege by men over women and children. Foucault (1972) called these strategic administrations of power 'discursive practices'. In the context of gender discourse two such discursive practices are shaming and humiliating.

Discursive Practices

Discursive practices are ways of talking, thinking, feeling and acting that, when enacted, serve to reinforce, reproduce or support a given discourse and at the same time deny, disqualify or silence that which does not fit with that discourse. These practices are informed by the archive which contains the specifications for these practices. Disciplinary practices can be performed on others; such as a man holding up another man to ridicule for not fitting with the gender discourse specifications for masculinity (such as by crying when hit), and on the self (such as the crying man feeling shame and humiliation at failing what he believes to be his own specifications of manhood and therefore personhood). The twin discursive practices of shame and humiliation are frequently employed in the regulation of men by other men and in men's self-regulation. This maintains the gender discourse that constitutes men's sense of 'self' and is further employed in men's regulation of women. This collection of discursive practices serves to maintain the strategic position of the dominant group, in this case, men.

Women also use shame and humiliation in their regulation of other women, their selves, and other men. However, this use of shame and humiliation does not challenge gender discourse, it is practised in such a way that it not only preserves, but reinforces it. For example, women employed as 'security' at clubs or sporting events may choose to deal with a drunk, aggressive man by shaming and humiliating him through questioning his manhood. This ridicule, if displayed in public, can produce additional derision from other men that deflates him. However, if done in private the same tactic might be met with his violence. This is not an example of women gaining a strategic position over men. Neither is it an implication that women are responsible, contribute to, or are in some way complicit with men's violence. Rather, it is an example of women's access to discursive practices of masculinity being restricted to those that serve to maintain the gender discourse that states what it is to think, act, feel and behave like a man. For Foucault (1990) this means that each of us has a sense of 'self' that is constituted by discourse and that in our enactment of discourse we are both the subject of discourse and its object. We are subjected to discursive practices and we reproduce them in a way that is consistent with the discourse and its archive. This 'double conditioning' engages both men and women in maintaining and performing the gender discourse.

A Discursive Approach in Practice

Within a discursive approach, it is the role of the therapist to explicate, situate and trace the history of the various discourses that are mediating the sense that those people who are consulting us in therapy are making of their experience. Naming the discursive practices of power that maintain certain discourses may open space for the consideration of alternative practices or counter practices. If in Foucault's (1990: 95) words 'where there is power there is resistance', then just as discursive practices constitute the exercise of power that maintains a discourse, a discursive approach to therapy can support counter practices that constitute resistance to a discourse. This notion can inform a therapy of change. What follows is a description of therapy in which a discursive approach is applied over six meetings with a man named Don. Don, and the other people's names have been changed in this account.

First Session

Don began by saying that there were a number of 'issues' that affected his life that he had decided to attend to. When I asked what these were he started to describe himself as being easily hurt and let down by friends. He said that when he felt like this he would withdraw and cut off all connections with other people. This would then leave him feeling lonely and isolated. He also felt that he was 'picked on' by other men at work and this made him very angry. When I asked Don about the areas of his life that this description did not encompass he spoke of feeling good about himself when he was dancing and socializing. He reflected on how this seemed to be the opposite of his previously described practice of withdrawal and isolation. He decided that he would like to work at creating and maintaining connections in his life, even in the face of potential hurt, so as to stop the momentum of alienation that it generated. On closer examination Don determined that he was not just responding to the particular event that he found rejecting or to the incident that hurt him, but to the entire momentum of aliena-tion which overwhelmed him with a whole history of hurt and rejection. This had him 'over-reacting' with anger and emotionally withdrawing. He described how this momentum convinced him that there was a conspiracy against him and that life had been unfair. I became interested in the possibility of his experience of alienation being the outcome of discursive practices of exclusion and so I asked him about the history of alienation in his life. He described his experience of moving a lot as a child and never feeling like he fitted in at school, so that eventually he adapted to alienation and isolation as a way of life. It had become a habit that mitigated against making connections. Reflecting on our discussion of this history, he made a decision to attempt to break this habit and to privilege connection in his life instead.

Second Session – One Month Later

When I asked about our first meeting Don said that subsequent to our conversation he had experienced at least two days of euphoria. This, he said, was because he had 'felt good about himself', a very uncommon experience. Following this, a feeling of depression returned which was an altogether more familiar feeling. He described this as being cyclical and identified it as an effect of the alienation. As alienation's momentum grew and he became increasingly withdrawn and resentful of life, his feeling of depression would grow. Eventually it would lift for a while only to return following the frequently occurring incidents in his life where he felt hurt, rejected or 'picked on'. However, the euphoria of feeling good about himself was new. Paying attention to feeling good about himself was also new for him as it was usually the feeling of depression that gained all of his attention. In giving our attention to this fact we began to talk about what possibilities there might be to affect this cycle by starving depression of his energy and attention and nurturing feeling good about himself instead. Don identified his ready sense of humour as being a real strength to him and told me of how he used humour to literally laugh at the depression. This helped him to diminish its effects. On reflecting on this fact in our discussion, Don made another decision. He decided that he wanted to take further action to break this cycle by diminishing depression through humour and to combine this with countering isolation and alienation through making and maintaining connections with others. These acts constitute practices of resistance that are counter to the discursive practices of exclusion.

Third Session – Two Weeks Later

Don said that he had been thinking more about the notion of inadequacy, particularly in relation to his experience of being a man. He described 'manhood' as being like a club and felt as if he had two choices. The first choice was to attempt to gain membership of the club. However, to qualify for membership he would be required to deny certain personal qualities he held dear such as a sensitivity to the feelings of others, a care and concern for others, a desire to share personal thoughts and feelings that might involve vulnerability and uncertainty and require trust. These qualities fall outside the gender archive's usual specifications for masculinity. This does not mean that a man cannot demonstrate these qualities. It means that when he does it may disqualify his eligibility for membership of the 'club of manhood' or, in other words, the masculine branch of the gender discourse. The other choice, for Don, was to forego membership. This would result in his rejection of the club of manhood and feeling rejected by it and moving to a position of isolation and anger. Thinking of manhood as a club, he began to question the validity of its existence and whether his rejection of it needed to result in isolation, anger and a rejection of connection in his life. When I asked him if he thought others might experience the same dilemma he told me of a number of men with whom he had a connection, who likewise did not appear to meet the requirements of membership to the club-of-manhood. It seemed to Don that what these men had in common with each other was that they were 'different'. They were their own person and they were happy being themselves. He decided that this could constitute a way out of the binary opposition of membership/isolation; he would privilege feeling happy about being himself and nurture connections with others who were also happy to be themselves.

Fourth Session – One Week Later

Don began by telling me of his success in 'shortcutting depression'. Instead of spiralling down into depression through feelings of anger and isolation, he had taken the twin steps of refusing to allow bad thoughts to have access to him when he recognized their presence, and he had made sure that he was in contexts where there was the opportunity for connections, and had then acted on that opportunity. These constituted further counter practices to depression and alienation. He felt that he was being successful and effective in breaking the cycle of rejection, hurt, isolation and anger. This success had fuelled his desire to go further and to have the courage to unpack the thoughts, feelings and experiences that informed the cycle that he was currently breaking. We were now moving beyond his experience of what was a problem to him to looking at what it was that allowed the problem to exist in his life. Not only had this the potential to challenge the effects of this problem in his life, perhaps it could be dismantled altogether. This, he felt, was more directly to do with feelings of inadequacy that stopped him from developing a sexually intimate relationship with a woman. Thinking of how this might be addressed by privileging feeling good and happy about himself, led to him being clearer about what prevented him from feeling this about himself. What stood in his way were feelings of shame and humiliation.

I asked Don what informed these feelings. He told me of a general and systematic process of feeling shamed and humiliated by not measuring up to the requirements of manhood, particularly in his experience of other boys at school whilst growing up. This had also been his experience of work where he believed that other men conspired to place him in humiliating situations where he would feel shamed. He would fume silently and harbour a growing resentment and anger towards them and towards life. It became clear that these feelings of shame and humiliation resulted from the discursive practices of the gender discourse. With regard to sex and relationships with women his sense of shame and humiliation had been informed by two incidents that he had never told anyone about before. They were, in fact, secrets that he carried around about himself and he believed that now was the time to finally 'confess' them if he was to extend the progress he had been making in feeling good about himself.

The first incident he recounted took place as a teenager in his room with his girlfriend and his male best friend. His best friend began to make sexual advances towards Don's girlfriend. Although she found these advances unwelcome, Don looked away and pretended that nothing was happening. He did not confront his friend's behaviour, nor support his girlfriend in protesting it. She was very angry with him and he then felt ashamed of his failure to support her and humiliated by his failure to confront his friend. At the same time he felt envious of his friend's 'male confidence and knowledge' that enabled him to make 'sexual advances'. This confidence and knowledge of the masculine gender archive and the expression of the confidence and knowledge in 'sexual advances' is a discursive practice that exercises the power that is male privilege. It was a confidence and knowledge that Don did not yet have and this incident reinforced his view of himself as inadequate and weak.

The second incident occurred in his later teenage years with a subsequent girlfriend, Belinda. She had become very angry with him and began to taunt him about his 'inadequacies'. He felt shamed and humiliated by her. She had access to discursive practices that enabled her to exercise power, but only in a way that supported gender discourse. It did not constitute a challenge to male privilege and it in no way meant that she contributed to, or was responsible for Don's response. He wanted to shame and humiliate her in return. He did now have access to that male knowledge and how to exercise power through the discursive practices of shame and humiliation and he did this through sexual violence. He used his greater physical strength to force her to have sex against her will. He subjected her to humiliation and shame. He raped her.

This notion of 'confessing' a secret is imbued with the religious dis-cursive practices of confessing sins in order to receive absolution and the practice of damnation for unforgivable sins. Foucault (1990) has identified how the confessional was a discursive practice that talked sexuality into a religious/moral discourse. In applying a discursive approach it was not my intention to talk Don's 'sins' into a religious/ moral discourse. This had already been done. Rather I was interested in talking it into the realm of ethics, with discursive practices of account-ability and responsibility. It was this interest that led to my asking Don some questions inviting him to speculate on the possible effects of his actions on Belinda. This included having a negative effect on her sense of safety in the world and her sense of personal worth; a vulnerability to feelings of shame, guilt, and humiliation; being traumatized, troubled by recurrent bad thoughts, and reliving the rape; believing that in some way she may have been responsible for the rape and feeling that people might judge her as being responsible; and feeling violated, abused, and losing a general sense of trust and well-being in situations and relationships.

Following the revelation of these 'secrets' we named the fact that Don now felt shamed and humiliated by my knowledge of these events. We talked about what effect this might have on him and our counselling relationship. We predicted the possibility that his initial relief in telling someone, in telling me, about this may turn to anger. He might feel judged by me, another man, and be resentful of my naming of his actions as rape, something he had not previously done. This was an acknowledgement that our 'therapeutic relationship' was not immune from reproducing the gender discourse through its various discursive practices. Naming this was a counter practice and opened space for engaging in other counter practices. Don decided that if those feelings arose he would privilege his desire to feel better about himself over feelings of shame and humiliation and that he would stay with his feelings rather than fall into a cycle of anger, rejection and isolation no matter how uncomfortable this was, in the hope that his life would continue to change for the better.

Fifth Session – Two Weeks Later

Don said, as we had predicted, that he had felt good for a couple of days following our meeting. He had felt unburdened of the secret but had then felt consumed by humiliation and shame. He had also felt very angry and resentful towards me for my naming of his actions as rape. However, our prediction of the possibility that the gender discourse might act upon him had helped him to stay with these feelings and continue meeting with me instead of being overtaken by the old process of shame and humiliation leading to anger and resentment and ending up in withdrawal, isolation and depression. He believed that these developments in his life were too important to stop now and that what he was feeling was not my judgement of him but his judgement of himself as being shameful and worthless. This was a naming of the way that the discursive archive informed his sense of 'self' to the extent that he did not need to be judged in order to feel judged. He was truly the object of the gender discourse not only when others judged him but when he judged himself. Don said that he was beginning to recognize that this view permeated every aspect of his life and had been reinforced by his judgement of his rape of Belinda as an unforgivable act for which he would never forgive himself. The 'punishment' for this, another discursive practice, was to never allow himself anything good in his life as he was unworthy of it.

We began to talk about the ways in which he carried out this punishment. Don said that it had permeated his experience of his career. He had worked hard all his life and had become financially successful but subsequently went bankrupt. Viewed through his recent realization it seemed to him that he brought about his financial ruin so that he would be disallowed financial success. His bankruptcy had acted to further reinforce feelings of shame and humiliation. He believed that he did not deserve friendships and so withdrew socially. He would not pursue personal relationships with women and had never had a sexual relationship because he was 'not worthy'. As a way of ensuring that history never repeated itself, he withdrew at the first sign of any woman showing interest in him. His way of ensuring that he never used sexual violence in a relationship was to never be in one.

The description of Don's life that our conversation drew out was constituted by gender discourse and the religious metaphor. It was a description of shame, humiliation and unworthiness and how he had never forgiven himself for his crime, sentencing himself to perpetual punishment instead. In seeking a way out of this absolution/damnation dichotomy Don had considered seeking the understanding of others but had then felt that if they forgave him instead of condemning him it would be morally wrong. So it seemed that absolution was not available. Within this dichotomy only 'eternal damnation' was left. I asked Don if it was possible to consider his life in ways other than through shame and humiliation, ways that still allowed him to take responsibility for stopping his own reproduction of these practices of humiliation and shame in subjugating others. Don could not become completely free of the gender discourse, however he could move from being a site of its discursive formation towards being a site of resistance to it. This resistance could be informed by a notion of ethics. This 'worthy way' could lead to his pursuit of relationships based on respect and care, free from his reproduction of men's discursive practices of shame and humiliation. In applying a discursive approach I was not concerned with how Don could be forgiven for his crime. That is the dilemma of the absolution/damnation dichotomy he had been trapped in. Rather, I was interested in how he could develop a worthy way of being that freed him from being both the subject and object of men's practices of shame and humiliation.

Sixth Session – Two Weeks Later

Part of a step toward feeling good about being himself and allowing himself to be in a relationship was to identify why he had raped Belinda and to consider what process led him to use practices of domination. If this led to him no longer accepting being subjected to practices of shame and humiliation and no longer reproducing them by subjecting others to these practices, he would be less likely to rape. We also began to consider what steps Don might take to begin an attempt at redressing some of the effects of his rape of Belinda. This rape had occurred some fifteen years ago. Although both their communities knew of what had happened, Don was not charged with an offence or held accountable in any other way. He never contacted her or spoke with her about it again. Subsequently he heard that she had died a few years ago as a result of an accident. He had wanted to be able to contact her to acknowledge the effects of his actions on her, although he did not know whether any such contact would have been acceptable to her. With her death he now thought it was too late. However, he believed that if he could not apologize to her in person he could at least attempt to honour her memory and began to craft a letter. This document was an apology and an attempt to acknowledge what effects Don's action may have had on Belinda. It was not a request for forgiveness. This, of course, is not all that he could do to continue to take responsibility for his actions. As well as continuing to take steps to refuse the sort of shame and humiliation that is part of the cultural practices of male culture, he could look at his responsibilities as a man in addressing these practices and their effects on both men and women in a whole range of areas. For example, he could choose to become more actively involved in community initiatives that attempt to help men take responsibility for stopping sexual violence and those that provide support to those that have been subjected to sexual violence. In fact this is a challenge for every man.

A Return to Dilemmas

In lieu of a traditional discussion I decided to ask Heather Elliott, who had been kind enough to read and talk with me about this paper a number of times, to interview me about some of the questions it raised for her. Her questions are related to the dilemmas listed at the beginning of this chapter.

As a man raised, like Don, in a culture that supports and reproduces ideas of male privilege and domination over others, what precautions have you taken to ensure that these ideas do not prevail in your conversations with Don?

Naming some of our experiences in terms of discursive practices and practices of power rather than it just being in our heads, allows the possibilities of their being more visible and open for critique rather than just accepted or unnoticed. It makes it possible to predict and plan a response to the discursive practice of shame in Don's experience of my knowledge of his rape of Belinda. This makes it more possible for me to experience and convey my respect for Don as a person whilst not respecting the way in which he has reproduced discursive practices of shame and humiliation. Not only does this make it less likely that ideas of male privilege and domination over others will prevail in our conversations it also provides a context in which it is more likely that Don will step in to take responsibility. The standard shaming practice in relation to rape is to pathologize and exclude with no way back in. A person who rapes another is a rapist and a rapist is a monster. A monster is sick, perverted, less than human and needs to treated with fear and loathing and excluded from society. Seeing men who rape in this way allows other men who have not raped to see themselves as having no connection or responsibility for the actions of the monsters. If this is the only identity available to Don, it means that asking him to take responsibility for his actions is requiring him to view himself as a monster. This issue of the discursive construction of identity needed to be addressed in the work with Don in order to avoid us reproducing the discursive practices of the gender discourse.

The shunning of certain persons and practices is a form of punishment practised for many thousands of years. In order to maintain a just society, can we get away from the forces of shame and humiliation or are they the unfortunate consequences of any society?

Shame and humiliation are discursive practices that are not inherently good or bad. However, they have effects that can be judged as good/ bad, helpful/unhelpful, just/unjust, effective/ineffective. If a person refuses to take responsibility for their actions then shame and humili- ation could be used as a form of social control to ensure the safety of others. However, it can also be used in a way that contributes to the problem by furthering a person's sense of alienation, resentment and anger that may result in them being more of a risk to the safety of others. For example, if a parent shames a child for their transgression but leaves no way back in, no way of making amends, they do not have a guar- antee that the child will not transgress again. In addition, the child is left with undesirable feelings, no way of dealing with them and a strong invitation to construct their identity, their sense of self, as being a bad person. But if the parent were to talk about the effects of a shameful act that the child had committed and collaboratively look for ways to redress these effects, a process of incorporation rather than alienation/ exclusion can occur. In this way, shame and humiliation are not inher- ently good or bad it is whether they are practised in a context of exclusion or re-incorporation. This point is probably best illustrated by the fact that the exclusion of people through imprisoning them does not reduce the probability of the offence being repeated. What difference would it make to have a genuine process of re-incorporation on leaving, or instead of prison?

Have you thought about how this work might have differed in terms of the focus or outcome if the therapist had been of a different gender, race, class or sexual orientation?

It would look different as different discursive practices that relate to different discourses and contexts of power could be reproduced, supported or challenged. If it is possible and safe in that particular context then naming and addressing the discursive practices has the potential of addressing the effects of inequity and privilege. However, it could be unhelpful and potentially abusive if they are simply reproduced and reinforce inequitable power relations.

When working alone with men who abuse women, how do you maintain accountability to those women who have been abused by men?

Often, I do not work alone. I would work with other women as co- therapists or reflecting team members. When I do work alone I look for ways to involve other men and women such as conducting theraputic conversations in training contexts and by having conversations with other women such as this one with you. When I am working alone with a man I also carry with me a history of conversation with women around these very issues. To a degree the voices of these women are internalized. This invites me, at times, to consider how other women may experience what is occurring in the therapy. I am not suggesting that this constitutes my being accountable to those women but it does help me to be self-reflexive on the issue of gender ethics.

How do you think feminist therapists working in the area of domestic violence and abuse will view this work?

Firstly I would recognize that listening to this story of rape as a woman, as a woman or man who had been raped, or who have known a person who has been raped, could evoke many feelings including anger, outrage, sadness, hurt and pain and for many people it may not be possible or even desirable to hear Don's own experience of pain. For some, hearing this story and asking them to attend to Don's pain would be an abuse of them. In terms of my work with Don I would have a range of concerns that I imagine many who would read this would share. Am I attending to Don's experience at the expense of the woman whom he raped? In devoting this writing space to Don's experience, am I privileging his experience over that of others? How do I attend to that and still utilize this writing space? Do I stop writing about Don's experience and start writing about other people's experience? If this is work in progress does it mean that it hasn't progressed enough for me to be writing about it yet? Or, if I wait, does this mean that I am rendering the issue and its dilemmas invisible by not writing about it? What does it mean to render my discomfort invisible? I would hope that this work could be seen as a genuine attempt to address male violence/abuse in a responsible and ethical context and an awareness of the dilemmas that this entails.

What is it that you draw on that enables you to walk that tightrope of dilemmas with Don?

I draw on my experience of hearing him articulate his greater understanding of the effects of his rape on Belinda; putting his experience in the politics of the discursive practices of gender, shame, humiliation and exclusion; hearing him name the way in which he reproduced these practices through shaming and humiliating her through the act of rape; hearing him articulate that understanding and how his experience of other men and women are changing. That makes me hopeful that we are in a context that names the practices of power in relation to gender and that contributes to his having a better experience of his life. I also draw on the belief that Don agreeing to his story becoming partially public is a political act against the usual discursive practice of secrecy. That act makes it harder for us all to get into the thinking that there are 'good' men and 'bad' men and that rapists are monsters. It becomes clearer that this is a discursive practice that implicates all men and invites us, as men, to ask ourselves how we may have reproduced these discursive practices even if we have not committed the act of rape. Finally, I draw on the knowledge that Don identified the naming of shame and humiliation as a gendered discursive practice as making a big difference to him. As a result of this, he had a better idea of the intentions of other men. He no longer saw it as being personally directed at him, it was about what men do to other men in general. His response to these acts changed from anger to disappointment and so he no longer looked for revenge. What he was most fearful of in a relationship with a woman was not rape, he said he would kill himself before repeating that act, but his anger. So going from anger to disappointment was a shift in how he acted as a person towards others and felt as a person in relationship to himself.

Note

Heather Elliott is a family therapist and training provider based at Yaletown Family Therapy in Vancouver, Canada. Heather writes and presents on feminism, postmodernism and narrative therapy (Elliott, 1997).

References

Bly, R. (1990) *Iron John: A Book about Men*. Reading, MA: Addison Wesley.

Burman, E. (1994) *Deconstructing Developmental Psychology*. London: Routledge.

Derrida, J. (1976) *Of Grammatology*. Baltimore: Johns Hopkins University Press.

Elliott, H. (1997) 'En-engendering distinctions: feminism, postmodernism and narrative', *Gecko*, 1: 52–71.

Foucault, M. (1972) *The Archaeology of Knowledge*. London: Routledge.

Foucault, M. (1977) *Discipline and Punish: The Birth of the Prison*. Harmondsworth: Penguin.

Foucault, M. (1982) 'The subject and power', in H. Dreyfus and P. Rabinow (eds), *Michel Foucault: Beyond Structuralism and Hermeneutics*. Chicago: University of Chicago Press.

Foucault, M. (1990) *The History of Sexuality. Volume 1. An Introduction*. Harmondsworth: Penguin.

Gray, J. (1994) *Men are from Mars, Women are from Venus*. New York: Harper Collins.

Law, I. (1998) 'Family therapy with children: a discursive approach', unpublished manuscript.

Law, I. and Madigan, S. (1992) 'Discourse not language: the shift from a modernist view of language to the postmodern analysis of discourse in family therapy', *Dulwich Centre Newsletter*, 1: 31–6.

Law, I. and Madigan, S. (1998) 'Identity, problems and the 'self': a discursive approach to therapy', unpublished manuscript.

Newman, F. and Holzman, L. (1997) *The End of Knowing*. London: Routledge.

Parker, I. (1997) *Psychoanalytic Culture: Psychoanalytic Discourse in Western Society*. London: Sage.

Weedon, C. (1987) *Feminist Practice and Poststructuralist Theory*. Cambridge: Blackwell.

White, M. (1991) 'Deconstruction and Therapy', *Dulwich Centre Newsletter*, 3: 21–40.

White, M. (1995) *Re-Authoring Lives: Interviews and Essays*. Adelaide: Dulwich Centre Publications.

White, M. and Epston, D. (1989) *Literate Means to Therapeutic Ends*. Adelaide: Dulwich Centre Publications.

9

THERAPY AND FAITH

Wendy Drewery with Wally McKenzie

Faith is a strange word to find in a book which has its genesis in both postmodernism and critical theory. Not only is the viability of faith brought into question by much postmodern theorizing, but the notion of faith raises all kinds of implications concerning fundamentalism and truth, each of which I take to be rendered problematic by the intellectual movements which have given rise to this book. However, it seems appropriate to acknowledge at the outset that the practices of psychotherapy are historically closely allied with many of the practices of religious faith, and with the good intentions and structured power relations these invoke, including Christianity. But although the people who share their problems in the extracts used in this paper are fundamentalist Christians, it is not the practices of such Christians alone to which I turn my attention in this chapter. Rather, I want to consider the problem of authority in relation to psychotherapy and the possibility of personal change. Just what kind of a miracle can anyone hope for from psychotherapy?

Faith can be a problem for therapists if it is understood as a non-negotiable belief in a greater authority, especially if the therapy is thought to be about changing something which is under the jurisdiction of that authority. In this chapter, with the aid of verbatim generated in therapeutic practice by my colleague Wally McKenzie, we will show how the desire for external authority and truth can be used to meet the desire for personal agency, in a form of therapeutic conversation which takes advantage of the creative possibilities for the evolution of understanding which can occur in dialogue.

Locating Ourselves

Wally and I work in a team which teaches a graduate programme in counselling. Over the years the programme has had various flirtations with Psychology, but our insistence on acknowledging the importance of other disciplinary orientations has kept us in Education. Our programme does not provide its graduates with registration as a psychologist, and many of them (though not all) work in voluntary or low-paid positions upon graduation. Like elsewhere, in New Zealand the matter and practice of psychotherapy are closely allied to the political situation. New Zealand is small enough that many members of the community of counsellors and psychotherapists know one another – which encourages a blurring of the boundaries among our practices. But we know too that there is a pecking order (of authority as well as monetary reward) which has psychiatrists at the top, next come psychologists (and there is a hierarchy within this lot, depending on the declared theoretical basis of their practice), then there are the psychotherapists, and then come the counsellors. Each of these groups has its own professional association. The New Zealand Association of Psychotherapists (NZAP) is a fairly recent arrival on this scene. It represents a deliberate attempt to distinguish psychotherapy from counselling, and to give psychotherapists the kind of veneer of respectability which allies them with the more medical models of professional practice. Apparently uncontroversially, many members of the NZAP are also members of NZAC – the NZ Association of Counsellors. This latter body disgraced itself in recent years by accepting as members persons who come from backgrounds in social work and community activism, and some of these are not even 'trained'. Without going into detail, the political situation in NZ is such that there is now pressure on the NZAC to distinguish those members who are 'accredited' practitioners, thus creating another hierarchy within the association. As in the United States, bureaucratic moves to contain costs serve to align psychotherapy with medical models of treatment.

Personal Change

The possibility of personal change is a presupposition of the practice of psychotherapy. It is presumed that personal change can be brought about by therapeutic technologies. To put this another way, the psychotherapist anticipates that he/she will bring about, or at least facilitate, change which is 'therapeutic' for the person seeking help. The notion of personal change is seen as unproblematic, since most psychotherapy is also underpinned by a notion of developmental possibility – by the idea that people can change and the presumption of directionality which imbues the idea of developmental change. The literatures of counselling and psychotherapy are however riddled with confusion as to whether the therapist or the person seeking help in effect brings about the desired change. The prevailing idea of course is that change is best when it is brought about by the people themselves. Therapists, like teachers brought up in the same mould, arrange the conditions in order to optimize the possibility of learning and/or personal change, in a process which is often called 'empowerment'.

Different approaches to psychotherapy, then, can be seen as different technologies for facilitating personal change in relation to particular problems or areas of discomfort in a person's life. Such ideas appear to run counter to the notion of therapy as treatment, which invokes a metaphor of the therapist 'doing to' the client, using a drug, say, or some mechanical form of technology. Personal autonomy and personal control are a central feature, one might say a central objective, of many forms of psychotherapy. Ways of conceptualizing the self, most often as a unitary thing or subject which can be in some way pointed to and spoken about, a kind of 'prime mover' or originator of action (see Drewery and Winslade, 1997), feature in pretty well all the major psychotherapeutic approaches. Mostly these ideas of self are presented as unproblematic.

Such notions are not confined to therapy. The idea that personal control or autonomy is possible is also a presumption of liberal politics (and taken to extremes by neo-liberals and the New Right). It is an important idea; Kant for example suggested that the possibility of moral being is predicated upon the possibility of free choice or autonomous functioning, and so imbued is Western society with this idea that our courts will not convict someone who can be shown to have no control over their own actions. This very important idea is severely challenged by the defence offered by many a soldier accused of committing a war crime that he (almost always he) 'was only following orders'. Such a defence almost never works in favour of the defendant because it is seen as a fundamental condition of humanness that even soldiers must take responsibility for the orders they choose to follow. For reasons pertaining to their relationship to authority and their presumed restricted capacity for choosing their own actions, persons who defer to religious authority in fundamentalist ways can provide a serious challenge to the psychotherapist. Indeed, there is a sense in which any form of fundamentalism is directly opposed to the liberatory moment of psychotherapy. It is no doubt on the basis of such an understanding that pastors frequently 'check out' suitable therapists before referring their constituents, and for similar sorts of reasons that we are seeing growth in training programmes for so-called 'Christian' therapy. The temptation (from outside such discourses) is to see such moves as attempts to police the kinds of suggestions which might be made within therapy, preserving the faithful to their faith. On the other hand, and perhaps more charitably, it could be said that Christians are wary of therapy which attempts conversion, or which challenges their faith in an external authority, a god.

Discursive psychology offers a way of conceptualizing these relationships to authority which allows us to think more freely about alternative possibilities, without necessarily challenging the authority of a god, or even of a commander in some form of discursive framework such as the army. From a 'narrative' perspective, 'therapy' is seen as indicated when a form of agency over one's own life has been lost (Drewery and Winslade, 1997). Therapy in this mode is about restoring, finding, or enabling agency on the part of the 'client'. In what remains of this chapter I shall consider the (problematic) idea that agency is central to healthy functioning in the world, and look at what kind of account we might give of agency in a post-structuralist framework. I shall bring together the politics of therapy and the practice of narrative therapy by examining some verbatim from actual therapy sessions with people who have strong Christian beliefs. In this way we can give an account of how it is possible to both acknowledge external authority or power and invoke personal agency.

Modernity and Dependency

Psychotherapy can be seen as a technology which invokes the authority of the promise of human progress – that same promise which is a part of the attraction of medicine and many other technologically informed solutions to human difficulties. But there are traps with this. One of the main issues raised by the application of technology is the problem of dependency, and how to deliver aid in appropriate ways. One of the ways in which this problem arises is in the potential loss of agency which goes with the desire to hand over the power to solve one's problems – the desire to 'get it fixed' or be rescued. Another potential difficulty is the desire of the helper to solve those very same problems – the desire to 'fix it' or to rescue. In my view, the major problem which characterizes post-Modernity [sic] resides precisely in this issue: how to deliver technological solutions in ways which do not deprive the helpee of their capacity to act on their own behalf. Resolving this problem seems to me to be a matter of reworking some dominating stories about development and the impulse to help. In making this claim I do not distinguish personal development from human development.

In terms of the language which is used to describe them, problems which bring people to seek therapy are usually constructed in ways which deny or despair of the capacity of the person to deal with them. The temptation, when seeking this form of help, is to think (expect, hope) that the therapist, using their expert training, can work some kind of magic to make it better. When problems are approached in this way, people look for 'solutions' which will 'fix' their lives. It is a helpless, dependent position. From a narrative perspective, this is the state of the person when he or she comes to counselling: the stories they are telling about what they are trying to achieve do not position them with sufficient agency to act upon or against the problem. Often, these stories derive from definitions given by others, and the person seeking help is often in the situation of needing to 'fit' into a familiar discourse in which they are experiencing discomfort. The task of the 'narrative' therapist is to look for ways in which the dominating discourses can be challenged, so that the person can reposition themselves in an overlapping discourse from which they can engage with their discursively inscribed situation on their own behalf. And so one of the first tasks of the narrative therapist is to learn about the discursive world of the person who is working with them.

Constructionism

The way we are developing narrative therapy at Waikato involves a strong invocation of social constructionist ideas. This theory is built on two central pillars:

1. An epistemological commitment, namely, that knowledge is claimed on many different grounds. Whatever reality is, our interpretations and even our explanations of it are always open to revision. Thus we can say that different people have different 'realities'.
2. A personal/political commitment, namely, that all people who come to counselling have the necessary capacities, strengths and wisdom to take charge of their own lives. This means that counsellors approach their counselling practice with an unshakeable belief in clients' capacity to know, understand and improve their situations themselves. It does not mean that people never need support.

The implications of these ideas are far-reaching:

3. The power to interpret meaning is primarily located in socially derived (usually tacit) agreement, rather than in the personal power of individuals. There are many such agreed histories, and many of these contradict one another.
4. Some stories in a person's life are rehearsed a lot and some are less often heard. Those which are often heard come to be taken as dominant and may even be thought of as the only possible story or way of speaking about certain things.
5. Speaking is an act-in-the-world. The effect of one's speaking can be understood as a function of the position from which one speaks in relation to the dominant story at the time and in the place of speaking.
6. Personal authority is of at least two kinds: a) that which is derived from these social histories, rather than vice versa; and b) that which derives from our human or ethical capacity to act in the world.

This last point derives logically from the construction of meaning as conventional (that is, born of agreement): unless we are able to agree to behave as if words have meaning (to cooperate), we are little more than automata. A form of ethical agency is presumed by this version of constructionism. It is in this sense that we also assert that human being must be understood primarily as a social phenomenon, and that the idea of individuality, or even identity, emerges from social being. But that is another paper.

Therapy and Authority

One of the most difficult implications of these central ideas for many people is the account we might give of the continuity of people's lives – of their personhood. There are many writings on the notion of multiple selves (e.g. Shotter and Gergen, 1989; Gergen, 1991), and some writers have proclaimed the idea of 'the empty self' (Cushman, 1990). Such ideas are shocking especially (but not only) to those who have come from a religious or humanistic background. In a religious framework such as Christianity, the notion of ongoing personal identity is central to the possibility of life after death and the Christian's relationship with God. Similarly, from a humanistic perspective, the possibility of a self which can be experienced in its purity is fundamental to health. The common thread here is what interests us in this chapter, namely, the idea that people can be autonomous actors and agents of their own lives. We presume every person to be capable in principle of moral action. We understand therapeutic conversation as conversation which derives from the client's discomfort in relation to an area of their life where they have lost, or do not have, power to act on their own behalf. A therapeutic conversation is a dialogical conversation of a particular kind. It has the objective of changing the problematic positioning of a person, re-establishing an agentic position in relation to the area of concern. The process of therapy is a collaborative process of negotiation over the meanings of a person's life. It is also a relationship which is inscribed by the expectations of therapeutic discourse.

Working with Christian clients (for example) who expressly relinquish all control to God can assume frustrating proportions. The professional history of many different psychotherapeutic traditions has been shaped by a humanistic world view which places a high value on (an under-theorized notion of) personal control. To the therapist trying to work empathically within the client's own framework, it may seem that therapeutic possibilities for such people are severely constrained. Openness is a value of most therapists, and it can appear that some strongly held beliefs close off, and run in direct opposition to, therapeutic values. Nevertheless, the suffering of these clients cannot be denied, nor can their desire for a change in their problematic life situation. The issue for therapists, then, becomes one of how to work within the client's framework, using good and effective professional practices, and at the same time not to deny the client's values – indeed to send the clients forth, validated as people.

In a constructionist framework, the authority of a god is never complete. From this perspective, power resides in various authorities whose dominance is discursively produced. We understand discourse as a mode of action – one of the ways in which people act upon the world (Fairclough, 1992). Such acting is less like being the cue which moves the first billiard ball, and more like 'throwing your tuppence worth' into a conversation among several people. Conversations can influence what we think about things, and hence what we and others do, in both momentous and unremarkable ways. All discourse is formed through language, but we emphasize that the language people use *constructs* their world, and themselves, in important ways. In particular, language constrains some possibilities, and opens others. However, 'we can only ever speak ourselves or be spoken into existence within the terms of available discourses' (Davies, 1991: 42). Because language use is primarily a social activity, no single individual (and no single 'faith') has complete control over the meanings which are conveyed by the language he or she uses. Individuals are thus both the site and the subject of a discursive struggle for their identity. This struggle is never final, and so one's identity, or to use a preferred term, one's subjectivity, is never beyond challenge (Weedon, 1987).

The focus of narrative therapy is not to give the client personal control over their entire life, but to install the client as an agent of their own life stories; to expose and enter into the struggles over the meanings in their lives where this is relevant to the problem brought to therapy. This personal involvement in the struggle for self-interpretation is crucial to personal well-being. This form of agency is very like that which Davies (1991: 51) describes: the therapist struggles to develop a discourse around the 'problem' in which the client has access to a subject position in which they have the right to speak and be heard; is author of their own meanings and desires, rather than having them given by others; has the sense of themselves as being able to go beyond the meanings of the given discourse.

The therapist's role is to develop a discourse within the therapy which is cast in the terms of the client's own frameworks, but which extends and challenges these everyday understandings where appropriate.

Therapy and Faith

Within therapy it can sometimes seem to be the case that the person asking for help has entrenched beliefs, and that these beliefs themselves may sometimes seem to be 'the problem'. Direct review of strongly held beliefs can be very difficult, and new ideas can be very hard for some people to entertain. This apparent inflexibility can be extremely problematic for family therapists who are approached by such people for help. A particular value which we hold about meeting others, in therapy and elsewhere, is that we do not believe we have a right to deny the deeply held personal values of others. We believe this code of practice is shared by many therapists, and for this reason many therapists would prefer to refer people seeking help who hold very different beliefs from their own, to therapists who are more 'compatible'. We no longer believe that this is necessarily the case, for we no longer see the issue as being about competing values, one set of which (the client's) must be given up in order that therapy may occur.

In distinction from this constraining orientation, we have come to understand difference as a condition of human existence, and every client to be, in some sense, a mystery. Although we can make some informed guesses about it on the basis of our own cultural knowledge, we cannot assume anything much about the ways in which the discursive world of another person is knit together. Our guesses always need to be checked out. Therapy, then, becomes a kind of systematic research project, loosely cohering around three phases or objectives: an intentional (and ongoing) exploration of the discursive world of the client; challenging and deconstructing the stories in which the client is so positioned that they cannot get a purchase on the problem; and reconstruction of alternative stories in which the person seeking help has repositioned him or herself so that they are able to act against the problem on their own behalf.

It is unreasonable to expect clients to enter the world of the therapist, so to some degree at least the therapist must enter the world of the client. For this reason it is important that the therapist have some knowledge of the way the dominating discourses in the client's life operate. In the case of clients who have fundamentalist Christian beliefs, Wally's experience of professional success suggests that his in-depth knowledge of their particular belief system can be useful in the therapeutic context. However, in accepting referrals from pastors, Wally is always clear that he does not share these beliefs. He is also very careful to convey his awareness of the personal importance of their beliefs to clients, and his lack of interest in attempting conversion within therapy.

Therapy as Deconstruction

Therapeutic conversations often take the form of philosophical discussion. The therapist is not required to be an expert on anyone else's life but rather, to maintain an attitude of respectful curiosity. This deconstructive approach is effected largely through the kinds of questions which can be asked of the client. We attempt to 'undo (the problem) from within by drawing attention to elements of it that are susceptible to change' (Davies, 1991: 46). For example, as we have already noted, the issue of control is important in the lives of Christians, and the therapist may be called upon to discuss the nature of change, responsibility, and relationships with God. The therapist enters into this conversation not as an expert on Christianity, nor as a non-directive counsellor, but as an interested (and possibly expert) co-enquirer.

The therapist may be viewed as entering into a process of *deconstruction* within the discourse(s) which is(are) seen as producing the person's problem (White, 1991). The objective of deconstruction is 'to uncover the working . . . of . . . the particular and local (i.e. irregular and discontinuous) operation of the actual power relations at work in structuring social forms in the modern world' (Parker and Shotter, 1990: 4, interpreting Foucault). No personal story is so self-consistent that it is not open to such challenge in its own terms (White, 1989). Thus the discourse of therapy must take into account in some effective way the discourses within which people we are working with 'speak themselves into existence', and be mindful of the ways in which these discourses structure themselves and their lives. So deconstruction in this context can take several forms, for example:

1. The therapist is curiously interested in the presuppositions, usually unstated, which enable the person whom they are working with to make this sense rather than some other kind of sense of their life at this time.
2. The therapist actively resists the common thinking pattern which blames some internal attribute of the person for 'failure'.
3. The therapist relentlessly conveys the assumption of the capacity of the person who is working to change their life.
4. The therapist is always listening for alternative ways of being which are already happening within the person's life, and which contradict their dominant understanding of the problem story.

The context, language and content of challenges must be couched in the language of the belief structure of the client. The re-examination of ideas and their *reconstruction* also must be developed within the belief structures of the person working to change their life, who is very much a senior partner in this process, considered to be the expert on how their life is constructed at all times.

The semantic form of the language used by the therapist is crucial. We do not think that it is always necessary to 'counterpose another discourse' (Davies, 1991), but at the very least the positioning of the subject in the sentence – the semantic form of the sentence – is very important. In the examples which follow, the therapist is Wally, with Gareth and Murray; the two men have both given their permission for us to use these examples in this way. In particular, we invite you to look at the form of questions used by the therapist. In each case, the intention is to position the person as the author or subject of the story – the actor, rather than as its object – the acted upon.

Murray

Following is an extract from a therapeutic conversation which is already well advanced. Wally has challenged some of Murray's ideas about what God wants for him, and Murray is struggling to come to terms with his perceptions of what God wants for his life. In the first statement, Murray positions himself as the passive object of God's agency. From this position he has no room for his own intervention:

> M: I think one of the last things I said to you before I left was, I felt that, I wondered why . . . [*looking for an acceptably respectful form of words to describe his right to question*] It seemed that God had allowed me to sort of dawdle along or stumble along through life over the last few years. Oh it's hard to explain, maybe I felt that He . . . God is God perhaps he could have intervened ten years ago and said, 'Look here, you should be going here not here, this direction. You need to see somebody beyond the church or whatever to unscramble you' or something. [*Murray clearly does not want to criticize God, nor does he invite this from the therapist.*]

The therapist does not challenge this construction directly. He asks an open question which does not presume anything more than that Murray has been working on the problem as he sees it, thus positioning Murray as someone who is an active participant in resolving the problem – implicitly challenging Murray's own positioning of himself as a passive receptor:

> W: Have you been thinking about it?
> M: I've been aware of that kind of thought for quite a long time . . . You said to me just before I left last time that you thought that it, perhaps it wasn't God's fault or my fault, and I wondered how you felt about that?

Murray still wants to take up a passive position, tending to give the problem away, asking for a solution. Wally's response is to enter directly into the Christian discourse with a respectful philosophical point.

> W: I've wondered sometimes, if we want God to intervene in our lives how do we set the intervening point? We can let God know, 'God, I don't want to spend my life stumbling along, I'd like you to be more useful than that to me. So when I reach this point of stumbling will you please intervene and give me a break?' How are we going to tell God when to intervene?

Wally has positioned Murray in an active, dialogical relationship with God, rather than the one-way model he had presented originally.

M: People cry out to God in extremes of circumstance don't they?

This is the relationship of helper to helpee which Murray brought to counselling: it positions the helpee as powerless, the helper as all-powerful. Wally enters more fully into a philosophical discussion, drawing on his own ideas about God and helping, and using some of the contradictions in Murray's ideas. It is important here that the therapist is not challenging the underpinning belief in God's power, but rather, looking for a story which would enable Murray to move from his powerless position and leave his beliefs in God's power intact. This is a part of a process of deconstruction. The questioning of the therapist does not challenge his faith, rather it invites him to reflect on the beliefs he already has that are congruent with his experiences.

W: I heard a man say that he wasn't sure what he should ask God for help with and what he shouldn't ask God for help with. Like he can really understand that for really major things in his life that he could ask God for some guidance and help. But then the puzzle was when did he stop doing that? Like, should he also ask God for guidance and help about which shoe to put on first? He said that might seem ridiculous but we make decisions about things, like which way we go to work, and all sorts of things. And he found it quite perplexing as to where to draw the line, and it seemed to him to be a very reasonable question. Do you have any thoughts about that?

M: No, no, that makes a lot of sense. It's a little bit along the lines of the fact that maybe Christian people don't use their mind enough, or they rely on God to get them out of a situation they in effect got themselves into by not thinking ahead of time or thinking forward. So why call out to God to get them out of it? So God's not going to always bail people out.

This response shows a significant (therapeutic) shift: Murray is accepting agency on his own behalf and readjusting his Christian discourse slightly, opening up space in which he can act on his own behalf. Wally pushes the point a little:

W: I don't know whether it's God not bailing people out or whether it's, where is the cut-off point. Where is the cut-off where we take responsibility and where is the cut-off where God takes responsibility? It may be about that we make the most of the faculties that we have, and we make choices that we believe are the best that there are to make.

M: Right.

W: And I've heard you give me plenty of evidence that through your life you've actually made choices that were the best you could make with the information you had available.

M: Well I think that that's really hit the nail on the head. I guess I've always been under the impression that some kind of spiritual problem is going to be rectified in a spiritual way. I really hadn't considered the possibility that maybe I can do a few things just by thinking about it, in my own mind so to speak. That is a new concept for me. Because frankly you don't get a lot of Christians telling you, oh, talking to you like we are talking now. It would be something like deliverance or a spiritual thing.

Murray has caught on and takes up the deconstructive process, taking up an agentic position and checking it out in relation to his other beliefs.

W: They would be wanting to give it back to God all the time?
M: Yes, yes.
W: To solve?
M: Yes to pray about it. That's what happened before I came to you, that people prayed about it.
W: And I certainly have no problem with that.
M: No . . . I guess I was always under the impression that my problem would be solved somewhere down the track by spiritual means. Either God would intervene you know somewhere down the line or one day he'd rid me of these horrible fears . . . I guess I've been thinking a bit this way since I've been coming to you because I thought well I seem to be making real progress here, and why didn't this happen years ago? I wondered, why didn't God engineer things that I met you or somebody else ten years ago, so that I would have had ten more productive years? So I thought well why does God allow us to fumble along? [*He has been expecting a 'fix it' answer – a kind of miraculous intervention.*]
W: I don't have a clear answer for that . . .
M: I don't feel as though anybody really . . . there was always this spiritual emphasis. You're not doing this or you're not doing that, that's why you're not getting anywhere sort of thing.

Wally is not saying that those Christian people Murray talks of were wrong. He is continuing to help Murray think about (deconstruct) past experiences by the process of questioning. There is also an important affirmation of his Christian faith. Wally is also interested in Murray's future relationship with God, and this is a part of the reconstruction. But the main focus, the therapy, consists in repositioning him, in his own story, as an active producer of his own solutions. In the sense that they are engaging in a conversation about beliefs which have a central place informing Murray's life, the therapeutic conversation is a living occurrence in his life – including his life as a Christian. We believe that the overt respect of the therapist for this dominating discourse in his life is an integral part of this therapeutic encounter.

Comment

Before we go any further perhaps we should speak a little more about the relationship of the therapist to these dominating discourses in the client's life. When we speak of overt respect, we do not intend to suggest that the therapist overtly recognizes the 'truth' of those doctrines. Instead, what we feel is necessary is recognition that those discourses are important to the client. In addition, we believe it is important that the therapist demonstrates curiosity, rather than knowledge, about how these discourses operate in the life of the client. And above all, there is no let-up in the therapist's expectation that the client is capable of taking, and expects to take up, an agentic position in their life.

In some senses there is not a great deal of difference between this form of deconstructive, therapeutic conversation, and more traditional forms of 'cognitive therapy'. The big difference is the unremitting belief of the therapist in the agentic expectations of the client, and the process of achieving this. Cognitive therapies have a focus on control, and the processes they utilize tend to be techniques for establishing more agentic thought patterns. Underpinning cognitive therapy is the idea that the therapist is an expert who can offer techniques which, if the client uses them, can 'help'. Wally uses these techniques too, but he starts a little further back – that is to say, he does not assume the role of the expert, and instead works to install the client in that role.

Gareth

This next extract is from a series of interviews with a client who described himself, and had been described by a psychiatrist, as depressed. Wally worked with him to combat his habitual worries in social situations by encouraging a consciously self-authoritative positioning. The following exchange occurred towards the end of a session:

W: Has this been helpful us talking about this today?
G: Yeah. It's been helpful. Yeah. It's made me realize that I am doing some stuff that's good to help this whole thing. I guess the way I feel though, I don't feel very confident that that's going to always help me, you know. I guess that's just the way I feel at the moment. I can see that there are some good things in it.
W: So what you have just talked about – will this be helpful to you over the next while?
G: Yeah, because I can work at . . . at . . . at the time. I can start working at things at the time. I've sort of realized that I can do that a bit more instead of waiting for it to happen and then looking back, I can now . . . OK, it's happening, let's do something about it, let's stop comparing myself with other people, stop . . . marching to the beat of someone else's drum, just do what I want to do. You know, ask myself those questions.

In our view, the voicing of his agency over the problem is therapeutically more important than the self-talk. This positioning eventuated in Gareth reading a book on depression and joining a gym as a result.

W: You seem to be talking more about what you want to do. Like you just said to me 'I don't know whether I want to do that or not'. When I first met you you never talked about what you wanted to do . . . Last time there were things happening and you decided some people wanted you to do some things, but you decided what you wanted to do. Is that happening more as well?

G: Yeah. Yeah definitely. I can see how that, you know those questions, what do I want to do right now, and is that good for me? I guess I haven't been asking myself that as regularly but I do do it when something like that crops up. I think, hey! Yeah, I really did that consciously the other day. I sat down and thought, Now, I'm getting those feelings that I want to pull out – is that what I really want to do? Am I staying in this group because there are people wanting me to, or am I staying because I want to? I really consciously thought that over. But I realized that my emotions would probably be exaggerated because of everything.

At this point in the therapy, Gareth is becoming more fully in charge of his own healing. Of course, it is also extremely important that the therapeutic conversation proceeds in the terms of Gareth's life, and not Wally's. The following extract shows how Gareth conceptualized part of his problem, and how Wally picked up the terminology for therapeutic ends. Gareth continued:

G: But I had a chat with a real close friend of mine last night. He's quite a spiritual leader in my life and he thinks a lot of stuff I'm going through . . . he thinks that the devil is using this . . . He's not saying that this whole thing is caused from the enemy, but he thinks he is definitely getting in and using the situation to get at me and bring me down as a Christian.

W: Like to take advantage of you!

G: Yeah. And I actually fully agree . . . (describes a nightmare) . . . And I was talking to (friend) about this and Mum and everything and they were saying how that is a bit of spirit . . . and I don't need them to tell me. That's when I started to realize that there is spiritual warfare going on in my life, and the devil is using the situation to get me, and the main thing I've realized this week is that he's telling lies . . . And I know that's not the whole thing – a lot of it is my thinking and that's why I've been coming to you. But I have seen that part of it . . . and last night . . . I went to a Bible study group (describes feelings of inspiration) . . . and afterwards I stayed back and I just felt this incredible urge to get (the leader) to pray for me and to really pray against how the devil is using this in me . . . So there's been a few turning points you know, and that's a good one for me. But at the same time I'm not . . . I realize that that's not the full answer – that that's part of it and that spirituality is part of it.

W: Are you saying that you think that God expects you to do your part in all this?

G: Yeah, definitely. Because a lot of it is my, you know, the things we have been talking about – my wrong patterns, my wrong . . . you know, marching to the beat of everyone else's drum, you know, all that sort of stuff. I realize that that's why I am coming to you, because if it was just this spiritual thing I wouldn't have come to you . . .

In a later interview, Wally is concerned to investigate and describe with Gareth the process by which Gareth has enabled himself to combat depression. The use of the phrase 'reclaim yourself' indicates the sense of depression as a loss of self. However, in a theoretical sense we suggest it would be more accurate to describe depression as a loss of the capacity to act in creating his own life. The therapy has sought to restore that capacity, within Gareth's own framework. For example:

W: . . . What qualities have you got . . . that maybe God would be aware of . . . that have enabled you to reclaim yourself? To begin this process and get well down the track in reclaiming yourself again after all this time?

G: I think that . . . I have a fairly in depth sort of character . . . I mean, I'm not, I mean I'm not just like – I'm not a shallow person even though sometimes I like to be shallow and on the surface you know. I'm not always going to . . . I always get really in depth with things and I guess I really have to see that as a strength. Whereas up to now it's been such a weakness. I don't want to be like that . . .

W: So one of the qualities that you have that God would notice is that strength that you have?

G: Yeah – of character.

G: Yeah . . . I don't know whether it's Christian teaching or not . . . because I mean definitely recently over the last few years I haven't had that. Yeah, maybe in the past, yeah. But I certainly don't believe that now, no. I believe that God created us in his image and we . . . yeah I really think that the importance of self-esteem and that is . . .

W: Like I was taught to be humble all the time, and that you couldn't be humble and proud at the same time.

G: Yeah, I've probably had a bit of that sort of thing.

W: Whereas . . . some people have taught me that you can actually be humble but you can take a pride in yourself and you just do that to yourself – you don't need to shout it to the world.

G: Yeah, I really believe that. I really believe that's what God wants. What he wants us to do. What he wants us to be. But I don't think I've really been able to do that too well in the past.

W: So there have been quite a number of ways that you have been missing out on yourself. [*A therapeutic moment!*]

G: Yeah.

W: And maybe God has been missing out on you too.

G: And maybe other people have been too because the fact that I haven't been able to accept that and work on those strengths . . . how can other people . . . how can I . . . influence other people if I don't believe it? Maybe. I don't know . . .

Wally has helped Gareth reposition himself in relation to his God, and in his world, and they have done this within the terms of Gareth's own beliefs. Throughout this conversation, the therapist never once showed less than total confidence that Gareth was working to understand his world and to act with integrity within it. Wally did not address issues of 'self-esteem' or other technical constructs such as 'low mood'. Gareth himself spoke of self-esteem, in passing. What the therapist has been working for is a depth of self-appreciation which does not conflict with Gareth's religious philosophy. In so doing, he has opened up space into which Gareth can move with more confidence than he is used to experiencing, space which he can enter with integrity.

Comment

Constructionist thinking as a basis of therapy is not in any way about competing 'truths' or even about 'getting it right'. The person coming for therapy should not feel that their deeply held personal beliefs are being undermined, or that the therapist is entering into a process of 'conversion' to the therapist's (better?) ideas. I think we could show that people who come to therapy from different cultures can have similarly 'disempowering' experiences on the basis of the therapist's expertness – but that is another paper.

Deconstruction of a problematic story comes about by at least two means which complement each other and work together: first, the repositioning of the client as the agent or active subject, rather than the passive object of the discourse within which their subjectivity is inscribed. This process is demonstrated in the first example. A second means of deconstruction in conversation involves noticing mutually self-contradictory understandings which have lain dormant, unnoticed or taken for granted in the person's own understandings of the world, and highlighting these. This 'therapeutic intervention' produces challenge: moments of personal struggle, (in)decision, and eventually, new understandings which show up as changes in feeling and behaviour. It is not the kind of challenge which shows how wrong you are. It is not a magical intervention or even a technical one in a Modernist sense. It is a use of language which takes seriously the idea that we create our worlds in conversation, and that this process can also be challenged because it is ongoing. The 'therapeutic' aspect of 'narrative' conversations lies in the deliberate focus of the therapist on the active, constitutive and productive nature of the language which the client uses, the listening for and entering into the discursive world of the client by the therapist, and the unremitting belief in the capacity of the client to deal with the 'problem' brought to therapy. Of course, ordinary conversations can have these characteristics, but what distinguishes therapeutic conversations is that they set out to produce a therapeutic shift in an intentional way. Ordinary conversations change us too, but there is often less clarity about the power relations inhering in the discursive interplay. We do not have to speak in ways which disempower people, but we often do.

Respectful Curiosity

Here at Waikato we are convinced of the value of respectful curiosity. By this we do not mean a curiosity about things that do not relate to therapy, or a curiosity that has a sense of prying or nosiness about it. Foucault suggests that curiosity evokes concern; it evokes the care one takes for what exists and could exist; a readiness to find strange and singular what surrounds us; a certain relentlessness to break up our familiarities and to regard otherwise the same things; a fervour to grasp what is happening and what passes; a casualness in regard to the traditional hierarchies of the important and the essential. (Foucault, 1989: 198)

The therapist who works curiously thinks and notices differently from the more conventional modes of therapy. Not only will the therapist benefit from this, but other people also are drawn into a curiosity about their own lives, knowledges, experiences, beliefs, choices, and options. This leads on from a reassessment of themselves and their previous understandings to wonderings and speculations about future possibilities for themselves.

We suggest that respectful therapy is characterized at least by an absence of any attempt at conversion to a 'right' way of living and thinking. Indeed, we would go further, and suggest that this principle applies to any situation where the struggle for meaning is going on, and not simply to therapy, with Christians or anyone else. This process describes a non-confrontational style of (political) struggle, and suggests the establishment of interpersonal relations which do not require domination by one party over all others. It presumes goodwill – a faith in the capacity of humans to engage in conversation about what is good and worth doing, and to struggle for agreements about our purposes. It does not presume that we could all possibly agree, but it takes limited successes in small collaborative action as signs of life – of moral being. It is both simple and complex. We are starting small: there is a lot more work to be done investigating the application of post-structuralist ideas to therapeutic conversation, but we are sure that the semantic structure of sentences, in particular the positioning of the semantic subject, is an important factor in 'empathic' communication. Increasingly in counsellor education we find ourselves making what seems a deceptively simple recommendation: watch your language!

References

Cushman, P. (1990) 'Why the self is empty', *American Psychologist*, 45 (5): 599–611.

Davies, B. (1991) 'The concept of agency: a feminist post-structuralist analysis', *Postmodern Critical Theorising*, 30: 42–53.

Drewery, W. and Winslade, J. (1997) 'The theoretical story of narrative therapy', in G. Monk, J. Winslade, K. Crocket and D. Epston (eds), *Narrative Therapy in Practice: The Archaeology of Hope*. San Francisco: Jossey-Bass.

Epston, D. and White, M. (1989) *Literate Means to Therapeutic Ends*. Adelaide: Dulwich Centre Publications.

Epston, D. and White, M. (1990) 'Consulting your consultants: the documentation of alternative knowledges', *Dulwich Centre Newsletter*, 4: 22–35.

Fairclough, N. (1992) *Discourse and Social Change*. Oxford: Polity.

Foucault, M. (1989) *Foucault Live*. New York: Semiotext(e).

Gergen, K.J. (1991) *The Saturated Self*. New York: Basic Books.

Parker, I. and Shotter, J. (eds) (1990) *Deconstructing Social Psychology*. London:
Routledge.

Shotter, J. and Gergen, K.J. (eds) (1989) *Texts of Identity*. London: Sage.

Weedon, C. (1987) *Feminist Practice and Poststructuralist Theory*. Oxford:
Blackwell.

White, M. (1989) 'The externalizing of the problem and the re-authoring of lives
and relationships', *Dulwich Centre Newsletter*, Summer 1988/1989, 3–12.

White, M. (1991) 'Deconstruction and therapy', *Dulwich Centre Newsletter*, 3: 21–
40.

10

INSCRIPTION, DESCRIPTION AND DECIPHERING CHRONIC IDENTITIES

Stephen Madigan

Identity, within the context of the institution of psychology and psychiatry, might be conceived as being *who* you say you are, through what *they* say you can be. This chapter offers an examination of the production, reproduction, and possible transformations of psychological culture within the organization of therapeutic life. I will situate my practice of therapy through a story about 'Tom'. I will position my experience of him, alongside his experiences within the institution of psychiatry, as a way to render my theoretical position transparent. Structurally the paper is indented to divide off the practice example from theory, however, the margins between theory and practice are usually blurred.

My experience is located within and against the institution of psychology. Having worked inside, outside and alongside the institution of psychology and psychiatry for some time, emphasizing and respecting difference, and analysing therapeutic relational politics and power, has proven helpful in my ongoing attempt to make the practice of therapy meaningful.

Inscribing Identity

The dominant Western understanding of identity is based in great measure on a liberal individualist framework which is maintained, and shaped through institutions, discourse and archives of science (Law and Madigan, 1998). Since the seventeenth century, science has 'owned' the study of the body. Psychiatry, psychology and other helping professions – such as social work and family therapy – have welded themselves onto the scientific project and appropriated their slice of proprietorship. For the disciplines of science, to obtain 'title' on the body has required the body's meaning be represented as utterly transparent and accessible to the qualified specialist (assisted by the proper methodology and technology) and, adequately opaque to the client and their community of supporting others.

Hospital ward based clients, characteristically deemed to have unspecialized knowledge of the body (of their own and of other person's bodies), are divided off 'spatially and socially' from the community through the support of methodological and technological practices (Parker, 1989; Madigan, 1992). More specifically, the patient of the psychiatric ward is discursively embodied and managed as a *Patient without Knowledge* (PwK). Knowledge that is afforded to the person (now PwK) by those in administrative power, is often viewed as 'bad' or 'wrong' knowledge – in opposition to the normal knowledge of science/society – and pictured as contributing to the inscribed disorder itself.

Recently I received a call from a local psychiatric ward asking if I would consider 'counselling' Tom, a man the hospital staff had 'tried everything on'. He was described as 'suicidal and depressed'. 'Everything' included thirty Electro Convulsive Therapy sessions within a twelve-month period, six varieties of medication within a twelve-month period, and a year's worth of group and individual psychodynamic therapy. The doctor explained that the therapy staff had 'all but given up' on Tom – a 66-year-old white, middle class, heterosexual male. He said that Tom had been living 'off and on' (more on than off) within the hospital as an 'unsuccessful patient' for over one year. Although Tom had been administered all the psychiatric technologies of normalization the hospital had to offer, 'nothing seemed to work'. Throughout the twelve months of hospital contact, Tom had participated in the hospital's ongoing systematic creation, classification and control of 'anomalies' in his social body.

From my discussion with the hospital staff who had worked with Tom through the year, it became clear that Tom's chronic body had been attributed and situated within particular sets of psychological meaning. His body was fitted categorically within memorized moments of psychological history, read through the archives of certain expert others and transformed into documents (when I first met Tom he weighed in with a 'six-pound file').

Tom was unanimously described as a chronic depressive personality, suggesting to me that the documented Tom, or the Tom of-the-file, was viewed as containing an essential, interior (modern) self. The live conversations and the conversations translated through the case files about Tom helped to locate the context of the staff's expertise of knowledge.

Specialized Codes, Interpretation and Deciphering

Rose (1989: 42) writes: 'We are governed through the delicate and minute infiltration of the dreams of authorities and the enthusiasms of expertise into our realities, our desires and our visions of freedom'. The psychiatric ward's raison d'être came from historical claims of being able to precisely pinpoint and isolate anomalies, such as depression, and its promise to normalize them.

Tom had endured the conditions of the hospital's relationship with him in full. I remember wondering how he had managed to survive the ECT, the various medication regimes, and the unfortunate therapeutic rituals of condemnation that occurred when the professional team became frustrated with his 'lack of progress'. At the point where Tom's therapeutic team was defeated the word 'chronic' finalized the hospital's examination; the psychiatric examination is the procedure that brings together surveillance and normalizing judgement. In Tom's case the inscribed 'condition' was chronic depression. The obvious contradiction was realizing that, on the one hand they condemned him to a life of (chronic) identity death, while at the same time desired him to 'recover' through their technology. He could not please the team as their technological practices did not work for him. As the hospital's meagre description of chronic depressive might suggest, Tom was inscribed as both cultural object and intellectual product of the institution.

Within the model of scientific medicine that psychology is situated in, the body of the subject is viewed as the passive tablet on which disorders are inscribed. Deciphering that inscription is usually a matter of determining a 'cause' of the disorder; and, quite often, the more popular technologies of psychology require an interpretation of the symptoms. With over four hundred possible ways to be considered abnormal (Caplan, 1995), the worldwide web of pathology-oriented psychologists rarely have difficulty plotting the person's entire life story within the text of the *Diagnostic and Statistical Manual of Mental Disorders, Fourth Revision* (the DSM-IV).

The process of being inscribed into the DSM-IV text always requires a trained – that is to say, highly specialized – professional whose expertise affords him or her the opportunity and privilege to unlock the secrets of the disordered body. The specialized knowledge, power, and professional status psychologists are afforded, is negotiated and distributed through the institution and its archives to control who gets to say what about who is normal and who is not, and with what authority (Foucault, 1970).

Central to a deconstructive critique of the modern psychological DSM-IV platform is an analysis of who is not allowed and afforded legitimate speaking rights because they have not acquired the proper rational inquiry brought on as a result of systematic thought and orderly investigation (Shotter, 1990). The PwK (viewed as operating without a context, but classified within gender, race, sexual preference and their relevant 'dysfunction' category), may only acquire legitimized speaking rights through a specified institutional grid and matrix that distributes and negotiates (in this case psychological) knowledge, power and storytelling rights (Epston, 1988).

Difference and Reflexivity

Because much of modern psychology ignores differences, its practice searches for something that is essential and substantial about the thing-in-itself rather than the thing-in-relation. Derrida (1991) argues that the recognition of difference forces us to abandon any essentialism or foundationalism in our search for the real thing since language constitutes meanings not in terms of the essence of a thing but in its difference from other things. Derrida looks instead at the movements of difference that constitute the world. His subversion of essentialist thought acts to undermine psychology's logocentrist claim of being able to speak 'the truth' about something or another through an available unmediated knowledge of the world.

Prior to meeting Tom, I pondered the discursive restraints used to inscribe and privatize Tom's body as chronic (Madigan, 1992; Madigan and Epston, 1995). I wondered what the pervasive knowledges and power relations were. What was the meaning of the site chosen for inscription? Could his body be somehow claimed back and de-territorialized (Fox, 1994)? Upon what kind of body does this kind of inscription occur, and how is it administered? What did it mean to Tom and his community of others to have a chronic body – a spoiled identity?

I pondered who it was that was able to say what and with what authority about Tom's body. Useful here is Foucault's writings which focus on the history of the body – how it became what it became, not biologically but in relation to power. I also asked myself reflexive questions (Madigan and Goldner, 1998), and spoke with my colleagues in an attempt at not reproducing the inscription and not introducing my own sets of debilitating expert knowledge. These questions were also intended as a performance of accountability to Tom. I asked myself: In what ways will I act to further perform and perpetuate Tom as a PwK? To what extent will my own set of expert opinions reproduce an Expert With Knowledge position? How will I go about soliciting pertinent medical information regarding the long term affects of ECT and how might this information affect my relationship with Tom and with the hospital? How might I help to deconstruct the hospital's version of Tom (and his partner Jane) without totalizing all relationships that Tom and Jane have encountered within the hospital? What are the discursive restraints (Madigan, 1992) of my own trainings in psychology, gender, class and age that will limit my conversation with Tom and Jane? How can I not respect the totalizing description of chronic inscription while remaining most respectful to this couple?

Co-Producing Each Other . . .

To have an identity is not to have a special essence that is one's own as characterized by the Western Enlightenment's creation and production of the self-contained individual and its search for a singular, unifying fundamental governing principle. An alternative view builds upon the idea that any identity grows from its relations to other identities; nothing can be itself without taking into consideration the kinds of relationship by which the 'self sameness' is constituted (Sampson, 1993).

Discursive influences like the Health Maintenance Organizations (HMO), Oprah and DSM technologies, are sculpted through intricate and ritualized power plays, all of which are set up to control the discourse (Madigan, 1996). All 'knowing' within this community context is viewed as mutually shared and shaped (Bordo, 1993).

Bakhtin suggests that '(I) get a self that I can see, that I can understand and use, by clothing my otherwise invisible (incomprehensible, unutilizable) self in the completing categories I appropriate from the other's image of me' (quoted in Clark and Holquist, 1984: 79). Bakhtin's view is that the other plays a central role in constituting the individual's self. Without the ongoing relationship to the other, our selves would be invisible, incomprehensible and unutilizable. The other gives us meaning and a comprehension of our self so that we may function in the social world. The knowledge we have of ourselves appears in and through social practices – namely, interaction, dialogue and conversation with others' responses. These interactions do not make us passive nor are the discourses without a rhetoric of intent (Billig, 1990; Sampson, 1993).

Bakhtin writes that we

> address our own acts (addressive quality) in anticipation of the responses of real others with whom we are currently involved; imagined others, including characters from whom we are currently involved; historical others, including characters from our own past as well as from cultural narratives; and the generalized other, typically carried in the language forms by which a given community organizes its perceptions and understandings of its members, which we have learned to employ in reflecting us back to us. (quoted in Sampson, 1993: 106)

We are equal contributors to each other's emerging identity, and we can see this in the relations that constituted Tom, and that we were able to mobilize together to reconstitute his identity.

I saw Tom and his partner Jane in therapy eleven times over the course of three months. The three of us met together at my office each session, except for two sessions when we went out for a walk to 'admire the gardens' around town – as Tom was a lover and a 'long-time student' of gardening – and we met as a foursome twice when two of Tom's six children were in Vancouver on business – it occurs to me that my meeting of persons outside of the designated therapy space is quite rare, as it does not follow from the rules of organized therapy which include the ritualized dialogic structure of the interview, the geographical rules of therapeutic office design, a session's temporal organization, client billing and other relational politics often left as unquestioned practices and performances of power.

In the first session Tom relayed – through a slurred medicated speech – that he had been feeling 'depressed' since his retirement, one and a half years earlier, and had twice tried to 'off' himself without success. I asked Tom if the word depressed was a term of his own or did it belong to someone else. He relayed that it was a 'hospital word' and what he was 'really feeling' was 'bored and unaccomplished'. In the first session I asked Tom the following questions (Tom's answers are in brackets):

Tom, do you think this bored and unaccomplished sense of yourself is a final description of yourself? (Perhaps, yes, maybe not.)

Tom, do you think this bored and unaccomplished feeling is a recent development since your retirement or is it a bigger comment on your entire life? (My entire life, well sometimes I feel like I didn't and wasn't any good at anything and people would be better off without me.)

Are these the times when you think about offing yourself? (Yes only these times, but I feel like this a lot.)

Do you think that other men your age also begin to feel bored and unaccomplished when they retire? (Yes, there is another guy on the ward my age, and another in one of the groups I went to.)

Why do you think that retiring men might begin to think in unaccomplished ways? (We don't know what else to do – you feel useless and angry.)

From what you have experienced what do you think might be helpful to these men? (Places for them to go I guess and something to do.)

Jane joined the conversation and we spoke for quite a while about the specialized inscriptions and practices of retirement. The conversation of bored and unaccomplished feelings was situated within men's culture and training, expectations, economics and love. We moved onto a discussion about the hospital's description of him.

Tom, why do you think this bored and unaccomplished sense of yourself may not be a final description of yourself? (It might be the shock treatment, because it makes me slow and I can't remember much and I feel like a rock on the end of a piece of rope.)

Tom, is the hospital's description of you as a chronically depressed person an accurate description of you? (I think they helped me get worse and never asked me about my work and retirement.)

Are there ways that the hospital has helped you to feel worse about yourself? (Well being with them a year or so I haven't gotten any better and I think that they are giving up – this is why they sent me to you [laughs], you're the last stop and they weren't much help anyway – most of them are nice but you know.)

Tom, do you think the hospital staff has hope for you in coming to see me? (Well they told me you helped someone else like me, so my guess is yes.)

Why do you think they think you can be helped? (Because I don't think they know what they are doing and I get mad at them for shocking me and doping me up as much as they do.)

Jane, are you mad as well? (Yes I am mad and I am glad we are here because my sister's niece told her that you were different, that you are good at what you do.)

Do you think Jane thinks there is hope for you overcoming this unaccomplishing boredom retirement has helped bring into your life? (Yes.)

Are there other people in your life that you think might be pinning their hopes on you beating this boredom. (Probably, yes.)

Can you name a few of these hopeful people? (Well my kids, and the neighbours and I don't know, Jane, and the occupational therapist.)

Do you have any ideas what all of these people witness and remember in you that you have somehow forgotten about? (The shocks have made me forgetful but maybe they could tell you a thing or two.)

Tom, do you feel that there might be parts of who you are as a man and a husband, father, employer, friend, worker, and gardener that you might remember once enjoying, but now these other yous have somehow fallen into silence? (Maybe, yes they are there but hidden.)

It was through sets of 'discursive questions' (Law and Madigan, 1998) that certain hospital and cultural certainties were undermined to open space for other possibilities and discontinuities constituting the storied inscription of Tom. The therapeutic conversations between Tom, Jane and myself tracked the threads of the institution's discursive practices and destabilized the hard chronic conclusions placed on Tom's body. In taking away expert knowledge from the site of the hospital we enlarged the degree to which alternative other knowledges might be taken up and performed.

Just a Gaze

Foucault described both the mutuality of knowledge and power and the extent to which all ways of knowing are exercises of power (1975). This power is not reducible to interpersonal domination, but is constitutive of social life and culture generally. Power, Foucault suggests, is not only 'repressive' but 'traverses and produces things, induces pleasure, forms knowledge, produces discourse' (cited in Dreyfus and Rabinow, 1983: 61). Power is, in this sense, 'decentred' and not the property of any subject. Power is normalized, rendered into discipline, practised routinely by subjects upon themselves as they re-enact the premises of their culture (Calhoun, 1995; Madigan and Epston, 1995). Even still, all is not equal.

For Foucault (1979), modern (as opposed to pre-modern sovereign) power does not derive from a central authority, is non-conspiratorial, and indeed non-orchestrated; yet it nonetheless produces and normalizes bodies to serve prevailing relations of dominance and subordination. Understanding this new sort of power requires two conceptual changes. First, we must cease to imagine power as the possession of individuals or groups – as something that people have – and instead see it as a dynamic or network of non-centralized forces. Second, we must recognize that these forces are not random or haphazard, but configure to assume particular historical forms, within which certain groups and ideologies do have dominance – dominance here is sustained not by decree or design 'from above' (as sovereign power is exercised) but through 'multiple processes of different origin and location' regulating the most intimate elements of the construction of space, time, and desire (Foucault, 1979).

Foucault is particularly helpful at this juncture for a social and historical analysis of the relationship between psychologist and subject. Where power works from 'below', prevailing forms of selfhood and subjectivity are maintained through individual self-surveillance and self-correction of established norms. Foucault writes,

> there is no need for arms, physical violence, material constraints. Just a gaze. An inspecting gaze, a gaze which each individual under its weight will end by interiorising to the point that he is his own overseer, each individual thus exercising this surveillance over, and against himself. (1979: 155)

Throughout our sessions Tom and Jane began to inscribe themselves back towards local, historical, cultural and social knowledges, all and the cultural discourse around the person who retires lost within the hospital's discourse. I witnessed how subversive responses were possible under even the most oppressive conditions. Our conversations afforded forms of resistance and transformation that were a part of a historical process.

We analysed and began to situate the discursive threads of 'retirement', 'shock treatment', 'men's identities', 'psychiatry', 'fatherhood', and 'relationships'. The more our readings of the dominant norm were investigated the more we seemed to position ourselves against the grain of the popular, taken-for-granted and chronic. As we moved away from the disciplinary practices of living as a retired or hospitalized person, the more Tom began to gain back aspects of himself once forgotten through boredom and feelings of an unaccomplished life.

Foucault also emphasized that power relations are never seamless but always spawning new forms of culture and subjectivity, new opportunities for transformation. Where there is power, he came to see, there was also resistance (Foucault, in Dreyfus and Rabinow, 1983). Dominant forms and institutions are continually being penetrated and reconstructed by values, lifestyles and knowledges that have been developing and gathering strength at the margins.

At one point in therapy we resurrected a 'therapeutic' letter campaign (Madigan and Epston, 1995; Madigan, 1997) whose purpose was to reconnect Tom to the local knowledges of his community of concern and care. We wrote the campaign letter at the end of the fifth session – three weeks after our first meeting – and while Tom was living on the ward. The letter read as follows:

Dear friends of Tom and Jane,
My name is Stephen Madigan and I have been working alongside Tom and Jane for the last three weeks. As Tom sees it, he has been taken over with a 'great sense of boredom' and feeling like he never quite 'accomplished enough' throughout his life as a father, friend, husband, worker, neighbour. Tom's feelings of boredom accompanied by an unaccomplished life seemed to have 'boxed him into a corner' to the point where it twice convinced him that he was not worthy of living. Tom says that being confined in the hospital for so long made him feel like giving up, but lately, Tom says that he 'might have a chance'.
   Tom, Jane and I are writing to you to ask if you would write a letter on Tom's behalf that might add an alternative description to the story that the boredom, the feelings of living an unaccomplished life, that a few of the hospital staff are telling about Tom.
   In the letter could you relay an experience that you have had with Tom that you see as neither boring or unaccomplished, and indicate what kind of future you would like to enjoy alongside Tom.
   Tom, Jane and I thank you for your help in this matter, and Tom wants all of you to know that he is feeling 'a bit better' these past few weeks.
   Warm regards,
   Tom, Jane and Stephen

Therapeutic letter-writing campaigns assist people to re-remember lost aspects of themselves. The campaigns assist persons to be re-membered back towards membership systems of love and support from which the problem has dis-membered them (cf. Barbara Myheroff, 1982).
   Letter-writing campaigns have been appropriate for persons as young as six and as old as seventy-six. They have assisted persons struggling with an assortment of difficulties including anxiety, abuse, bulimia, depression, perfection, shame and fear. The campaigns create a context where it becomes possible for people struggling with problems to bring themselves back from the depths of totalizing discourses, harmful disciplinary practices, and therapeutic violence (Madigan and Epston, 1995).
   Persons receiving letters – campaign contributors also include pictures, collages, tapes, videos and poems – often rediscover a discourse of the self that assists them to re-member into situations from which the problem has most often dis-membered them from. These include claiming back former membership associations with intimate relationships, school, sports, music, walks, careers, and family members, and

reacquainting themselves with aspects of themselves once restrained by the problem identity.

Over the years I have encouraged massive international writing campaigns that netted literally hundreds of responses, and have had equally successful three-person discursive blockades. Over this time, letters of support have arrived from some very curious authors. For example, family pets, teddy bears, cars, dead grandparents, unborn siblings, sporting heroes, and storybook characters are among the variety of encouraging campaign contributors.

Letter-writing efforts can take on a variety of shapes and forms, but the most standard campaigns involve the following:

1   The campaign emerges from a therapeutic interview when alternative accounts of who the person might be are questioned, revived and reremembered. The person is also asked to consider whether there are other people in his/her life who may regard the person differently from how the problem/professional group describes them – these different accounts are then spoken of. I might ask the following questions: 'If I were to interview ⸺ about you, what do you think they might tell me about yourself that the problem/ professional group would not dare to tell me?' Or 'Do you think your friend's telling of you to me about you would be an accurate telling, even if it contradicted the problem's/professional groups tellings of you?' Or 'Whose description of you do you prefer, and why?'

2   Together, the person seeking therapy and myself (along with the parents, family/partner, friend, therapist, etc., if any of these persons are in attendance) begin a conversation regarding all the possible other descriptions of the person as a person that she/he might be, could be, would want to be, but has been restrained from remembering due to a discursive inscription's powerful hold over her/him. We dialogue on who the client might be, who the client would like to be, and who the client used to be well before the problem took over her/his life. We recall their forgotten alternative lived experiences of herself/himself that the client may have forgotten through the problem's restraining context.

3   We then begin to make a list of all the persons in the client's life who would be in support of these alternate descriptions. Once the list is complete, we construct a letter of support and invitation.

4   If finances are a problem I supply the envelopes and stamps for the ensuing campaign.

5   If privacy is an issue, we use Yaletown Family Therapy as the return address.

6   The client is asked to bring the letters into the therapy session and to read them aloud (and sometimes a letter writer is invited into the session to recite their letter in person and to act as a witness of their own and the letters written by others).

7   I will offer to read the letters back to the client and/or the letter writer so that both may experience a textual re-telling of these written accounts (and other support persons might be asked to come to the session as witnesses to this re-telling remembrance).

8   The person seeking therapy is asked to go through the collection of letters as a way of conducting a 're-search' on herself/himself. A research model based in qualitative research theory is used and the client is asked to scour through each letter and begin to establish familiar themes and categories commonly found within the letters. These counter-categories are then re-produced and written into a return letter to all the people who took part in the campaign.

Campaign Contributors

The repercussions of problematic discursive practices will often push persons to dis-member themselves from the support systems that surround them, and will coerce them toward isolation, detachment and withdrawal. Similarly, problems may compel support persons to move away from the persons' struggling, by encouraging hopelessness, anger and despair.

Our experience has shown that once support persons have received a letter inviting them to contribute to a campaign, they will often feel compelled to write more than once (three and four letters is not uncommon). Customarily, contributors have had the experience of feeling 'left out' of the helping process by the professional institution. Being left out will often leave them with the opinion that they are 'impotent' and 'useless'. Frequently they report feeling 'blamed' and 'guilty' for the role they believe they have played in the problem's dominance over the person's life. They suggest that many of these shameful feelings about themselves have been helped along by various professional discourses as well as self-help, religious and pop culture literature.

The writing of a re-remembering text offers family members and other support persons with an opportunity to break free of the problem's negative dominance in their own lives, and allows for an alternative and active means for renewal and hope. Therapeutic letter-writing campaigns act to re-remember alternative accounts of a person's lived experience that the institution of psychological practice will often separate them from. Therapeutic letter-writing campaigns are designed as counter practices to the dis-membering effects of problem lifestyles and the isolating effects psychological discourses often create in people's lives. The letters form a dialogic context of preferred re-membering, re-remembering and meaning.

The campaigns are but one therapeutic method of honouring, re-collecting, and re-acquainting persons, families and communities with their local knowledge that often 'lives' outside the dominant domain of psychological theory and practice.

Conclusion

Within a Foucauldian framework it is pointless to view the 'psychologist' as the villain, as psychologists (viewed as persons) find themselves embedded and implicated in institutions and practices that they as individuals did not create and do not control – and they frequently feel tyrannized by. This position is not in any way suggesting that we divert our attention away from psychology's continued patterns of exclusion, subordination and normalization. It is also important that we view our active participation (recruitment) within psychology as recursive, reproductive and socializing. However, it is important that Foucault not be interpreted as supporting a view that suggests 'all players are equal', or that the positions of dominance and subordination are not sustained within networks of psychological power.

In four weeks' time Tom had received forty-one letters supporting him with hope, and counter-stories confirming him as anything other than a chronic body. Tom decorated his hospital wall with the campaign letters, cards, poems and pictures, and began to start up campaigns of resistance with other hospital ward members. We viewed the letters as counter documents that stood against the 'word of the file' and the Expert with Knowledge. The letters ritualized, confirmed and performed Tom, Jane and their community of concern as Persons *with* Knowledge.

We celebrated the discursive victory and resurrected knowledge with a Persons with Knowledge party, complete with cake and honorary degrees. Tom walked away from the hospital eight weeks after our first conversation together – and he never went back to being who they said he was. These days, Tom volunteers with a homeless shelter two days a week and currently holds the status of 'gardener-in-residence' in his new community.

Psychologists are not the enemy, but they often have a higher stake in maintaining institutions within which they have historically occupied positions of dominance over their clients/subjects. This might be why the psychological establishment has often felt like the enemy to clients struggling within its textual borders, and those of us struggling to change its institutions, archives and practices. Moreover, the fact that cultural resistance to psychological practices is continual does not mean it is on equal footing with forms that are culturally entrenched. To struggle effectively against the coerciveness of these psychological forms it is first necessary to recognize that they have dominance.

Post-structuralist theory discloses that everything is political (Calhoun, 1995). Texts are written for reasons of power, and every reading of a text is an act of power. In the writings of Derrida and Foucault we are led to recognize that discourse is driven less by reason than by power. Without a consideration of the cultural and socio-political context of any problem brought to therapy, therapy could be considered as merely reproductive of culture and its institutions, and as such uncritical. In other words, the therapeutic questions we ask or don't ask, the texts we read, the files we keep, the interpretations we make, the knowing unchecked professional nods we nod, the chapters we write, who we include and exclude at meetings and conferences, and how we consider the geography of our office space as a place of power – if left unknown, unwarranted, and unchecked – will act to help solidify traditions and techniques of psychology's power (Madigan, 1996).

Between the time when Tom left the hospital and when Tom and Jane decided to 'move a little eastward', they played a vital role in our family therapy training programme. Paid on a par with other therapeutic consultants their knowledge continues to circulate, subvert and resist.

An array of cultural alterations have made significant changes to the conditions of therapeutic life, changes which need to be named, described and understood. Discontinuity, displacement and destabiliza-tion may be terms of postmodern academic accessorizing, but they also point to 'real' elements of contemporary therapeutic experience.

Note

I would like to acknowledge personal communications with Michael White, Imelda McCarthy and Nollaig Byrne on the subject of re-membering and dis-memberment.

References

Bakhtin, M.M. (1986) *Speech Genres and Other Late Essays*. Austin, TX: University of Texas Press.

Billig, M. (1990) 'Collective memory, ideology and the British Royal Family', in D. Middleton and D. Edwards (eds), *Collective Remembering*. London: Sage.

Bordo, S. (1993) *Unbearable Weight*. Berkeley, CA: University of California Press.

Calhoun, C. (1995) *Critical Social Theory*. Oxford: Blackwell.

Caplan, P. (1995) *They Say You're Crazy: How The World's Most Powerful Psychiatrists Decide Who's Normal*. New York: Addison-Wesley Publishing.

Clark, K and Holquist, M. (1984) *Mikhail Bakhtin*. Cambridge, MA: Harvard University Press.

Derrida, J. (1991) *Writing and Difference*. London: Routledge.

Dreyfus, H and Rabinow, P. (1983) 'The subject of power: interview with Michel Foucault', in *Beyond Structuralism and Hermeneutics*. Chicago: University of Chicago Press.

Epston, D. (1988) *Collected Papers*. Adelaide: Dulwich Centre Publications.

Foucault, M. (1970) *The Order of Things*. London: Tavistock.

Foucault, M. (1975) 'The eye of power', in *Power/Knowledge*. New York: Pantheon.

Foucault, M. (1979) *Discipline and Punish*. New York: Vintage.

Foucault, M. (1989) *Foucault Live: Collected Interviews, 1961–1984*. New York: Semiotext(e).

Fox, N. (1994) *Postmodernism, Sociology and Health*. Toronto: University of Toronto Press.

Hoagwood, K. (1993) 'Poststructuralist historism and the psychological construction of anxiety disorders', *The Journal of Psychology*, 127 (1): 105–22.

Law, I. and Madigan, S. (1994) 'Power and politics in practice', *Dulwich Newsletter, Special Edition*.

Law, I. and Madigan, S. (1998) 'A discursive approach to therapy', unpublished manuscript.

Madigan, S. (1992) 'The application of Michael Foucault's philosophy in the problem externalizing discourse of Michael White', *Journal of Family Therapy*, 14 (3): 265–79.

Madigan, S. (1996) 'The politics of identity: considering community discourse in the externalising of internalised discourse', *Journal of Systemic Therapy*, 47–63.

Madigan, S. (1997) 'Re-considering memory: reremembering lost identities back towards re-membered selves', in D. Nylund and C. Smith (eds), *Narrative Therapies with Children and Adolescents*. New York: Norton.

Madigan, S. and Epston, D. (1995) 'From spy-chiatric gaze to communities of concern: from professional monologue to dialogue', in S. Friedman (ed.), *The Reflecting Team in Action*. New York: Guilford Publications.

Madigan, S. and Goldner, E. (1998) 'A narrative approach to anorexia: discourse, reflexivity, and questions', in M. Hoyt (ed.), *Constructive Therapies*. New York: Jossey-Bass.

Middleton, D. and Edwards, D. (eds) (1990) *Collective Remembering*. London: Sage.

Myerhoff, B. (1982) 'Life history among the elder: Performance, visibility and remembering', in J. Ruby (ed.), *A Crack In The Mirror: Reflexive Perspectives In Anthropology*. Philadelphia: University of Pennsylvania Press.

Parker, I. (1989) 'Discourse and power', in J. Shotter and K. Gergen (eds), *Texts of Identity*. London: Sage.

Rose, N. (1989) *Governing the Soul: Technologies of Human Subjectivity*. London: Routledge.

Sampson, E. (1993) *Celebrating the Other: A Dialogic Account of Human Nature*. San Fransisco: Westview Press.

Shotter, J. (1990) 'The social construction of remembering and forgetting', in D. Middleton and D. Edwards (eds), *Collective Remembering*. London: Sage.

PART III

DECONSTRUCTING PSYCHOTHERAPEUTIC DISCOURSE

11

THE THERAPIST AS CLIENT AS EXPERT: EXTERNALIZING NARRATIVE THERAPY

John Morss and Maria Nichterlein

Dear Nat,

This letter may come as no surprise to you since we share the same beliefs regarding the process of change and therapy as a narrative. Still, I couldn't restrain my need to share with you some of the reflections that assaulted me after you left my consulting rooms. And to be honest, the conversation with you was most challenging: it is not common that the theme that is brought to therapy by my clients hits so close to the heart of my professional practice, to the core of my doing. I guess I am not sure to what degree what I'll be writing is a reflection of your concerns or a reflection of my fears . . .

Like other chapters in this collection, we are concerned with exploring the idea of deconstruction in relation to narrative therapy. We use the term 'narrative therapy' rather loosely, to include later developments of the systemic approach, and the non-expert approach of Goolishian and Anderson (Anderson, 1997), as well as the approach of White and Epston, et al. Like other authors here, we greatly admire the narrative approach: for its respectful attitude to clients, whether child or adult; for its attention to the power dynamics of therapy; and for its attempted suspension of expertise in the therapeutic relationship. One of us employs narrative techniques in day-to-day therapy (Law, 1997). In this context, we feel that narrative therapy's appeal to deconstruction is potentially a very fruitful one but also one that requires scrutiny. In particular, we feel that a consideration of the potential of deconstruction may help us to clarify some pitfalls in the practice of narrative therapy. For deconstruction is by its nature resistant to expertise. It has a tendency to undercut authority, including that of its user. If there is any possibility that narrative therapy may not have succeeded in entirely distancing itself from the expertise model, then deconstruction should help it to do so. This chapter is a letter to narrative therapy: it is also an externalization.

First we should explain what we do and do not mean by deconstruction. What we do not mean is a systematic critique or analysis of a text, a life, or a 'problem', seeking to reveal hidden processes or discourses. The way that Foucault's work has been appealed to by theorists of narrative therapy sometimes seems to take this linear, cognitive and instrumental form. 'Deconstruction' is just not a helpful word for this kind of discovery process – there are many more familiar words. What we mean by deconstruction is, rather, something like what we think Derrida is doing in his commentaries on texts: a setting in motion, an unsettling, a disturbing, a liquidizing – something like what happens to solid rock in an earthquake or bomb test. Surprisingly perhaps, there are political implications here. The process of rendering fluid may not be in itself political activity, but may be a prerequisite for political activity. Indeed, activity intended to be political – emancipatory, for example – may be doomed to failure (or worse) without such preliminary work. For all that may be possible without it may be the minor rearrangement of existing structures, the redeployment of existing vocabularies, and some self-deception by the political activist. In Derrida's words:

> Asking oneself questions, including ones about the questions that are imposed on us or taught to us as being the 'right' questions to ask . . . and not only questioning, but thinking through the commitment, the stake, through which a given question is engaged: perhaps this is a prior responsibility, and a precondition of commitment. On its own it is not enough of course; but it has never impeded or retarded commitment – quite the reverse. (Derrida, 1994: 40)

To present the argument more starkly, we might suggest that (as on a bicycle) wheels must be in motion before gears can be changed (and even for the cyclist to remain upright). The spinning of the wheels itself involves work. What it may generate is a kind of space of possibilities, and some effects (such as chaos-type effects) that only emerge with motion. Deconstruction may be a matter of turning up the heat beneath the kettle of text, or of life.

Such a warming or freeing-up process may not be immediately reminiscent of the work of Foucault, more popular than Derrida in contemporary narrative therapy. Foucault's intellectual style has sometimes appeared glacial. The comprehensive and relentless nature of surveillance in modern societies is laid out in chilling detail. His well-known account of the panopticon (summarized and discussed very clearly in White, 1988/9), for example, presents us with an analysis of modern life that is striking and highly persuasive, but which scarcely invites negotiation. However, Foucault's larger agenda may perhaps be seen in the terms we are proposing. His work in the areas of the medical, legal and social sciences, as investigations into the history of truth, was surely intended to contribute to a process of general unsettling in (the history of) philosophy. Support for this more mobile interpretation of his attitude may be found in Foucault's own account of his intellectual path. In *Power/Knowledge* (Rabinow, 1984: 51), Foucault has described why he chose to work on the histories of psychiatry, medicine, the prison, and so on, rather than on the histories of the natural or mathematical sciences. This choice does not appear to have been motivated by either a sentimental or an emancipatory interest in social activity as such. Rather, he seems to have felt that the 'harder' sciences had for too long been assumed to represent the proper subject-matter for serious work in the philosophy of knowledge. In order to make it possible for political change (changes in subjectivity) to be thought, the philosophy of knowledge had first to be shaken up. This process seemed impossible in terms of the physical sciences. Socio-legal sciences, and to a lesser extent medical sciences, remained something of a soft underbelly of the philosophy of knowledge. Foucault's choice was a strategic one.

Foucault therefore seems to have been advocating a necessary problematization of commonplace presuppositions concerning social life. Subsequent to this disturbance, his own very real political commitments (and presumably those of others, both convergent and divergent) would have a chance of expression. But his theoretical work was not predicated on the legitimacy of his political commitments as such (in terms of political activism his message perhaps was 'do as I do, not as I say'). Rather as in an (idealized?) image of democracy, process does not presuppose outcome. What we are suggesting is that, although not in the service of a specific political programme, Foucault's intellectual work may still be considered politically strategic; and that the same may be said of Derrida. In both cases, if our analysis is at all correct, the intellectual work is done without certainty of outcome, emancipatory or otherwise. This uncertainty is perhaps of the essence of political activity. Deconstruction does not seek to control the future. In this respect it may be thought of as playful. But it may also be thought of as melancholic (the figure of Walter Benjamin is perhaps representative here). It is tentative, doubt-ridden, as questioning as it is manipulative: in a word, *non-expert*.

In this sense deconstruction can be thought of as a kind of setting at risk, a relaxation of control and of the enforcement of stability: like the sending of a missive on a voyage whose outcome is not totally certain, such as that of a postcard sent through the mails (Derrida, 1987). Derrida's discussion of posting recalls, in more than superficial ways, the letter(document)-writing technique of narrative therapy (White and Epston, 1990; White, 1995). The narrative therapist's letter to her client might always get lost en route, or remain 'submitted for typing'; its recipient-reader is controlled in his reading much less than with a verbally expressed message within the clinic, allowing (and trusting in) a much wider range of responses. And after all, what is an 'externalizing' letter other than one (benevolent) extreme of a continuum, at the other extreme of which is situated the conventional appointment [post]card, with its word-processed label with identification number, and which carries its own (oppressive?) messages ('you have a fixed place and time in our system' . . .)?

We wish to examine narrative therapy in a deconstructionist style of this kind. But this chapter is not itself narrative therapy. Rather, we are *writing about* therapy, which is to say writing about the therapist. The therapist takes the role of client in relationship to us, the authors of this chapter. As authors, we must in turn be prepared for our own expertise suddenly to become negotiable. We must resist becoming what Harlene Anderson has called a 'narrative expert'. As she suggests,

> When a therapist [claims to be] a content expert – a knower of the human story and how it ought to be told or formed and retold or re-formed – he or she implicitly takes the role of a narrative expert whose function is to edit – to guide or revise a client's story . . . Even therapists who purport to fight certain dominant social discourses inadvertently and paradoxically marginalize a client when they assume their [the therapist's own] counternarrative (for example, social injustice, gender inequality, institutional colonization) is better for a client. (Anderson, 1997: 96–7)

We will not therefore seek to impose our own particular 'counternarrative', as if presuming to make an authoritative and final judgement on narrative therapy. Rather, we intend to play with the externalizing technique of letter-writing in order to highlight (in)consistencies in some aspects of narrative therapy: specifically, issues of power, knowledge and control. For the narrative therapist may not find it easy living up to the high ideals of the paradigm, may feel assailed by doubts concerning his or her professional activity, and may even seek therapeutic assistance in connection with such concerns. We therefore suppose ourselves to be a therapist ('Marion'), working with a rather challenging client: namely, a narrative therapist ('Nat'). Marion is of course also a narrative therapist. To continue:

First Letter

I wrote a letter to Nat after the first session:

Dear Nat,
This letter may come as no surprise to you since we share the same beliefs regarding the process of change and therapy as a narrative . . . I guess I am not sure to what degree what I'll be writing is a reflection of your concerns or a reflection of my fears. I have no doubt that you'll consider these ideas with the respect that has characterized your practice and that, together, we will be able to develop some understanding and – why not? – a statement (perhaps even a paper) in relation to these issues. As you can see, part of the reflections that I want to share with you today are about the excitement, the energy generated by these issues. But before I continue any longer with my response, let me try to reproduce what we discussed in this session:

Nat, you came to talk to me almost 'dragging yourself'. You were very quick in stating your great sense of futility in coming to explore the issues that were distressing you. Not that you considered the issues by themselves futile. Rather, the futility had arisen from the belief that this problem was almost unsolvable, that rather than a problem, it was a *condition* of therapy. You no longer believed it possible to achieve an understanding of therapy that defined the client in empowering and respectful ways. Instead, you felt that what you needed to do was to come to terms with power structures that are inherent to therapy: to reconcile yourself with therapy's 'dark side'.

You then told me about your struggles to become the therapist you wish to be. You told me about the deep commitment you have to help people that are experiencing suffering. You also told us about your deep commitment to social justice (commitment that is well-known in the community since it presents itself in all of your activities) and respect for the client and their entitlement to be recognized in their world (as they live it). You told me of your disappointment when you started your studies, of the incredibly tedious and (totally?) unrelated issues discussed in your university years ('rats! . . . and more rats!!').

You also told me about your excitement when you heard about narrative approaches. These ideas resonated so fully with your experiences and they presented themselves as full of optimism and completely committed to the values that you held so dear that you couldn't but participate with this enthusiasm. You describe the experience as 'blissful' and you felt that the years of searching were over, that there was a way – clean and elegant – to help those in suffering.

Yet, this blissfulness didn't last long. Things started to get complicated once more when you read more about that 'protean' concept called post-modernism. But the concerns were not only coming from the theory, from abstract concepts, but also from clients. You were specially taken aback by Judith who came to you after having seen another counsellor whom she felt betrayed by. Not that 'feeling betrayed by one's therapist' was new to you. Like many of us, you are extremely aware how so many clients feel betrayed by the pathologizing tendencies of traditional therapies. Rather, Judith was so disconcerting because her sense of betrayal came from her therapist believing that she was the victim . . . a victim of the neglect of her parents ('they were doing the best they could,' Judith said), a victim of the boy that raped her for six years until she turned thirteen ('he was only four years older than me . . .' Judith said) or her school ('school has to have standards,' Judith said). What was disconcerting was that what Judith found oppressive was the therapist's insistence that she was being subjugated by her circumstances, by the politics of capitalism and gender. What was most disconcerting was that Judith found oppressive our explanations of oppression. What was disconcerting was that our 'saving tools', for her, were oppressive . . .

So your search for a respectful therapeutic approach started to crack and, as it did, you became increasingly aware of the complexities and the fears involved in such a dream.

As you talked, I started to have this image of X Pert as being at the root of your despair. X Pert, a monster who insidiously enters into all aspects of your practice and entices you away from your desires of being respectful and empowering in your relationship with your clients. I couldn't but resonate with your sensation of being trapped. And who wouldn't? X Pert is no simple monster, it has two (if not, several) heads. One seduces with knowledge: with the righteousness of years of training, readings and supervised practice that invites you to believe, as you stated during our conversation, that one could understand human behaviour or, at least, human suffering. This face of X Pert kept on telling you that you could help your clients much better 'if only' you could be allowed to use all your training and experience. Surely, he kept on saying, you should not deny your clients the benefit of your 'hard-earned' expertise.

X Pert's second face traps you through emotions. This is perhaps the most sneaky of X Pert's presentations, the most difficult to discern until it is too late. But, as you wisely stated, could one take the risk of not stopping or challenging the client who is crying that, out of pain and hurt, they are going to kill their fiancé? Or what about the other client who, with tears in their eyes and a trembling voice, begs you for a statement that tells them what is wrong with them, an expert voice that could define the malady that has been spelt in their lives so that they could go to the pharmacy and buy the medicine? (or, 'which is the monster that is haunting me'?). Could one ethically not respond to their pain and share with them the knowledges that you have acquired through the professional training, knowledge that entitles you to a title and an honorarium?

Yes Nat, the questions you have brought to our conversation are not easy ones. As I said before, they touch the core of what I do and I feel as disconcerted as you do when I am visited by them. Yet I also feel excited with the idea of exploring these rather dark/shadowed spots in the landscape of our practices . . . Thanks for your willingness to share these vulnerabilities with me and I cannot but be curious about how this story unfolds.

Take care, lots of care,
Marion

Narrative therapy represents a significant shift from traditional approaches to therapy. Its origin cannot be lineally traced to a couple of thinkers (even when there are certainly certain preferences and certain gurus . . .). The question of the foundations of the therapeutic praxis can go back to Bateson and his second order cybernetics, the constructivist ideas of von Foerster and von Glasersfeld (among others) which were introduced into America by the MRI Institute (mainly through the work of Watzlawick), followed by reference to Humberto Maturana and Francisco Varela and their questioning of external realities (Gergen, 1994; Anderson, 1997). The conversations held by practitioners (mainly from a family therapy background) around the ideas presented by such authors were simultaneous with conversations held in academia regarding the social construction of realities. Postmodern, post-foundational descriptions were insidiously intruding into the traditional practices of therapy, and prompting practitioners to re-evaluate their praxis.

Instead of seeking to discover/diagnose and remediate/treat pre-existent ailments – ailments whose definition positioned the client as an object of the knowledge/expertise of the professional – therapists started to see therapy as the art of writing stories collaboratively: stories that position client and therapist as brothers-in-arms in protest against the client's problems.

Notwithstanding the advances represented by this shift, this approach still finds no space for any negotiation of 'the basic facts'. The therapist is clear and decisive in understanding the client as oppressed by the problem that brought him/her to counselling. In this clarity, the therapist joins the client in protesting against the subjugating effects of the dominant (problem-saturated) stories of their lives. And could we do otherwise? In the immediacy of the pain, the suffering of the client, the therapist sees no other ethical option but respectfully to join the client in their struggles. To conceive this attempt as totalizing, as rendering the client passive before the description of the therapist, seems disrespectful of the need for committed action. After all, the anorexia is eating away the client – should we not get frustrated with it and challenge it? Should we sit and wait for the client to have the clarity to understand that this can cost them their lives? How far can we go with the negotiations?

Second Letter

This letter to Nat was written after the third session:

Dear Nat,
I know you were not very impressed with my first letter ('too clichéd', you said, 'even when the themes that you touched in it were very much the relevant ones . . .'). Still, I couldn't restrain my urge to write and share with you my excitement when seeing the progress that you have made in your relationship with X Pert. Congratulations!

It is only three sessions ago that you came to consult with me regarding your struggles to become the therapist you wished to be. At that time, I was speechless, almost pulled down with you in the despair.

Yet, today, you surprised me. You came with a more relaxed presence and said that things were starting to move in positive ways, that you had more space in relation to X Pert and that even when he was very much present in your daily life, you felt stronger vis-à-vis him.

As you stated during our conversation, this change is still in its early years and you are cautious about its long-term life. At the moment however, it feels like a breath of fresh air that has helped you to regain some (much needed) energy. I couldn't but be surprised by the way this movement took place. It started when working with a newly arrived immigrant woman. As you said, it was the immediacy of the difference that kept X Pert at bay. X Pert was overwhelmed by the scale of the difference between it and her – his knowledge was of no avail, for the first time he became aware of his own limits. Not that his knowledge was devalued or undermined, but rather that it suddenly became negotiable, open for inspection and scrutiny by the client . . . she had the last voice. Strangely enough, this was not threatening to you, rather and in mysterious – almost inexplicable – ways, it was liberating and exhilarating. You couldn't but continue experimenting, you said. So you tried something similar with your other clients. And to (this time) your surprise, the same sense of space, of lightness and of possibility, was present in the conversation.

As you said before, we have to be cautious about the long-term life of this discovery. Yet, it feels like a breath of fresh air, which has given you new energies in your struggles with X Pert. We cannot but wait in suspense and curiosity to witness the unfolding of this story.

Once again, take care, lots of care,

Marion

Why has narrative therapy (since Goolishian) placed so much emphasis on the expertise of the client, and the not-knowing position of the therapist? It surely reflects a recognition of the ubiquitous, subtle and ambivalent effects of professional knowledge in the context of the helping relationship. With or without appeal to Foucault, this concern reflects an awareness of the controlling and regulating effects of knowledge when its distribution is asymmetrical. However well-intentioned, the deployment of expertise cannot but place the less-informed (or less-credentialled) person – the client – at a disadvantage. But knowledge and expertise cannot be simply given away. The therapist who believes that he or she has done so may instead have replaced one form of expertise with another: the temptations to do so are very great. De-experting may instead, as Glenn Larner (1996) suggests, involve the rendering negotiable (or fluid?) all the expert's knowledge; an indication of a genuine preparedness to put all of one's knowledge 'on the table', piece by piece if not all at once. This in itself must be extremely difficult to achieve. In treating the narrative therapist as client, we as authors must be prepared to go at least as far. How do we do so and at the same time assume the authority to write this chapter?

What is meant by expertise in the client? It does not simply mean that the client has a privileged 'insider's' view of his or her world and the suffering suffusing it. As pointed out in the literature of social construction (Gergen, 1994), a person's access to their 'feelings' has to be thought of as mediated by discourses, values, vocabulary and so on. When we treat the therapist as client, therefore, we are not attributing to the therapist an authentic story of the reality of the therapy situation, as if we sought to eavesdrop on this story. Rather we are indicating that the therapist (as client) is at home in the complexities of the situation, perhaps recognizing very little of it as complex; whereas for us, all is strange and alien. In the narrative therapy relationship itself, the therapist must accept his or her vulnerable position as novice in the client's experienced world; as a stranger cast adrift in a confused seascape, where none of the familiar rules and regulations may apply, and where there may be no stars to steer by. The therapist (as therapist) must not cling to familiar structures and systems but must step outside the comfort zone (perhaps, out of the consulting room). When we as authors place the therapist in the role of client, it is we who must cast ourselves adrift. As the eddies and currents pick us up and swirl us around, we have a (slim) chance of discerning the shapes of those force-fields. Going into the encounter with preconceived ideas about the shapes of those force-fields – with knowledge about prevailing dis-courses in our society, for example – may well undermine the process. Our therapist-client has a daunting task. He or she is constantly beset by temptations, which arise in a baffling array of forms. Safety offers itself in the form of familiar shorelines, or familiar pieces of conceptual apparatus floating by. Familiar forms of language offer themselves. All must be subjected to the assaying process of the client's experience, because all comprise expert knowledge. The DSM is not the only totalizing system of vocabulary in the clinic.

Another of the many temptations that assails the narrative therapist is the temptation to emancipate. Like the sirens' lure to the familiar yet deadly shallows, the odyssey of emancipation draws its appeal from the good intentions of the therapist. It suggests that emancipation is not only possible (itself a big claim) but that it is achievable if correct techniques are adopted, with appropriate sensitivity. It leads to clients' expressions of gratitude and their avowals of personal growth being interpreted as the lineaments of liberation. This process is itself an unremarkable one. Most forms of psychotherapy and psychiatry adopt forms of intervention that define a vocabulary for outcomes as well as for 'problems'. Many define successful outcomes in terms specific to their own approach, so that the evaluation of therapy is highly theorized and the whole process is a coherent (if not a circular) one. But the circumstances in the case of narrative therapy are more specific than this. The perception that outcomes are emancipatory is very heavily loaded. There is an enormous contrast between the pessimism of the social analysis – the analysis of deep, oppressive effects of surveillance in modern societies – and the optimism of the therapeutic contract. Where else have we encountered such extremes of black and white, of death and life? In fundamentalist religious movements, and in fundamentalist political movements; in crusades against alcohol, against drugs; salvation, redemption . . .

It has been pointed out by Kathleen Stacey (1997) that successful client outcomes have been defined in terms dominated by the metaphor of *resistance*. That is, successful transaction results in a strengthening of the client's will and competence to resist some power-structure consensually agreed to be operating. As Stacey points out, resistance is only one of several ways in which a client's relationship with a problem situation may be improved upon. Co-existence, grudging toleration, contempt, amusement, are all possible options. Why then does resistance hold such a privileged place in the narrative therapist's vocabulary (as privileged perhaps as the different process indicated by the same word in another kind of therapy)? Our re-framing of the therapist may clarify things here. It would appear that resistance best fits with a particular self-image of the therapist – that of a guerilla in the war against oppressive discourse. This is the romantic image of the small, cunning hero, almost childlike in some respects, relying more on wits than on brute strength. David against Goliath; hobbit against necromancer; Jack the Giant-killer. A fantasy of the power of the small individual over an immense and highly resourced enemy (the last arrow must fly to the heart of the dragon, the final missile to the heart of the death-star). Along with the dream of emancipating the client goes the fantasy of overthrowing the monstrous system, more or less single-handed. Almost a fantasy of omnipotence . . .?

Finally, Then, a Letter to the Reader

Dear Sir/Madam,

You have told us about the problems that Academic Arthur has caused you. Whenever you felt that you had made some progress, begun to understand something – never over-estimating such understanding – Academic Arthur has always turned up with a critique, with a 'yes but', with a new twist . . . It is almost as if Academic Arthur's main purpose in life is to make you feel small. And yet you can't help feeling that, so often, there is just a fragment of what he says that indeed makes new sense, that challenges in a way that is ultimately helpful. What you may have to consider is that however much he may be a creature of narrative externalization, Academic Arthur is also an intrinsic part of you; a part that you must acknowledge, just as Dr Frankenstein had to acknowledge his monster as part of himself. He is, at least, as much a part of you as he is a part of us.

yours <u>very</u> sincerely,

Maria and John

No doubt about it, the therapist as client is living a highly vulnerable life. Her story is a heroic one, battling against diverse enemies and striving to retain her innocence at all cost. For a certain dogged kind of simplicity is required of the narrative therapist. Knowledge must be painstakingly built up with the client, each block scrutinized, weighed, compared. No pre-cast components may be utilized, and no trusted tools employed: the tools, also, must be fashioned anew, in each new encounter. An austere and challenging vocation indeed.

Note

John wishes to express thanks to John Kaye, to Elmarie Kotze and to Tim Linzey. Maria wishes to express gratitude to Gabriel Reyes, Gloria Kunstmann, Christina Harmstorf, Marta Lohyn, Geraldine Slattery, Robyn Boord, Sue Lintern and Helen Mares whose differences of style made her think.

Bibliography

Anderson, H. (1997) *Conversation, Language, and Possibilities: A Postmodern Approach to Therapy*. New York: Basic Books.
Anderson, H. and Goolishian, H. (1992) 'The client is the expert: a not-knowing approach to therapy', in S. McNamee and K. Gergen (eds), *Therapy as Social Construction*. London: Sage.
Derrida, J. (1987) *The Post Card: From Socrates to Freud and Beyond*. Chicago: University of Chicago Press.
Derrida, J. (1994) 'The deconstruction of actuality, an interview with Jacques Derrida', *Radical Philosophy*, 68: 28–41.
Gergen, K. (1994) *Realities and Relationships: Soundings in Social Construction*. Cambridge, MA: Harvard University Press.
Larner, G. (1996) 'Narrative child family therapy', *Family Process*, 35: 423–440.
Law, I. (1997) 'The politics of knowledge and its dance within therapy: an interview with Maria Nichterlein', *Gecko*, 1: 72–83.
Morss, J. (1992) 'Making waves: deconstruction and developmental psychology', *Theory and Psychology*, 2/4: 445–65.
Rabinow, P. (1984) *The Foucault Reader*. Harmondsworth: Penguin.
Stacey, K. (1997) 'Alternative metaphors for externalizing conversations', *Gecko*, 1: 29–51.
White, M. (1988/9) 'The externalizing of the problem and the re-authoring of lives and relationships', *Dulwich Centre Newsletter*, 3–21.
White, M. (1995) *Re-Authoring Lives: Interviews and Essays*. Adelaide: Dulwich Centre Publications.
White, M. and Epston, D. (1990) *Literary Means to Therapeutic Ends*. New York: Norton.

12

CAN (AND SHOULD) WE KNOW HOW, WHERE AND WHEN PSYCHOTHERAPY TAKES PLACE?

Eero Riikonen and Sara Vataja

This chapter is a dual and well-intentioned attempt to create non-knowledge where there was knowledge before. What we do could be called 'deconstruction of the concept of psychotherapy' combined with an effort to (partially) deconstruct the idea that deconstruction is a basic process in psychological healing. First, we try, a little provocatively, to show that there isn't anything which should be called 'psychotherapy'. Second, we attempt to give some grounds for not making too much of deconstruction in this field. What we mean by the latter expression will become apparent only in the very end of the article (we hope).

We start with our (rather Baudrillardian) effort to show that 'psychotherapy' in a very real sense is not in need of deconstruction – because there has never really existed any *definable* activity deserving that name. There are so many schools of therapy and so many varieties of activities calling themselves 'psychotherapy' that it is not easy to even start to look at their differences and similarities. The situation is made even more complex when we observe that many of these activities can hardly be separated from what people do continuously in their everyday lives. In fact, people talk of their problems and interact with others in more or less beneficial ways, mostly with non-therapists.

Outcome studies do not give any relief here. Psychotherapy and related activities should be beneficial interaction par excellence. But do we know what makes certain psychotherapeutic interactions successful? We don't. Different schools of therapy and counselling each make claims regarding the specificity of their methods and their effectiveness in achieving results. Because the creation of distinctive packages of practices makes economical sense, there has so far been relatively little interest among therapists themselves to examine things like common elements or shared backgrounds. However, a great number of psychotherapy outcome studies have shown that the results of therapies mostly correlate with the quality of the interpersonal relationship (measured by factors like 'warmth of the therapist', 'trust', 'hopefulness', 'a constructive nature of conversation', 'feeling understood', etc.), not with factors like the methods used, or the length of training of the professionals involved. The so called 'non-specific factors' have generally proven to be at least as important, if not more than the 'specific factors' (which supposedly relate to particular methods targeted at defined 'symptoms' or 'personality structures'). Additional but important complications are the sheer impossibility of non-ambiguous descriptions of any human interaction and the healing elements it contains and the presupposition that the effects of certain beneficial interactions take place immediately after these interactions – something which happened thirty-five years ago could, at least in theory, very well trigger significant changes today.

We believe that 'psychological healing' – the supposed activity/result of effective therapy – very seldom takes place in those relatively regulated settings called 'therapy' and that people generally do not notice moments of mental or psychological healing. In fact, healing (we could as well talk of 'generation of mental well-being', or things like that) seems to mostly happen in everyday contexts and situations which most therapists would have difficulty in recognizing as relevant at all. We do not think that this devaluation is an innocent result of the poor observation skills of people. It is more likely that the situation could be explained by the continuous overvaluation of the expert's actions typical of many psychotherapeutic theories and a corresponding devaluation of the well-being generated by everyday interaction.

Psychotherapy process researchers have attempted to avoid some of the critique by creating more detailed descriptions of therapies, and some have chosen the road of developing full-fledged manuals. We are very sceptical when it comes to giving univocal descriptions – of anything. This suspicion is well supported, we think, by writings of various authors and thinkers representing discursive perspectives to psychology. What is common to these views is the idea that whatever takes place in the interaction should be looked at as examples of the use of 'discursive resources', as creative use of tools for accounting for expressions, experiences and deeds. We are convinced that it would be useful to subject phenomena like 'therapy' or 'psychological healing' to a treatment by 'discursive psychology' (e.g. Edwards, 1997). However, it would seem useful for us to use the word 'resource' here also in a wider sense. We could talk of 'discursive resources for the creation of well-being'. It is, in fact, rather strange for us that this perspective, strongly implicated by discursive views, has not been more systematically developed.

So, it seems to us that the project of various schools and groups of therapists to claim and safeguard forms of interaction and call them 'therapy' – in opposition to other forms of interaction thought to be less beneficial – is counterproductive and even dangerous. The biggest problem is that the idea of expert-driven therapy gives the competence to the professionals and leads to believing that only expert-defined actions are useful or effective. It is an example of spiritual hubris which can easily be turned to material profit.

To summarize so far: for us there is no reason to think that we know *what psychotherapy really is*. This creates obstacles to our deconstructive urges – to deconstruct illusory things could be a very complicated matter indeed.

From Facts to Imagination

The idea and experience of repetition is inherent in the concept of problems. Most of the options for psychological help try to transform the repetitive and given to something changeable and 'created'. If the task of therapy is seen as turning constraints to opportunities we should be very interested in understanding more about constraints and possibilities from a discursive perspective. This theme has links with a previous text, *Re-Imagining Therapy* (Riikonen and Smith, 1997). This book contrasted dialogical and monological forms of interaction and tried to show that changing constraints to non-constraints in most cases presupposes a dialogical and metaphorical orientation to situations. Another topic which was not developed very far in the book but must be discussed here concerns links between unitary knowledge, conceptualism and attempts to create a scientific basis for psychology or psychotherapy. In the latter task some of the most recent writings of Jean Baudrillard are helpful (Baudrillard, 1994).

Re-Imagining Therapy drew particularly upon social constructionist views, Bakhtin's ideas about dialogue, and Wittgenstein's ideas of language, specially to look at *language-in-the-speaking* as opposed to texts, theories or abstractions of language (Wittgenstein, 1953: nos. 130, 132; Shotter, 1993a; Shotter, 1993b). We also wanted to connect some recent discussions of the therapy world to wider issues and dialogues. It also seemed to us that the perspectives and ideas we talked about could be applied to much more general issues regarding interaction, service cultures and even human rights. We tried to avoid looking at therapy through individualistic lenses and use or develop relational perspectives and metaphors. In accordance with these views we saw words primarily as tools, gestures and actions, not as labels for objective things. Examining Mikhail Bakhtin's ideas about dialogue and dialogical understanding (see Bakhtin, 1981; Morson and Emerson, 1990; Wertsch, 1991; Shotter, 1993a) made us convinced that the world of therapy could indeed benefit from looking more closely at how we relate *to* and *with* language.

Both Shotter and Bakhtin make it clear that knowledge of relationships cannot be given a descriptive form. Shotter claims that relationships between people base themselves mostly on a special kind of knowledge he calls 'knowledge of the third kind'. It is not external or objective knowledge. This type of knowledge has to do with experience and with how we relate to our situation or circumstances. It is closely connected to emotions and felt invitations of situations and has its appearance only in moments of interaction. It is thus something people constantly need in order to go on and get on with other people (see Wittgenstein, 1953: no. 154). Understanding 'knowledge' in these ways allows new possibilities for understanding therapy and counselling.

The concept of metaphor was central for *Re-Imagining Therapy*. First, we took Wittgenstein's view of methods of (philosophical) research quite seriously and applied it to our own thinking and writing. Like him we saw that the main task of research is to find *images and metaphors* which arrest the flow of automatic thoughts and actions and make taken-for-granted metaphors more obvious. These kinds of images and metaphors make new connections, possibilities or more productive metaphors. According to this view, therapy is largely about new connections and distinctions becoming visible through dialogue – about finding new ways of relating to things. These 'new ways of relating' may refer to the relationship to the 'problem', but also to life, to experience, to other people – or to oneself. One of the implications of these views is that therapy is about creating *shared* visibilities, about promise seen *together* and about *connectedness*. It is (when it works) a continuous development and reshaping of shared, providential (promising, inspiring) realities. These realities are clearly not attributes of individuals. They are *not in people* but rather something in which the persons themselves are in and to which they act and react. They are genuinely dialogical phenomena produced jointly by the participants, and yet something which cannot be totally controlled by them. This type of joint action is more than the sum of its parts (see Shotter, 1993a).

We saw it as our task to re-imagine therapy: to see it in imaginative ways, to re-equip it with imagination, to 're-metaphoricize' it. This task was not made easier by various existing attempts to create systematic, detached and overarching conceptualizations of therapeutic interaction, deconstructive or not. These forces are often unquestioned, so it is worth elaborating on the assumption of systematic understanding (Johnson, 1993). For many reasons, it seemed useful to look at psychotherapeutic interaction in a way which respects its metaphorical, fragmented, imaginative and momentary character.

Purely referential views of language have impoverished not only our ways of understanding human life but also *words themselves*. And this is not a problem only of language, because our conceptions of language and words have a close connection to the kinds of relationships which *can* exist between people – and between us and other things. Modernist conceptions and uses of language tend to lend support to more limited, linear, utilitarian and goal-oriented approaches both to people and to the natural world. It is noteworthy that these uses of language – factual talk of disappearing facts – are typical also for the literature of deconstruction and social constructionism.

In trying to pursue these ideas we were struck by the immediate difficulty of how to avoid being monological when writing for academic audiences. We soon noticed that to succeed in our project we had to speak differently, metaphorically, even strangely. We had to use different styles and to give words and concepts slight twists, to exaggerate and to even use 'wrong words'. Because words and voices are living things, we could not be satisfied with only writing *about* them, we also had to include some of their life. Similarly, we could not stick to describing only the *results* of our thinking, but had to show real pieces of the process.

From Limiting Facts to Providential Gaps

There are obvious links with monological types of interaction, violence and 'conceptualism'. Conceptualism and attempts to gain unitary knowledge are linked with the idea of control and predictability (see Maffesoli, 1996: 26–44). Freshness and metaphoricality – which of course have many links – are in this sense basic social resources which are needed to keep interaction interesting and morally regrading to *all* participants. To make all this more understandable it is perhaps useful to focus for a while on the role of imagination and natural providence in keeping dialogue alive.

People who write about imagination and possibilities sometimes refer to the philosopher Giambattista Vico who lived in eighteenth-century Italy (e.g. Shotter, 1993a: 57–72). A central concept for Vico was 'sensory topic', the starting point of the shared worlds of people. Sensory topic is something pre-verbal, a feeling of being in some situation together. These places, 'loci' or 'topoi', the original sources of shared worlds, can be thought of as resources which people draw upon in shaping their actions and interactions.

Vico made it clear that the very character of our practical social activity is not finalizable. It always contains possibilities for continuous development and further shaping (Shotter, 1993a: 68–9). This doctrine of 'providence' or of 'natural provision' is interesting in a world like ours which generally idealizes finalized knowledges. The word 'providence', often used in religious contexts, refers to the finding of an abundance or a source of richness. Providential topics or objects can, like children's toys or a lover's eyes, be continuous sources of possibilities. It is important to observe that providence in Vico's sense is both unavoidable and conditional. The potentialities can be utilized only if they are seen. If Vico's ideas are sound, there is no final knowledge in the social sphere and we should give much more weight to the use of imagination as a way to develop the potentials of our interaction.

Vico's ideas of providence describe very well what happens in the field of psychotherapy. For various reasons (discussed later in more detail) the developers of models and methods seem to have a temptation towards unnecessarily early closures. What Vico is telling us is this kind of closure is always problematic. The complexity and inter-relatedness of things feeds continuous spirals of development. Developing any model or idea creates grounds for further questions, for seeing further connections.

We have been often struck how easy it is for therapists to talk of our methods or of how we are using *a* method or *a* combination of this or that method. It is also quite easy for us to make a distinction between using a method of some kind and not using a method – between doing and not doing psychotherapy. For many different reasons, many of them economic, it is useful for a person of authority in the field of psychotherapy to make claims of knowing what his or her method is, of its distinctness from other methods, of its modernity, of its academic credibility, and so on. It is better to have a clearly defined, respectable package which can be sold.

It is possible to visualize two extreme views of human action. The first assumes that people are like machines systematically following rules when they think, act and relate to each other. The rules are out there already, they just have to be applied in particular instances. The second is a resource perspective: seeing people as imagining creatures guided by a motive for inspiring interaction and using whatever discursive resources they can find or create for this purpose. Both of these views can be applied to psychological help.

The latter perspective can be linked to Wittgenstein's notions of the nature of (philosophical) problems as situations that occur when we do not know how to go on. The same view is valid for other types of human problems. When stuck, people start by themselves or jointly with others to examine the options, the possible next steps. This process requires imagination – imagination requires stepping outside the objective observations and actual situational limits. (It should be remembered at this point that activities like imagination or remembering do not have to be considered individual phenomena (see Middleton and Edwards, 1990), they are correlates of discourses and dialogues.) The responses orient towards what has happened previously, to what happens now, and to the future. They are varied and complex. The tasks of these responses are to make it possible to go on – this often means that they enable us to get along with others; they should (normally) maintain, or increase, the moral status of the person and others; they should also be intelligible. The combination of these tasks cannot be met by applying ready-made rules.

At this point it is useful to look more closely at the place where continuities and new directions are created in speech: at silences or breaks between utterances – 'interactive gaps' (Shotter, 1993b). This concept refers both to the progression of meaning and the contrasts between meanings. We could say that the bridging of gaps between responses and what precedes them not only produces meaning and continuity, it also creates the relationships between people.

The concept of 'interactive gap' can be related to what Bakhtin describes as 'own words' (Bakhtin, 1981: 293–4; Morson and Emerson, 1990). He speaks of own words as words and expressions in which there is *more freedom* than there is with others. 'Foreign words', carriers of truth and order, are meant to be passively received and preferably obeyed. Own words seem to make more of the potential space of interactive gaps visible, foreign words seem to obscure it.

Interactive gaps are moments during which meanings can be transformed. They can be sites where a steady progress of argumentative meanings is guaranteed, as well as playgrounds of contrasting and mutually effacing meaning. We could thus conceptualize parts of the workings of imagination in relation to interactional gaps, gaps between the utterances of dialogues or units of thought. In everyday life people are generally not at all conscious of the great amount of creativity that is inherent in their responses.

From Mental Health Promotion to Enhancement of Dialogue

It is our general belief that joyful and inspiring experiences are vitally important for people. The sources of joy and meaningfulness are of course quite variable. The question is: what kinds of elements are required and can they be described or regulated?

Our preliminary answer is that the search for these factors will lead outside the domain of psychological theories, as we know them. These kinds of experiences have a relationship not only with the 'sacred' (things transcending human control) but also with something which is directly in contradiction with science which aims at uniform knowledge and universal concepts.

Feelings and experiences of well-being link with very local, very unique circumstances, happenings and relationships. Despite their micro-nature these happenings can offer ways of connecting us to something transcending us (and transcendence in this sense does not necessarily imply religious interpretations of experience). We can get a feeling of being connected to the world, or to something felt more or less vaguely as meaningful, for instance when we are working with the dirt of our garden, walking our dog or when swimming in a communal pool. The important thing seems to be the capacity of something to make a feeling of machine-likeness (or a constraining quality) of life to disappear. We do not feel like cogs in a machine at those moments. A prerequisite of this is a feeling of 'gaps' or 'areas of emptiness' between what happens and our reactions to it – which generates a sense of 'freedom'.

From a discursive perspective 'problems' could be seen as interactional practices which increase the feeling of being trapped or, in other words, diminish perceived life-control or experienced competence. 'Problems' exist from this viewpoint when somebody interacts, thinks or talks in ways which leads to experienced loss of control, failure and incompetence (see De Shazer, 1985, 1988, 1991; Anderson and Goolishian, 1988). From this perspective 'a solution of a problem' is the disappearance of these forms of thinking and speaking.

The question is, are there general remedies for experiential and interactional traps, machine-likeness and cul-de-sacs? Our answer is negative. The nature of the interactional (micro-)phenomena we are talking about does not allow universal solutions. A joyous moment or moment of freedom is always a mystery to some degree, a good feeling must be a child of the moment.

To clarify these ideas further it could be useful at this point to make a short detour to a field where topics like mental health and mental well-being have been in the focus of intense thinking for years. This discursive domain is 'mental health promotion'. It goes without saying that mental health promotion, in most cases an interest of people concerned mainly with phenomena at the level of populations, focuses on developing general understandings about sources of mental health.

A crucial topic is of course is how the main target of mental health promotion is seen. What exactly should 'mental health promoters' attempt to influence? Health promotion is concerned with enabling people to maximize their 'health potential'. In WHO's famous 'Ottawa Charter' of 1986, health promotion was defined as a process of enabling people to increase control over and thereby to improve their health. The same document also states that health promotion aims at returning power, knowledge, skills and other resources relating to health to the community to individuals, families and whole populations.

Relatively widespread agreement concerning factors promoting and protecting mental health still leaves open many ways in which mental health and well-being can be conceptualized. These views are important because they suggest different approaches and lines of action. They also locate the responsibilities and resources differently, some of them, for example, encourage the action and active participation of citizens and users. A definition of the focus of activities attempting to promote mental health which fits the perspectives proposed in this article is to see the main target of mental health promotion as the *possibilities of clients alone and with others to create contexts, moments, experiences and life projects that generate well-being*. This relates to both client-professional interaction and to social interaction in general. These types of keys to well-being seem to have two important features. First, the users or clients are the true experts regarding them. Second, they can mostly be found in the happenings of everyday life. One of the benefits of this view is that it transfers the users and citizens to the sphere of normality.

The production of circumstances that generate well-being is a challenge common to everybody.

From Good Intentions to Good Interaction

What we have said so far points to the need to change our views regarding the principal targets of helping and supporting practices. Certain ways of talking, certain texts, and certain forms of interaction should perhaps be seen as the 'patient', not the clients or persons seeking help. What we have on our hands are 'sick', oppressing or inhuman interactional practices. This is not in any way to minimize the suffering that people are presenting or claim that everything is only talk. We just want to underline what we consider as a gravely neglected dimension of helping work.

But to what degree can better interactional practices be produced purposefully? We have already tried to show that the position of experts is difficult from the dialogical perspective described above. Well-being cannot be 'given' to somebody. It is a result of the multi-dimensional and complicated interaction of the person and his or her social and material environment. If there is a recommendation which could be given to professional helpers at this point, it is a very simple one: it is that the experts should be very sensitive to what clients see as promising and inspiring and build their action on this basis.

As we know so well, most Western countries are full of do-well organizations inventing guidelines and building programmes for better lives – for others. When we want to create good interaction or good moments for ourselves and our nearest, we start mostly from much hazier ideas and follow less consequent steps. Think of a good conversation with a friend. Good interaction and good conversations evolve naturally and often unpredictably. The real interest, the living spark is in the moment.

The same problematics concerns most efforts to consciously develop client-professional interaction. The idea of development in itself presupposes measurement and instrumental logic. The continuous and successful 'well-being work' or 'inspiration work' of our everyday lives can be developed and enhanced but the approaches to do that have to respect the nature of this activity. The methods have to be sensitive to the volatile preferences, developing boredom, desires, humour and spirit of the moment.

We have come to see 'mental well-being' or 'healing' as a process in which 'providential realities' are developed socially, in interaction and dialogue. The elements which together constitute enlivening, inspiring and enabling interaction are various and in complicated relationships to each other. They have natural links to even more amorphous concepts like 'metaphoricality', 'sacredness' and 'interactional freshness'.

Concepts like this are, however, easily understandable from the perspective of everyday life. They refer to ways of treating each other and oneself well.

From Desperate Analysis to Happy Language

The production of providential realities and interaction necessitates sensitivity and respect for many kinds of personal and interactional 'sonorities'; we are indeed dealing with personal and social poetics. Social poetics cannot be understood without examining metaphoricality and thematic variation or freshness.

Both metaphors and the idea of newness, surprise or freshness presuppose discontinuities and striking contrasts. This implies that professions interested in helping should be interested in ways in which people normally create inspiring moments and conversations. When we study any group of people in informal conversation, we see that they jump relentlessly from topic to topic and from one point of view to another; the old topics and perspectives often quite soon become stale. It is indeed typical of problematic and dehumanizing situations that some or all participants are denied the right to thematic variation and metaphoricality.

The 'dialogical approach' we propose links with some of Jean Baudrillard's recent ideas concerning the distinction between analytical and radical thought (1994). In his essay 'Pensee radicale' Baudrillard contrasts 'radical thought' with truth-oriented, univocal, analytical thought in the following way (all of the Baudrillard excerpts are from a downloaded Internet version of the text which is available from: http://orion.oac.uci.edu/~spk/baudrillard.html):

> Analysis is by its very definition unfortunate . . . But language on the contrary is fortunate (happy), even when it designates a world with no illusion, with no hope. This would in fact be here the very definition of radical thought: an intelligence without hope, but a fortunate and happy form. Critics, always being unfortunate (unhappy) in their nature, choose the realm of ideas as their battle field.

Baudrillard also tells that 'Radical thought is never depressing. This would be a complete misunderstanding'. And also that 'Radical thought does not decipher secrets of the world', it 'anathematizes' and 'anagramatizes' concepts and ideas, exactly what poetic language does with words. Baudrillard claims that the *passion* of radical thought relates to the rehabilitation of enigma and mystery. According to him this passion dominates in the 'free and spiritual usage of language' and only disappears when language is used for a limited finality, to deliver information, in 'communication' traditionally understood. For these kinds of reason Baudrillard tells us: 'it is better to have a despairing analysis in a happy language, than an optimistic analysis in despairingly boring and demoralizingly plain language'. Interestingly, Baudrillard wants to rehabilitate our interest in the *form* of language and writing. One of his main points is that we have been obsessed with the content and devalued the form (genre, style, rhythm, tone, irony, humour, 'Witz' etc.), which, however, is the main field of resolution of truths and oppressive forces.

We are so accustomed to seeing help as matter of content, not of style and form, that Baudrillard's views easily seem almost nonsensical. However, taking into account the points made previously, the centrality of '*langue heureuse*' seems to become evident. Baudrillard's views help us to see that the conversational activities we call therapy can be re-conceptualized as 'flourishing work'. Because of its dialogical nature the methods of this kind of work could be seen as Baudrillardian 'happy dialogue'. It is important to underline here that 'happiness' in Baudrillard's sense doesn't refer *only* to humour or lightness (it refers *also* to these things). The expression points rather to the general capacity of certain forms of language and dialogue to undo finalizations and too-perfect constellations of meaning. The happiness of dialogues is their power to refreshen, to bring about joy, to dissolve burdens and oppression.

From Conclusions to Openings (and to Pommetics)

After having said what we have, it would be strange to attempt to reach any final conclusions. The Baudrillardian ethos seems to demand some-thing different all together. Looking for something fitting we turned towards a developing manuscript of one of the authors (Eero Riikonen). This text, which could be defined as 'social science fiction' (or 'fictional history of future social science'), tells about a process of developing a new art/discipline called 'Pommetics'. Pommetics is all about ways to turn trivial things to interesting ones, together and alone. It is about transforming facts to something nicer. What we present here is a piece of one of the opening chapters of the manuscript of the report on Pom-metics. It might give some ideas of what a Pommetic and reconstructive turn in psychotherapy might mean.

So: What is this report really about?
This is a report about regaining not-understanding.
Knowledge can't be destroyed (it should not be wise either as will be learned later) but it can be made playable by *impossibilities* which helps us momentarily notice the nothingness which is a source of creation, to use a traditional expression (don't worry if you don't understand, it will become

easier, along the way, not to feel ashamed or guilty because of that). Impossibilities are the hammers whose hits refreshen the Mind.

Knowledge creates stone. What we are looking for are words and creatures that can create echoes and reflections making stone alive. We need to understand the language of swallows.

First there was logos (concept, thought, reason), then there was stone. From this stone houses and empires were built. To it the first laws were engraved. To understand the properties and capabilities of stone, science was created.

I have had the sensation of everything sometimes turns to a stone. I can, like the writer Milan Kundera, see swarms of agelasts, soul eaters, destroyers of laughter marching on our streets.

But what do we become if we stop hearing and seeing and feeling the meeting of the stone, warm evenings and swallows?

The time of writing stories has ended. The swallows never fly straight.

To not write stories we have to forget. Art of forgetting is art of life.

I speak of an error contained in pointing directly. But, as you understand, vaguely, I guess, I have to speak of this pointing and its alternatives indirectly. So what can I say: The heaven is for these who don't instruct, but there is always some room for half-serious teachers.

We need good, old, incomprehensible, not de-gapped words, words with invisible letters and big W's.

We should worship those moments when we find them – and there are many of them.

After the Openings

There are good grounds, we feel, for not seeing psychotherapy or psychological healing as a form of deconstruction. Deconstruction is an analytical, reflective activity. What we are proposing is the use of imagination to create holes to univocal knowledges *and* to the analytical and reflective machinery producing them. Deconstruction is movement from one knowledge to another. Pommetics is movement from knowledge to void and to the connectedness made possible by this emptiness and by the impossibilities producing it.

What we need is not psychotherapy nor deconstruction but cultivation of the art and value of life.

References

Anderson, H. and Goolishian, H. (1988) 'A view of human systems as linguistic systems: preliminary and evolving ideas about the implications for clinical theory', *Family Process*, 27: 371–93.

Bakhtin, M. (1981) *The Dialogic Imagination: Four Essays by M.M. Bakhtin*, ed. M. Holquist. Austin: University of Texas Press.

Baudrillard, J. (1994) *La Pensee Radicale*. Paris: Sense and Tonka.

De Shazer, S. (1985) *Keys to Solutions in Brief Therapy*. New York: W.W. Norton.

De Shazer, S. (1988) *Clues to Investigation of Solutions in Brief Therapy*. New York: W.W. Norton.

De Shazer, S. (1991) *Putting Difference to Work*. New York: W.W. Norton.

Edwards, D. (1997) *Discourse and Cognition*. London: Sage.

Johnson, M. (1993) *Moral Imagination: Implications of Cognitive Science for Ethics*. Chicago: University of Chicago Press.

Maffesoli, M. (1996) *Ordinary Knowledge*. London: Polity Press.

Middleton, D. and Edwards, D. (eds) (1990) *Collective Remembering*. London: Sage.

Morson, G. and Emerson, C. (1990) *Mikhail Bakhtin: Creation of Prosaics*. Stanford, CA: Stanford University Press.

Penman, R. (1992) 'Good theory and good practice: an argument in progress', *Communication Theory*, 2 (3): 234–50.

Riikonen, E. and Smith, G. (1997) *Re-Imagining Therapy: Living Conversations and Relational Knowing*. London: Sage.

Shotter, J. (1993a) *Cultural Politics of Everyday Life. Social Constructionism, Rhetoric and Knowing of the Third Kind*. Buckingham: Open University Press.

Shotter, J. (1993b) *Conversational Realities*. London: Sage.

Wertsch, J. (1991) *Voices of the Mind*. Hemel Hempstead: Harvester Wheatsheaf.

Wittgenstein, L. (1953) *Philosophical Investigations*. Oxford: Blackwell.

INDEX